WHERE IS SOUL?

PSYCHOLOGY IN MODERNITY

WHERE IS SOUL?

PSYCHOLOGY IN MODERNITY

Edited by

Greg Mogenson & Pamela J. Power

DUSK OWL BOOKS
London, Ontario, Canada

Published by
Dusk Owl Books
London, Ontario, Canada

Cover design, interior design, and typesetting by
Michael Mendis

ISBN 978-1-7388606-5-4

CONTENTS

ACKNOWLEDGMENTS

The text of Chapter One as printed in this book is the short oral version of a several times longer essay that is included as a chapter in the forthcoming volume: Wolfgang Giegerich, *How to Think Psychologically: With Jung Beyond Jung, CEP* 7 (Routledge), expected to appear during 2025.

The quotation from Elie Wiesel in Chapter Six of this volume is reprinted with the permission of the current copyright holder, I. Abrahamson © 1985, Newberry Library, Chicago, Illinois.

SOURCES AND ABBREVIATIONS

The following abbreviations have been used for frequently cited sources:

CEP*:* Wolfgang Giegerich, *The Collected English Papers of Wolfgang Giegerich*, 6 vols., New Orleans: Spring Journal Books, 2005-2013. Cited by volume and page number. All volumes have been republished since 2020 by Routledge.

CW*:* Carl Gustav Jung, *Collected Works*, 20 vols. Herbert Read, Michael Fordham, Gerhard Adler and William McGuire, eds., R. F. C. Hull, trans., Princeton: Princeton University Press, 1957-1979. Cited by volume and paragraph number.

MDR: C. G. Jung, *Memories, Dreams, Reflections*. Rev. ed., Aniela Jaffé. Trans. Richard and Clara Winston. New York: Vintage Books, 1989, cited by page number.

Letters: C. G. Jung, *Letters*. 2 vols. Ed. Gerhard Adler. Bollingen Series XCV: 2. Princeton: Princeton University Press, 1975.

Spring: *Spring: A Journal of Archetype and Culture*, New Orleans: Spring Journal Books. Cited by volume number, in some cases by year.

AUTHORS' BIOGRAPHIES

Paul Bishop is the William Jacks Chair of Modern Languages at the University of Glasgow. His books examine the history of ideas, psychoanalysis and analytical psychology with particular emphasis on Nietzsche, C. G. Jung, and Ludwig Klages. His publications include *Jung's Answer to Job: A Commentary*, the two-volume *Analytical Psychology and German Classical Aesthetics: Goethe, Schiller, and Jung*, and *Reading Goethe at Midlife: Ancient Wisdom, German Classicism, and Jung*.

———

Wolfgang Giegerich is a Jungian analyst now living in Berlin. He received his Ph.D. from the University of California, Berkeley and a Diploma from the C. G. Jung Institute Zürich. He has been writing, lecturing, teaching, and supervising candidates for many years. His work is the impetus and inspiration for the International Society for Psychology as the Discipline of Interiority, where he presented at its 2012 Conference in Berlin. He is the author of numerous books. Recent publications include *The Historical Emergence of the I*, *Working with Dreams*, and *Coniunctio: Reflexions on a Key Concept of C. G. Jung's Psychology*.

———

John Hoedl is a graduate of the C. G. Jung Institute in Zürich. He grew up working on the family farm and his first degree was in Physical Education. Prior to beginning his training, he worked for Child Welfare Services in group homes, residential treatment centers, and with families for children in care. He is a past president of the Western Canadian Association of Jungian Analysts and is a founding member and president of the International Society for Psychology as the Discipline of Interiority. He has a private practice in Edmonton, Canada.

———

Tsuyoshi Inomata qualified at the C. G. Jung Institute, Zürich, then worked in university, clinical and private practice. He is the author of Japanese books including *Historical Consciousness of Psychology*. Tsuyoshi is Associate Professor at the Tezukayama Gakuin University in Osaka.

———————————

Kenji Kaneshiro, Ph.D., was born in Okinawa, Japan. He is a clinical psychologist, a haiku poet and a member of the Haiku Poets Society. Formerly in clinical practice in psychiatry, pediatrics, and schools, he is currently Assistant Professor in the Department of Clinical Psychology at Taisho University. While practicing psychotherapy from the standpoint of depth psychology, he researches themes such as developmental disorders, language, and religion in Japan.

———————————

Philip Kime has an academic background Philosophy and later, Cognitive Science. He trained at the C. G. Jung-Institut Zürich, Küsnacht, where he is currently Vice-President. Since entering into the field of Analytical Psychology, he has been repeatedly somewhat alarmed by the lack of philosophical attention to ideas which fundamentally require, indeed stem from, a philosophical orientation. Such an orientation is not optional in Analytical Psychology, regardless of what one's personal preferences in this regard might be. Attempting to address and demonstrate this concretely to students is the focus of his current teaching work. He is particularly interested in employing structure and form as opposed to content in order to discuss psychology.

———————————

Jun Kitayama is a professor at the Faculty of Letters, Department of Psychology, Gakushuin University, Tokyo. He received a Ph.D. in Psychology from Sophia University in 2018. He is the author of *Clinical Psychology Practice with the Elderly: Commitment to the Spirit of those Growing Old*. He is a trained Certified Clinical Psychologist and a Certified Public Psychologist and has been practicing at a psychiatric clinic for more than 15 years. During psychotherapy sessions, he places great importance on the client's dreams, drawings, and sandplays, and focuses on the moment at which their sense of subjectivity activates.

Carmen Kobor is a Jungian analyst in private practice in Beverly Hills, California. She is a member of the International Association for Analytical Psychology and a member of the C. G. Jung Institute of Los Angeles, where she regularly teaches and supervises. She presented at the ISPDI conference in Dublin 2018, and her paper, "The Crucible of Soul Logos" is published in *Psychological Perspectives*, 2021.

Greg Mogenson is a registered psychotherapist and Jungian analyst practicing in London, Ontario, Canada. He is a founding member and past Vice-President of The International Society for Psychology as the Discipline of Interiority and the publisher of the imprint, Dusk Owl Books. The author of numerous articles in the field of analytical psychology, his books include *Vicarius Animae, Notional Practice, Psychology's Dream of the Courtroom*; and *The Dove in the Consulting Room*. He is also the author of the monographs: *Dereliction of Duty and the Rise of Psychology, as Reflected in the "Case" of Conrad's Lord Jim*; *That Glimpse of Truth for which you had Forgotten to Ask*; *Inwardizing Rilke's Dog of Divine Inseeing into Itself*; and *Jungian Analysis Post Mortem Dei*.

Joseph Maria Moreno holds a degree in Psychology, a Master's in Clinical Psychology, and a Master of Arts, Humanities, and Culture. He has more than 35 years of professional, clinical, and research experience, including private and institutional psychotherapy and consultation in Spain, the USA, and Mexico, and he has a clinic in Barcelona, where he offers therapy and counseling services. Psychoanalysis, Analytical and Archetypal Psychology, and PDI have shaped his thinking and practice. He is the author of *Symbolism of the houses* (ed. Arbor Scientae, 1987), and contributor of the chapter "Bitcoin, Utopia and Soul" in *Essays on "The Soul's Logical Life" in the Work of Wolfgang Giegerich* (Routledge, 2024).

Pamela Power, Ph.D. is a clinical psychologist and Jungian analyst living and practicing in Santa Monica, CA. She is a member of the Los Angeles Jung Institute where she teaches and supervises. She is also a member of IRSJA and IAAP and currently serves on the Executive Committee of ISPDI. Prior to becoming a psychologist, Pamela studied music theory and history at UCLA and was trained as a classical musician, playing and teaching cello. She is the author of *Transitions in Jungian Analysis: Essays on Illness, Death and Violence* (Routledge, 2024) and her essay "How Does Music Think?" is published in *Essays on "The Soul's Logical Life" in the Work of Wolfgang Giegerich* (Routledge, 2024).

Michael Whan is a Jungian Analyst with the Independent Group of Analytical Psychology, a member of the College of Psychoanalysts-UK. He is a senior associate at the Royal Society of Medicine, and a patron of the Department of Germanic Studies at the Institute of Modern Languages, University of London. Along with contributing chapters in several books, he has written papers for journals such as *Spring Journal, Harvest, Chiron,* and the *International Journal of Jungian Studies,* and is currently working on a collection of essays on the dialectic in alchemy.

Peter White is a Canadian songwriter and retired high school teacher of music, recording, philosophy, and native studies from Sault Ste. Marie, Ontario, Canada. He has contributed to *Jung Journal Culture and Psyche,* the book *Essays on "The Soul's Logical Life" in the Work of Wolfgang Giegerich* and most recently the introduction to the book *Human Dignity and the Garden of Eden Story.* He has served on the Executive Committee of the ISPDI since its founding in 2010.

PREFACE

More than a dozen years after THE INTERNATIONAL SOCIETY FOR PSYCHOLOGY AS THE DISCIPLINE OF INTERIORITY held its inaugural conference in Berlin 2012, I was involved in the planning of our anticipated return to Berlin in August 2024. As a member of the Executive Committee, I was privy to both the creative work of envisioning and the busy work of producing the conference. Led by our able president, John Hoedl, the conference committee consisted of Peter White, Gabriel Eckart, Harry Henderson, Jennifer Sandoval, Philip Kime, and me. There were many details, arrangements, contacts, and contracts to attend to, so many, in fact, that at times we had our fingers crossed that everything would come together. Our efforts were met by an enthusiastic response from long-time members of the society, interested newcomers, and invited speakers. There was a wealth of proposals to choose from in planning the conference schedule, more than time allowed. We were pleased that our honorary patron, Wolfgang Giegerich, agreed to be one of the keynote speakers.

Looking back, what a gathering it was! More like a "retreat" in which attendees spent time during breaks and after the formal presentations in discussions and social gatherings that sometimes went well into the night. Essential for bringing it all together was a deep feeling for the "psychology *with soul*" that has inspired us from the works of C. G. Jung and Wolfgang Giegerich. Even before the conference was over, the idea for a book of papers from the conference was conceived.

Subsequently ripened during the process of compiling and editing, this volume serves as a kind of "conference proceedings," although it contains only a selection from the many presentations. Beginning with an introduction by Greg Mogenson, the reader is brought into the sphere of that radical continuation of Jung's psychology which Wolfgang Giegerich has called, *Psychology as the Discipline of Interiority*. Speakers from the UK, USA, Germany,

Switzerland, Spain, Canada, and Japan were in attendance, unfolding our approach to psychology in a myriad of ways.

The announced theme of the conference, and now the title of this book, is "Where is Soul? Psychology in Modernity." One might wonder what that question even means. We speak of soul and psychology all the time. But in PDI, soul and psychology have been highly distilled, and these distillations require a different approach and understanding. The implications of "The Soul's Logical Life," as described by Wolfgang Giegerich in his seminal book of that title, leave one with many questions. This is because the tables have turned. As Jung originally stated, and Giegerich emphasized, we do not think of the soul as being "in us," but rather of our being "in soul." Likewise, psychology isn't "about us," but "about soul," which means that our job today is to learn where soul has gone and to discover thereby the "Soul in the Real." The various chapters in this book relate to these important ideas.

The critical challenge of taking the deeply intellectual works of Wolfgang Giegerich to heart is as demanding as it is liberating. We are helped in this venture by the numerous books that he continues to publish, and by the many books and papers from other authors in the field of PDI. This current volume adds to that growing number and will be of interest to those new to PDI as well as seasoned readers.

Pamela J. Power
Executive Committee Member of ISPDI

Where Is Soul? Psychology in Modernity

GREG MOGENSON

A dozen years ago, at our inaugural conference, I gave a little background on the origins of the ISPDI. How marvelous it is to now be gathering again in Berlin, our society having come of age in the meantime. As I look around the room this morning, I am gratified by the presence of both members of long standing and interested newcomers. I think with pride of the productiveness of our membership. Year after year, there's been a steady stream of stimulating seminars and conferences as well as a surprising number of articles and books published by our members. What a growth of psychological mindedness we have achieved in this venture together! What collegial bonds have been forged! How brilliantly we have been led through the years by our President, John Hoedl! And what gratitude I feel when I think of the dedication of our past and present executive committee members. Also remarkable, the freshness of anticipation I feel at the prospect of the new paper we will be hearing in a few minutes from our honorary patron, Wolfgang Giegerich. Despite our hundreds, and for some of us thousands of hours spent sharpening our wits against his texts as against a whetstone, a new paper of his can pretty much be counted upon to sharpen them still more. In keeping with the adage that Dr. Giegerich adopted as a title for one of his books, "the soul always thinks," psychology as the discipline of interiority never becomes old hat.

But how, it might also be asked, does psychology as the discipline of interiority look from outside its own purview? Jung taught us the importance of learning to see ourselves from outside.

Surely this applies also to our little guild and is at least partly mediated (though it is true, Jung had something more than this in mind[1]) by how we come across to others.

In stark contrast to the tribute I have just paid to our achievements, it is my impression that within the wider world of Jungian psychology our contributions are regarded by many as being excessively intellectual, needlessly arcane. How else to explain the question that was once put to Giegerich in the middle of a long interview, "What do you say to those who say, 'I cannot understand what Wolfgang is saying. Why doesn't he write in a simpler way so it is easier to understand him?'"[2] My reaction to this question, when first I came across it (and maybe this was a little arrogant on my part), was to be reminded by my annoyance of an observation Jung made with respect to the naive presumptions that are routinely displayed by all and sundry when it comes to psychology. In the early pages of *Psychology and Alchemy*, the great psychologist writes, "It is a remarkable fact, which we come across again and again, that absolutely everybody, even the most unqualified layman, thinks he knows all about psychology as though the psyche enjoyed the most universal understanding. But anyone who really knows the human psyche will agree with me when I say that it is one of the darkest and most mysterious regions of our experience."[3] Now as I transcribe this line into my talk, I note that the distinction drawn in it— between what everyone thinks they know about psychology and what the psychotherapist working analytically knows—evinces what

---

[1] C. G. Jung, *MDR*, p. 341: "He [man in general, i.e., each of us as the individual we are] has no objectivity toward himself and cannot yet regard himself as a phenomenon which he finds in existence and with which, for better or worse, he is identical." For a full discussion of this topic see, Wolfgang. Giegerich, *What Are the Factors That Heal?* (London, ON: Dusk Owl Books, 2020), pp. 82-94. See also: Wolfgang Giegerich, *The Historical Emergence of the I: Essays on One Chapter of the History of the Soul* (London, ON: Dusk Owl Books, 2020), pp. 311-315.

[2] Wolfgang Giegerich and Robert Henderson, "Love the Questions Themselves," in: Robert & Janis Henderson, eds., *Living with Jung: "Enterviews" with Jungian Analysts*, Volume 3 (New Orleans, LA: Spring Journal Books, 2010), p. 278.

[3] Jung, *CW* 12 § 2.

in our literature is called the psychological difference. Just as the alchemists stipulated that their gold was not the people's gold, so also our psychology; it, too, is not reducible to the common conception of psychology that everywhere prevails. But this said, let us hear Jung out. "There is no end," he continues, "to what can be learned in this field. Hardly a day passes in my practice but I come upon something new and unexpected. True enough, my experiences are not commonplaces lying on the surface of life. They are, however, within easy reach of every psychotherapist working in this particular field. It is therefore rather absurd, to say the least, that ignorance of the experiences I have to offer should be twisted into an accusation against me. I do not hold myself responsible for the shortcomings in the lay public's knowledge of psychology."[4]

Turning now to Giegerich's response to the question put to him, I find myself admiring how much more charitable this was than mine might have been.[5] Though it is obviously true that the intellectual calibre of his writings is very high, to some, even dauntingly so, the issue raised by the question is whether this really needs to be so. Oedipus, Schmoedipus, the interviewer wants to know why Giegerich doesn't write in a simpler manner. His assumption seems to be that Giegerich is indulging in a high-brow conceit, that he is making matters more difficult than need be. In response to this, Giegerich begins by saying that, no, this is not the case. On the contrary, he always endeavors "to write as clearly as [he] can, without flattening the issues to be discussed and losing their inner complexities."[6] The problem, he offers, may have rather to do with an expectation of some readers to understand things immediately. But reading takes work. It requires a stretching of the mind. After stating this, he then—and this is the part of his response that I want to highlight—fully opens himself up to, and lets himself in for, the outsider's perspective that his interviewer's question, and its manner of being put to him, brings. This he does (apropos of Jung's great line about our "meet[ing]

---

[4] *Ibid.*

[5] Actually, the same question was put to me by the same interviewer. For my response see: "When 'One' Becomes 'Two': The Vocational Character of the Mediating Other—An 'Enterview' [by Robert Henderson] with Greg Mogenson," *Spring 84* (2011): 241-243.

[6] Giegerich and Henderson, p. 278.

ourselves in a thousand disguises on the path of life"[7]) by setting
aside his identity as a writer and identifying himself with the position
of the interviewer, who seems to have such difficulty understanding
his texts. Like him, Giegerich is also a reader, and this, moreover,
very often of books that are over his head, too.

> In my [own] voluntary reading, I read only books I don't
> understand. Why should I bother with texts that I understand at
> first sight? What they would bring to me would have to be so close
> to how I already think that it could hardly be worth wasting my time
> on them. But when reading those difficult books, I harbor the
> *un*understood within myself and live with it, go pregnant with it,
> often for many years, until perhaps, at long last, its meaning
> discloses itself to me of its own accord.[8]

Having emphasized the difference between the unpsychological
expectation of immediate understanding, on the one hand, and the
understanding that may come from patiently carrying what he calls
the *un*understood to term in oneself, on the other, Giegerich then
offers that "Behind this difference there is another, deeper one":

> Has, underneath my not understanding, *the soul in me* already caught
> fire by what I read, but do not understand—or has it not? Only if a
> kind of passion is kindled about what is in the ununderstood—in
> other words, only if the soul has understood that *this* is something
> precious that simply needs to be understood—can I [as was said of
> the Mary of the Annunciation, to whom he made reference earlier]
> "keep all these things and ponder them in my heart" in the first
> place. The point here [he continues] is that, for a psychological
> approach, the question or the ununderstood is known to have
> everything in itself it needs, even the solution to it. It *is* already the
> solution from the outset (or else we are not dealing with a soul
> question in the first place, but rather with a technical one). The
> solution or answer is not a second thing, a new addition.[9]

Surely, as readers we are all familiar with what Giegerich here describes.
Starting out in my youth reading Jung, I understood very little. Maybe

---

[7] Jung, *CW* 16 § 534.
[8] Giegerich and Henderson, p. 278.
[9] *Ibid.*, p. 279.

a half of one percent. But the soul in me had caught fire. There was an implicit understanding. In dreams of that period, Jung appeared to me as a fiery wise sage, with flashing visionary eyes and wild, wind-filled, floating hair.[10]

It is a matter of feeling, this passion and catching fire that Giegerich describes. Long before our attaining intellectual clarity, we already feel the surplus value, the soul value, in the matters of interest that have galvanized our attention. And here, as I reflect upon this point, I am reminded of Giegerich's also having characterized feeling (in Jung's sense of it as a rational function involved in the discerning of value and the making of value judgments) as performing a bridging function across the psychological difference.[11]

Time and again, it happens like this. A subject matter or topic of interest is felt by us to be, not merely what the discipline most closely associated with it has claimed, but at once both less than that and more, a self-othering, ego-transcending, expression of the soul's out-picturing itself to itself. "This [...] has always claimed my deepest interest and my greatest attention," writes Jung:

> the manifestation of archetypes or archetypal forms, in all phenomena of life: in biology, physics, history, folklore, and art, in theology and mythology, in parapsychology, as well as in the symptoms of insane patients and neurotics, and finally in the dreams and life of every individual man and woman. The intimation of forms hovering in the background not in itself knowable gives life the depth which, it seems to me, makes it worth living.[12]

At the outset of my remarks, I cited Jung's observation that "everybody, even the most unqualified layman, thinks he knows all

---

[10] How different this from when, years later in our studies, our understanding, though greatly increased, has become too formulaic and assured. As late in his life Jung put it upon hearing about the debates that had arisen amongst his followers concerning how the concepts of his psychology should be conceptualized and conveyed, "From such discussions we see what awaits me once I have become posthumous. Then everything that was once fire and wind will be bottled in spirit and reduced to dead nostrums. Thus are the gods interred in gold and marble and ordinary mortals like me in paper." Jung, *Letters 2*, to von der Heydt, 22 December 1958, p. 469.

[11] Giegerich, *CEP* IV, p. 510.

[12] Jung, *Letters 2*, to Martin Flinker, 17 October 1957, p. 397.

about psychology." This is so because the layman, and not only he, but many in professional psychology as well, equates psychology with the immediate psyche. It is generally assumed that psychology has directly to do with what is going on inside people, with what in Jungian psychology is called "personalistic psychology." But following Jung and Giegerich in their observing of the aforementioned psychological difference, we in our guild know that psychology in the eminent sense is not about people, but about the soul. When Jung in the passage I quoted speaks of the experiences that his psychology is properly about, but of which the general public know little or nothing, he especially has in mind the experience that what may variously be referred to as consciousness, mindedness, or "the soul" has phenomenologically had of itself in the course of our collective mental history. And it is this that is reflected in all the various fields of study into which Jung looked for the forms, as he called them, that hover in the background giving to life its depth and worth.

Remember the story that Jung tells of a patient "who was neither a poet nor anything very outstanding, just a naturally quiet and rather sentimental youth," who, in response to being rejected by a girl, became captivated by a vision of the stars embracing in the heavens like lovers and then broke into an astronomy observatory where he was later arrested by the police?[13] Like him, the psychologist, too, is led by the fire in his heart to trespass into other fields.

> [...] [I]n treating the problems of psychic life[, writes Jung,] we perpetually stumble upon questions of principle belonging to the private domains of the most heterogeneous branches of knowledge. We disturb and anger the theologian no less than the philosopher, the physician no less than the educator; we even grope about in the fields of the biologist and of the historian. This extravagant behaviour is due not to arrogance [on the part of psychology and the psychologist] but to the circumstance that man's psyche is a unique combination of factors which are at the same time the special subjects of far-reaching lines of research. For it is out of himself and out of his peculiar constitution that man has produced his sciences. They are *symptoms* of his psyche."[14]

---

[13] Jung, *CW* 7 § 232.
[14] Jung, *CW* 8 § 752.

"Where is Soul?" Pertinent to this question, from which the title of our conference is taken, is Jung's comment that psychology has "no delimited field"[15] of its own, but rather, "fall[s] between [...] the academic stools" inasmuch as the human psyche "forms at least half the ground necessary for the existence of them all."[16] Little wonder, then, that the psychologist may feel puerile and inferior at times; like the youth that broke into the observatory, to be a hapless intruder and trespasser.[17] Expressing this sentiment, Jung once described himself as "the most accursed dilettante that has ever lived."[18] But this is as it must be. For our falling between the academic stools is at the same time an overreaching of their differences. We could also say, a seeing through to the reigning or existing concept that, as soul of the real, they and we are nested in at particular points in time. And this is why, negating the negation of his having dubbed himself a dilettante, Jung could also claim that "[a]lthough we are specialists par excellence, our specialized field, oddly enough, drives us to universality and to complete overcoming of the specialist attitude [...]."[19]

The one in us that wants things simpler, however, might here object: shouldn't psychology just claim the consulting room as its stool and leave it at that? The problem with this, according to Jung, is that only "the smallest part of the psyche [...] presents itself in the medical consulting room."[20] Further to this observation, I like to remember his saying as well that the psyche is not in us, but the other way around, that it is we that are in the psyche.[21] And surely it was because of his keen sense of this that he lamented the fact that "the doctors interested in psychotherapy have practically no knowledge of the general human mind as it expresses itself in history, archaeology, philology, philosophy and theology, etc. [...]."[22]

---

[15] Jung, *CW* 10 § 338, *CW* 9i § 112, *CW* 16 § 209.

[16] Jung, *CW* 16 § 209.

[17] For a discussion of the dialectic involved in "transgression" and "trespass," see: Wolfgang Giegerich, *The Soul's Logical Life,* pp. 248-249.

[18] Quoted in Sonu Shamdasani, *Jung and the Making of Modern Psychology: The Dream of a Science* (Cambridge, UK: Cambridge University Press, 2003), p. 22.

[19] Jung, *CW* 16 § 190.

[20] Jung, *Letters 2*, to Benjamin Nelson, 17 June 1956, p. 307.

[21] Jung, *CW* 13 § 75. See also: Jung, *Letters 1*, to Josef Goldbrunner, 14 May 1950, p. 555.

[22] Jung, *Letters* 2, to Benjamin Nelson, 17 June 1957, p. 307.

Zooming out from the patient in front of him (even as in *The Visions Seminars* he wrote of how, "behind the impressions of daily life—behind the scenes—another picture looms up, covered by a thin veil of facts"[23]), Jung endeavoured throughout his long career to equip himself with a much wider education. "It […] behoves us," he wrote, "unembarrassed by our shortcomings as amateurs of history, to go to school once more with the medical philosophers of a distant past, when body and soul had not yet been wrenched asunder into different faculties."[24]

Laboratory *and* library, consulting room *and* scholar's study: cancelling the difference between these spheres, the kinds of "experiences" that Jung's psychology was especially concerned with were the result of study, amplification, and seeing through.[25] Even when working with patients, it was by venturing along routes of resemblance between their material and the motifs of alchemy, mythology, religion, and the various other fields he mentions that he opened up the psychological difference in such a way that the transpersonal dimension in their dreams and life situations were thrown into relief.

What I am driving at here is the need for otherness. Without the mediation provided by another subjectivity, field, or discipline, psychology's scope is limited to the experience of the psyche as it is prepossessed by the patient's ego, on the one hand, and by it own naïve subject here/object there empiricism, on the other. Now it is important to add that the otherness that I just mentioned is for psychology always to be grasped as an internal other. Jung's studies of medieval alchemy, for example, though they involved much delving into antique manuscripts in the manner of objective scholarship, were ultimately about his psychology's presenting itself to itself as alchemy.[26] In a book of my own, likewise, I once reflected psychology

---

[23] C. G. Jung, *Visions: Notes of the Seminar given in 1930-1934*, ed. Claire Douglas (London and New York: Routledge, 1998), p. 14.

[24] Jung, *CW* 16 § 190.

[25] For more on the difference between the naïve expectation of experiencing the soul immediately and accessing it via such reflective modes as study, amplification, and seeing-through, see: Giegerich and Henderson, p. 269.

[26] For a fuller discussion of Jungian psychology's existing as an internal tension with the subject matters that it meets itself as and thinks itself through, see Giegerich, *CEP* V, pp. 371-373.

into itself in the mirror of the allusions that Freud and Jung had made in their writings to the law and the courtroom, as for example when Jung compared the individuation process to "an endless inner trial in which [one] is his own counsel and ruthless examiner."[27] And it is the same with the papers we present to each other at our conferences. Inspired by such diverse subject matters as music and the moon landing, modern technology and the nuclear bomb, each of these has ultimately to do with the soul as psychology producing itself, freshly and anew, via what I like to call a speculative heuristic. "We are not as naïve," writes Giegerich, summing up this stance, "as to want to take on the soul directly. We have understood that psychology is the study of the reflection in some mirror and not the study of *what* the mirror is the reflection *of*."[28]

Before I yield the podium to Dr. Giegerich for his keynote address, I only want to add that I am reminded by what I have had to say to you this morning, and by the title of our conference, of a dream of Jung's reported by him in his memoirs. In this dream the great psychologist finds himself at the grail castle of Arthurian legend. Excited by the prospect that, glory of glories, the ceremony of the grail is to be celebrated there, in one scene of this dream, which is of especial pertinence in our present context, Jung finds himself standing before a trellis that is affixed to the lower wall of the castle. This trellis, as he describes it, was made of "black iron artfully formed into a grapevine complete with leaves, twining tendrils, and grapes." Further to this

---

[27] Jung, *MDR*, p. 345.

[28] Giegerich, *CEP* IV, p. 132. With the metaphor of the reflection in some mirror, Giegerich intimates what is meant in our literature by the term "logical negativity." In a related passage, he explains that psychology's "only subject is the soul's speaking about itself. […] *Every* topic has (and has to have) fantasy or soul character in order for it to be a psychological topic, regardless of whether it is considered an empirical reality or as something transcendent. Psychology is concerned with the mother image, not with real mothers, with the motif of the virgin birth, not with virgins that give birth, with the fairy tale dragons, not with whether dragons exist, with myths of the underworld, not with a real underworld, with the God idea, not with an objectively existing (or not existing) God." (Giegerich, *The Historical Emergence of the I* [London, ON: Dusk Owl Books, 2020], p. 299.)

At intervals of six feet on the horizontal branches were tiny houses, likewise of iron, [which were] like birdhouses. Suddenly I saw a movement in the foliage [he writes]; at first it seemed to be that of a mouse, but then I saw distinctly a tiny, iron, hooded gnome, a *cucullatus*, scurrying from one little house to the next. "Well," I exclaimed in astonishment to the professor [with whom I'd been conversing], "now look at that, will you ...."[29]

What in Jung's dream is imaged as tiny birdhouses affixed to the lower wall of the grail castle—do these correspond to the privileged domains of the various sciences and disciplines that psychology transgressively ventures into due to its having no delimited field of its own? And the little hooded gnome jumping from one to another of these, does he, by the same token, not correspond to that patient of Jung's who, as we heard, was compelled by an impassioned heart to break into the observatory? For, surely, though Jung refers to him literally and on the objective level as a patient he had to deal with in his psychiatric practice, for us who read Jung, this youth may also be taken subjectively,[30] as a figure in Jung's text that is reflective of the fiery, exuberant, boundary-crossing impulse that is operative in his approach to psychology as a psychology with soul.[31] And in this

---

[29] Jung, *MDR*, p. 281.

[30] Even as, somewhat relatedly, Jung speaks in another context of his discovering that in him "[…] the small boy is still around, and possesses a creative power that I lack […]" (*MDR*, pp. 173-174).

[31] For a literary parallel, recall how in Peter Shaffer's play, *Equus*, an aging psychiatrist inwardly grapples with the envious longings he feels for the passionate life of a troubled youth who, it was discovered, would ride out on the moors at night, naked in the moonlight, on horses he'd stolen from a nearby stable. In a manner comparable to Jung's account of the patient of his who broke into the observatory, the ecstatic night rides of this youth are yet another way of depicting how, in the course of our studies, the soul in us, as we heard from Giegerich, may have already caught fire by what we have been inspired by, but do not as yet explicitly understand. How important it is, this carrying of the *un*understood in ourselves, no matter how sophisticated we may over time have become! How important, likewise, that care be taken of the youth in us who, against the materialistic prejudice of our times, and in the manner of such figures as the dummling in fairy tales and the Parsifal of the Grail legend, reads what he reads and studies what he studies because he wants to know the soul! Now I put it this way, referencing

connection, let us recall again Jung's statement about how as psychologists "We disturb and anger the theologian no less than the philosopher, the physician no less than the educator; we even grope about in the fields of the biologist and of the historian."[32]

In the final sequence of his dream, the movement of the hooded gnome scurrying from one little trellis-house to the next becomes Jung's own as he prepares to swim across a channel that divides the island in half. Housed on the other side of the island, the grail awaits. Jung's task, he realizes, is to fetch it back.[33] Giving an ear to the

---

the care that should be taken, to make a connection to Giegerich's teaching about our needing to impress upon our patients, and ourselves as well for that matter, that the way we are, our nature, so to speak, with all its gifts, weaknesses, vulnerabilities, and flaws, is like a ward that we are responsible for looking after (see: Wolfgang Giegerich, *Neurosis: The Logic of a Metaphysical Illness* [London and New York, Routledge, 2020], pp. 380-381; see also, Wolfgang Giegerich, *What Are the Factors that Heal?* [London, ON: Dusk Owl Books, 2020], pp. 84-85). And further to this, my deeper point is that this also applies to psychology as a theoretical pursuit. By this I mean (and here again I draw upon a passage from Giegerich), that the psychologist *as psychologist*, even if he is one of those who works with experiments, questionnaires, statistics, and the like, has also to acknowledge and care for the fact that what has attracted him to the field is "the promise of learning the secret of the soul" (Wolfgang Giegerich, *What Is Soul?* [New Orleans, LA: Spring Journal Books, 2012], pp. 20-21).

[32] Jung, *CW* 8 § 752. Here for the sake of balance we may additionally ask if there are currents in Jung's thought in which what he boldly affirms as psychology's disturbing and angering the theologian and the philosopher, etc., perpetrates an offence against his own field of psychology. Put another way, are there times in which his trespass into another field of inquiry, like his youthful patient's trespass into the observatory, is delusional? The answer here is, yes, when it comes to Jung's having allowed himself to become concerned with God as a literal reality in the ontological sense, when his business as a psychologist, as he well knew much of the time, was only with the question of what ideas and images of God and the gods reflect about the soul. (See: Giegerich, *CEP* VI, pp. 189-199.) Also pertinent and helpful in relation to this issue is Giegerich's stipulating that the dialectic of transgression, wherein psychology meets itself in and as its own other, has the character of "sober frenzy" (*The Soul's Logical Life*, pp. 258, 267).

[33] I have glossed over the detail, not pertinent in our context, that there is a twist in the dream. In its second half, the figure of Jung discovers that

presentations we shall be hearing at this conference, surely this is an apt figuring of our task here as well—not in the literal sense of bringing back the grail of olden times (Jung well knew that we cannot turn back the clock[34]), but in the sense of delving just as passionately into the topics and subject matters of our present world and finding into the soul of our own times thereby.

Introducing the Keynote Speaker

I have now the pleasure of inviting our keynote speaker to the podium. As the honorary patron of our society, which for more than a decade has been dedicated to the reception, appreciation, and stewardship of his immense contribution to Jungian psychology, Dr Giegerich hardly needs any introduction. I will only express to him, once again on behalf of our membership, how wonderful it is to have him with us for this event. Most of us, I am sure, have devoted many years to the study of his writings. Not only has the sheer volume of his works kept us busy, but the value of each one as well. As readers we are repeatedly drawn back to his writings. For me, the comparison that seems most apt is to that of listening to great works of music and to the viewing of great works of art. Just as we attend performances of the same time-honored symphonies again and again, so in a quiet hour and with a strong cup of coffee in hand, do I give myself over to one or another of his seminal texts. How many times have I read *The Soul's Logical Life*? How many times, his essay on Kafka's *The Penal Colony*? I don't know, I've lost count. And I am sure we could go around the room, introducing ourselves to one another, just by telling each other which essays of Dr Giegerich's we treasure most.—Why, it is quite as if we have learned from him a new kind of reading, some of us, likewise, a new kind of writing. Ordinarily, we read and write about our topics and subject matter as objects in front of ourselves, that is, from a more or less safe distance. But as Dr. Giegerich avers, psychology only exists in the

---

the grail is not presently in the castle, but in a small, uninhabited house in the North of England. His task, he realizes, is to fetch it back in time for the ceremony that is to be celebrated that evening (See: *MDR*, p. 280.)

[34] "One cannot turn the clock back and force oneself to believe 'what one knows is not true'" (*CW* 11 § 293)

first place through the inquiring mind's reflexively subjecting itself to itself in the objects of interest it meets itself as. Illustrative of this is the example he gives of the mythical hunter, Actaion, who, when he comes upon the Goddess Artemis bathing in the wilderness, is turned into a stag and torn to pieces by his own dogs. Something like his happens also to the reader of Giegerich and to the writer of texts in our field. Or, not to them, *per se* (though it may certainly feel that way), but more profoundly still to the conception of psychology they had hitherto assumed. Regarding this, let us call it, dismembering moment of truth, Giegerich declares that "[…] it is not just Actaion (or you or me) […] that moves into the forest. It is our psychology as such, its logic, that subjects itself to its own inherent necessities and to the complexities of its inner essence."[35] A radical insight! Actaion, the mythical hunter, is "the soul itself *as* human psychology approaching *itself* as truth."[36] His dismemberment, likewise (and ours as well as we study and read) is indicative of the fact that for a truly *psychological* psychology our very notion of soul and of the whole enterprise of psychology must be put at stake on each interpretive occasion. For as Giegerich explains (and this is the crux of what I want to get across in connection to our esteem of him as a psychological writer), the wilderness of interiority in which Psychology, in the manner of an Actaion, encounters itself in its truth, only *is* "if and when psychology totally (with *all* its hidden underlying assumptions […]) subjects *itself* to the process of a radical self-experience, which on principle must be allowed to overthrow any or all of those assumptions. Nothing must be exempt [he continues]. There is no wilderness, if the very idea of soul and psychology is not constantly at stake […] in every concrete psychological issue that is up for discussion."[37] And to this I would add, no PDI conference at Berlin's Crown Plaza Hotel either.

But here we are, about to listen to Dr Giegerich present to us on the topic of "Interiority and Accomplished Modernity." Putting ourselves and our psychology at stake yet again, please join me in welcoming him to speak to us now.

---

[35] Giegerich, *The Soul's Logical Life*, p. 214.

[36] *Ibid.*, p. 212.

[37] *Ibid.*, p. 211-212

Interiority and Accomplished Modernity

WOLFGANG GIEGERICH

The answer to the question of this conference, "Where is Soul?," could be given in the one word: nowhere. And the name of this nowhere is interiority. But what exactly is interiority? As a criterion that allows us to distinguish between when interiority has truly been achieved and when not, we can use Jung's dictum that for a truly psychological dream interpretation "behind the impressions of the daily life—behind the scenes—another picture looms up, covered by a thin veil of actual facts."[1]

The difference between "the impressions of the daily life" and "the other picture that looms up" points to the difference between two kinds of seeing as two fundamentally different styles of relating to reality. They could be illustrated by the difference between how a modern chemist and how a medieval alchemist would perceive the same chemical phenomena. The chemist as representative of the first kind of seeing will see the processes as the positive facts of the interactions of chemical substances. The adept, on the other hand, would view the same processes as a spiritual mystery and see in them, for example, the appearance of a green lion, or a salamander frolicking in the fire.

The first kind of seeing perceives nothing but the external looks, the shape, color, etc. In order to understand what the second kind of seeing is that gives us "the other picture" and takes us into interiority, let us examine a very special example, the event of a man's suddenly falling in love at first sight with a woman.

---

[1] C. G. Jung, *The Visions Seminars*, Book One, Zürich: Spring Publications, 1976, p. 8.

When this happens, the man is instantly flung out of his ordinary sense of life. In this moment he does not just see, with the first kind of seeing, this woman's external looks, her possibly existing beauty and erotic attractiveness. Such an external observation could not suddenly disrupt the conventionality of ordinary life. Rather, what happens to him is that he is struck by the flash that comes to him from her unveiled soul or innermost essential being. Indeed, we must here not shy away from admitting that what really flashes up for him is nothing less than the other person's *divinity*, nor must we sort of euphemistically play down the outrageous sense of this word by, for example, claiming that this is "*of course* only a manner of speaking." The divinity has been *seen* by him, although probably unbeknownst to him, because consciously he in all likelihood merely feels its emotional effect.

The *seen divinity* is what gives to the experience of falling in love its mind-shattering power and catapults him into the status of interiority or into the land of soul. Being hit and penetrated by the radiating shine coming from the woman's ultimately divine soul, he knows himself as being known by her soul and at the same time has also seen her innermost truth. Empirically he and she are two. And yet for him they are not two because in his status of interiority they are in one another. The factual (although only *subliminally* occurring) revelation of the divinity of the other person as her ultimate truth represents for us the supreme paradigm for what Jung called the looming up of "the other picture."

Usually, we view experiences of love as emotional happenings and attribute them to desire. The love I am here concerned with is, however, a strictly *cognitive* event, an event of a *true meeting*. He sees and *knows* her soul in its unveiled truth. The fact that this cognitive event is also accompanied by and results in powerful emotions does not change its primary cognitive character.

When speaking of a "true meeting," I do not mean the *psychic* meeting of the *two persons*, for then an unrequited love could not be a true meeting. What I mean by the phrase "true meeting" is the *psychological*, "diagonal" meeting of the one *person* with the *divine truth* of *the other* person.

Falling in love is an event of cognition or seeing that is in itself self-contradictory. One's *seeing* the other person's soul *comes* exclusively as one's *being* seen by the penetrating shine or gaze radiating from the other soul. In the second kind of seeing, one's forward-looking gaze is *contra naturam* not allowed to live itself out, to find its natural fulfillment by simply recognizing what is objectively to be seen. Instead, it is within itself *checked, halted*. This astounding possibility of the self-inhibition on the part of a person's impulse, instinctual desire, or general outward orientation against its natural course, here the self-inhibition of the first kind of seeing, is the human animal's singular distinction. Through this self-inhibition the forward-looking gaze is, as it were, dammed up and thus driven back deeper and deeper into *itself* so that its nature changes. It turns into a *recursive* forward looking. What this change of its nature, this its becoming in itself recursive, amounts to is that the second kind of seeing is now *pure receptivity*, free of any volition or desire. It is openness precisely for the inner *unknownness* of what is before one's eyes, for its innermost essential being or soul, for its inner *infinity*—in other words, for what according to Jung is "behind the scenes."

Having by means of the example of falling in love demonstrated what interiority in itself is, we can now turn to interiority in the *opus magnum*, the history of the objective soul. But before we get to it, we first need to clarify the nature of the human world-relation.

The moment *Homo sapiens* appeared on the stage of the world, he was the *existing* psychological difference, namely, animal *and* human, or biological organism endowed with psychic faculties *and* soul. That he is animal and has a psyche are empirical facts. But that he is truly human, that he is soul and that therefore he is fundamentally *more* than an animal is not an empirical fact. His being human, being soul, is given by nature only as an empty logical form without semantic filling, only as a mere promise or *calling*, a *transcendental* reality. *Homo sapiens* is in himself incomplete. He has to *create* his own humanness in the course of history and thereby himself bring about his missing completeness.

What it means to have his humanity only as an empty logical form is that *Homo sapiens* logically *extends a priori beyond himself*, outside of himself. He exists as self-transcendence. But where could this extending beyond himself go? It could only go to what there is beside himself, to the natural world. With his empty logical form of soul, the human animal has *logically*, *psychologically* a priori reached out over external reality and therefore overarches it.

The *human* animal and nature out there are consequently from the outset mediated with each other; *they* both have their place within this mediation. This in-ness in the mediation is what constitutes interiority. Only from outside himself, from his interaction with the world, can Man's empty form of soul receive its semantic filling and precisely not from within *himself*, not, for example, from his so-called unconscious. The content of his own essential being, his own humanness, has to *come* to him from the world of nature as a veritable subject that speaks to him and sends its gazes into him.

I claim that from the outset archaic Man's entire mode of being-in-the-world was that of what I called "the true meeting." Since the empty form of his innermost essential being overarches the world, he could not help looking into the world with "the second kind of seeing," that is, a looking from the stance of pure receptivity, the stance of openness precisely for the *unknownness* of the things in the world, for their *soul*, their inner *infinity*. And because Man's soul has *a priori* overarched the world as such, the things of nature would gaze at him and he would find himself struck by "*their* other picture": by the thing's inner divinity gazing at and into him. Thus, during those early ages, Man inevitably experienced numerous gods, demons, and nature spirits, indwelling in the trees, rivers, mountains, winds, the sun and moon, etc., as their own ultimate truth.

Originally, gods were, however, not permanently existing other-worldly beings who *sent* these gazes. Originally, they were only momentary flashes coming from the earthly things *themselves*. As Kerényi has pointed out, the *name* of the Greek god "Zeus" referred to the event of a momentary *flaring up of a light*. Only later did this name take on the meaning of the permanently existing originator of and behind this flashing up.[2] And Heidegger, connecting etymologically the Greek *theós* (god) with *theáomai* (to gaze at, behold), viewed the gods generally as *die Hereinblickenden*, the ones who gaze into our ordinary life.[3]

---

[2] Karl Kerényi, "*Theós*: 'Gott' auf Griechisch," In: *Idem, Antike Religion* (München: Albert Langen, 1971), pp. 207-217, here pp. 210–214.

[3] Martin Heidegger, *Heraklit*, Gesamtausgabe, vol. 55 (Frankfurt am Main: Klostermann, 1979), p. 8. See also: *idem., Parmenides*, GA, vol. 54, *ibid.* 1982, pp. 152 ff.

Animals, as exclusively *natural* beings, know only the first kind of seeing. During a thunderstorm they may certainly witness flashes of lightning and possibly be startled or scared. But nothing *gazes* at them from within these empirical flashes.

Because our discussion circles around the gazes coming from the inner divinity of things and the gods in them, we might be tempted to classify this whole topic of the archaic experience of "the other picture" under the rubric of "religion." But then we would fall for "the impressions of the daily life," for what it meant *for the people.* But we as psychologists must see "the other picture" behind this "religious" surface appearance, must see what the archaic experience of the world objectively means from the soul perspective.

Using modern sandplay therapy as a model, we could comprehend the ritual practices and mythology as a whole as the unwitting production of "sandplay pictures." Does not John Keats' statement, so important to Hillman: "Call the world if you please, 'The vale of Soul-making.' Then you will find out the use of the world,"[4] does this statement not sound like another formulation for the sandplay-like work of the semantic spelling out of Man's own other transcendental half? We call this ongoing production of Man's "sandplay pictures" the history of *culture.* The cultural process is a building of "castles in the air," in the *non-existing* sphere of the soul's logical life, the sphere of interiority, *but*—and this is what makes it sandplay-like—with a foothold or anchor in the empirical reality of the natural world.

For psychology the *true meeting* of Man and World has to be its theoretical starting point. We cannot begin with the one of the Two, the human individual. Only then has psychology truly taken its place in *interiority.* True interiority is not inside. It is above the heads of people in the height of the a priori mutual entwinement of Man and World. The soul has *two* parents, the human mind and the nature of the world.

Now I come to a historical revolution: the rise of monotheism in ancient Israel. It amounts to an epochal change. Again, as psychologists, we must here not simply fall for "the impressions of the daily life" by taking over the believers' self-understanding and

---

[4] James Hillman, *Re-Visioning Psychology* (New York: Harper & Row, 1975), p. ix, quoting H. B. Forman, ed., *The Letter of John Keats*, London: Reeves & Turner, 1895, p. 326.

thus see the appearance of monotheism as a *religious* phenomenon. As Jung told us, in its images, the soul is speaking about *itself*, and so I say that by means of creating such a fantastic idea as that of a monotheistic God, the soul *does* something to *itself*.

The idea of the monotheistic God must *psychologically* not be read as a theoretical claim, but as the soul's formulation of a *program* for its future. This is so because the crucial point of the emergence of the monotheistic God is that he is the soul's invention of a world-*external* creator of the *world*. Now the soul has all of a sudden dared to *think* a point outside of the whole, outside of its own containment within itself. The monotheistic God is the first dawning of the concept of an Archimedean point. By means of it the soul wishes to rise above itself, to catapult itself out of its original status of interiority. Now that human life as sandplay production has been given an external producer of the sandplay, the cosmos-*external* Creator of the universe, the previous interiority as the intricate in-one-another of Man and World is, in principle, over.

Keeping my model of sandplay production in mind we also see that there cannot be any "sand" and "toy figure" to represent *this* God in the sandplay picture. Indeed, this God comes even with the explicit prohibition to make a graven image of him. Such an image would be visibly present in the world and thus undermine his own essential distinction: his being a pure *thought* without worldly substrate.

From God's point of view, the natural world is now logically on principle encapsulated, "pocketed," indeed, no more than a toy version of the world. Nature as "Mother Nature" has been rendered obsolete.

But practically, *for the people* in ancient Israel, these changes were for the most part still only *semantic,* just a new belief system. The *syntax* or *logic* of life, Man's interiority in the world, did not really change much.

The syntactic realization of the monotheistic program required, centuries later, another epochal change, the appearance of Christianity. In it the soul articulated a new program, that of the incarnation, God's becoming man. Today, I unfortunately do not have the time to describe the Christian revolution with its two phases, the medieval and the early-modern one. So I just indicate, all too briefly, what the final result reached during the early-modern period was, which ended at the time of Hegel and Schelling. It had brought about the autonomous I as *thinking*-substance and existing concept. With this I, the project of the incarnation and indeed the project established with the idea of the monotheistic God had become fully realized, because in the form of this I the world-*external* Archimedean point existed now in man *living on this real earth.*

In addition, the I had also become the Lord of the gaze.

The period brought about by the soul's Christian epochal change was not simply *followed* by a new period. Rather, it had itself explicitly brought about its own *conclusion*. Such a conclusion *is*, however, *in itself* already the next epochal change: the change to modernity.

At the end of the early-modern period the soul could feel absolutely *elated* since it had arrived at its goal. But then, when it woke up the next morning and had to face the coming day, it found itself thrust into the modern world, and felt in a hole. Why? I list four reasons.

(1) Having as I at long last *become* the Archimedean point, modern Man had lost his *having* an Archimedean point or Pole Star for itself to orient itself by in life.

(2) Man's transcendental essence having actually arrived in him, he had also lost his *purpose and direction*. Now, he could no longer expect any higher and essential fulfillment to come to him from anywhere.

(3) Having already come home to him, Man's transcendental truth did no longer reach out over the world, with the consequence that now *fundamental otherness* ruled over his world-relation. For the I as the world-*external* Archimedean point, the natural world could not be anything but radically other; nature had now logically turned into the realm of positivistically apperceived physical facts in their naked materiality and thus as open to unrestrained exploitation. Man had lost the interiority in the mediation of Man and World and along with it his *containment in meaning*.

(4) The function of the monotheistic God as the Archimedean point had been to syntactically serve as a lever to lift Man out of his archaic containment in interiority and install him in the new *modern* world-relation of fundamental otherness. But by now, God had done this his work, so God could go. In fact, logically he had already gone. No longer: *Vocatus atque non vocatus deus aderit*. The loss of God, however, meant that existence had lost its metaphysical *ground*.

On account of all these losses (of ground, orientation, purpose, containment in meaning) a gaping abyss had opened up for *modern* Man. The 19th century called it nihilism.

But in truth, this abyss exists only for a consciousness that is *not adapted* to the new reality, and it is not adapted because it keeps clinging to the pre-modern expectations. In itself, the epochal change to modernity is simply the flip-flop-like switch from interiority to externality and from the primacy of the second kind of seeing to that of the first kind of seeing,[5] to Man's new world-relation in terms of positivism.

Contrary to people's initial feeling of having lost all direction and purpose, the *opus magnum* that the soul pursues in modernity is still determined by a clear goal-directedness and purposiveness, merely a different one from before. In fact, modern Man is even propelled forward by an enormously powerful force in the direction of externality. All love and passion of the soul flow to the physical world in its materiality and positive facticity. We could perhaps even speak of a deep *devotion* in the religious sense, but one of which Man is systematically kept unwitting. De-votion had an original downwards sense, it meant, before a battle, a commander's consecrating himself together with the whole enemy army to the underworld. Seen in this light, the motto, taken from Virgil, under which Freud placed his *Interpretation of Dreams* could with some justification be said to be the secret motto of the soul's program in modernity: *Flectere si nequeo superos, Acheronta movebo.* Stripped of its mythologizing *façon de parler*, this quotation clearly expresses the resolute switch away from the commitment to higher spiritual ideas and divine powers to the new devotion to naturalistic causes and mechanisms, to externality in general.

There is in the modern world indeed such a passionate downwards orientation, namely, an ever deeper immersion in the material world, in physical reality, above all through physics, biochemistry, nanotechnology, down to the smallest particles and even beyond all particles. With constantly accelerating speed science and technology are swept forward by an immanent will that wants to get to the end.

---

[5] Rather than how people experienced it, namely, as the flip-flop switch from the early-modern elated feeling of fulfillment to the modern feeling of loss, emptiness, and of an abyss.

The end, the ultimate goal, seems to be for the mind to become able to synthetically produce life and to understand (or even go back behind) the Big Bang, in order to bring about, in empirical Man, an approximation of the knowledge and technical skill that would at least in principle enable him to re-create the world—in short, to have in this way, at least in principle, caught up with the idea of the Creator God.

The same passionate downwards drive is also at work in Man's self-relation. Man nowadays feels the strong need to view and define himself as (higher) *animal*, as biological organism and individual body, as naked ape, as in two thirds of his DNA-sequence being closer to chimpanzees than to gorillas. His deepest effort goes to his understanding himself from beneath, in terms of biological evolution and physiological processes, and to explain all his higher functions (such as empathy, consciousness, language, thinking) strictly naturalistically, be it neurobiologically from the brain, or be it as the evolutionary further development of rudimentary functions in animal precursors, or be it as natural results of early Man's social behaviors in response to practical necessities.

Externality as radical otherness of Man and World even surpasses itself in Man's *outsourcing* some of *his own* most precious distinctively human faculties. In remote sensing, the modern I delegates its own "being the observer-standpoint" to satellites and their sensors, and in the automation of processes and in robots it delegates its own "being subject" and "being self-determined, self-responsible," to external machines. Through "Artificial Intelligence" apps Man unburdens himself of his own faculties of thinking and being artistically creative, a tendency that amounts to a kind of de-selfing on the part of Man and to a celebration of externality *per se*. Even the self as such of Man is logically externalized into the ephemeral, utterly superficial selfies.

While *semantically* seeing himself more and more as decidedly earthborn, Man has *psychologically* already left the earth. Psychologically he has now his real home in Virtual Realities[6] and in outer space,

---

[6] The difference of Virtual Reality from the world of the mind and the imagination is that Virtual Reality aims for *experiences by the senses* and thus depends on physical devices like Head-Mounted-Displays. It also involves the bodily interactions of the experiencing person. The mind, however, although dependent on the audible or silent sounds of language, uses the

although according to "the impressions of the daily life" he is obviously still living on this planet. By the same token, he longs to be swept away by strong emotions and to get into an altered state of consciousness in order to find self-oblivion. Even in practical reality, the natural world as a whole is increasingly becoming replaced by a technically produced artificial world. As the New Testament says: "Behold, all things are become new" (2 Corinthians 5:17).

I started this presentation with the assertion that the answer to the question, "Where is soul?," could be: "nowhere," and that the name of this "nowhere" is interiority. Now I must modify this statement by adding that it is only true for the bygone past. In modernity, *the soul* is precisely present in the "nowhere" or absolute negativity of the force that drives human existence ever deeper into externality and the sensory.

No doubt, there is also one exception: the discipline of interiority. But this interiority is a methodologically produced one, not an interiority as a mode of being-in-the-world prevailing as a matter of course. That nowadays interiority has to be methodologically produced confirms that the discipline of interiority is itself under the rule of externality.[7]

And then of course, modernity is also a time and a fertile field that lets sprout up numerous political, religious, spiritual, and psychological movements promising deeper meaning or salvation. Formally, they may give a place to interiority. But they are not in the service of the soul. They are clearly the ego's response to the challenges presented by the

---

sounds only as a kind of springboard to push off from, and, negating them, frees itself precisely from this sensory basis so as to enter and exist as the dimension of spirit and meanings.

[7] Here we might remember Jung's crucial insight that psychology as a scientific field became only possible as well as necessary as a consequence of the disappearance of religion or metaphysics as a living and lived reality, we could in our context also say, the disappearance of interiority as Man's mode of being-in-the-world in the Western world. Jung's insight holds true for all three types of psychology: (1) the positivistic and technically oriented psychologies; (2) psychologies as ersatz religion and consolation for the loss of meaning; and (3) psychology as the discipline of interiority.

modern reality of the objective soul and cater to the subjective emotional needs or longings of people's psyche.

$\boxed{\textbf{2}}$

Where is Human Dignity in Modernity?

PETER WHITE

Where is human dignity in modernity? It is an interesting question and indeed, when casting a look around the world today, one that seems to demand an answer. Being back in Berlin for the first time since the inaugural ISPDI conference in 2012 brings the topic into sharp focus. At that time, I attended a concert where a unique confluence of cultural threads came together in a beautiful expression of music in a performance of Beethoven's 5th symphony by an orchestra comprised entirely of Israeli and Palestinian musicians, a performance given in a venue originally built for the 1936 Olympics, the Waldbhune amphitheatre. Such a poignant gesture toward a real desire for human dignity, setting aside the very worst and striving only for the very best in one of humankind's greatest works of art! And now, here in 2024, despite the continued performances of that orchestra and the endless beauty of Beethoven's music, the old conflicts have erupted anew and one gesture that marks the difference between 2012 and 2024 is a May 5th report of pro-Palestinian protestors appearing at a yearly Jewish memorial march at the former Auschwitz death camp.[1] As individuals we have many thoughts and feelings about these ongoing conflicts and the political and cultural attempts to resolve them. But none of that is of any concern to our purpose today, which is to ask how, in the concept of human dignity, is the soul in modernity talking about *itself*? Not I as an individual

---

[1] Rafal Niedzielski and Vanessa Gera, "The yearly memorial march at the former death camp at Auschwitz overshadowed by the Israel-Hamas war", Associated Press, May 7, 2024, https://apnews.com/article/poland-march-of-living-auschwitz-a7996e224bb4be1c76059b6fafbbd19d.

asking what human dignity *means* to *me*, not mankind as a collective asking what it *means* to *us*, but what *is* human dignity from the standpoint of *soul*. It is only by asking *this* question that we can explore how human dignity is seen from the standpoint of psychology as the discipline of interiority and, from there, begin to determine "where" human dignity is in modernity.

Now, my stipulating that what people think and feel about human dignity in relation to world events is of no concern to a psychological stance is a real rejection of what seems natural, and this in itself is an affirmation of an important methodological principle of soul-making, that it is an *opus contra naturam*, a work *against* nature. When it comes to interpreting phenomena like dreams or myths, this working against nature or one's natural expectations is well understood. The dream image that presents itself as one thing is really about something else. As Giegerich states in *The Soul's Logical Life*:

> According to JUNG, sexual images must not be taken literally; they are metaphors; they do not necessarily talk about actual sexual behavior, sexual problems, sexual desires and fantasies. For JUNG, the sexual is one particular (and perhaps a preferred) means of expression ("medium") among others for something categorically different [...].[2]

How challenging, though, to think along these lines when our subject matter is loaded with social and political implications. Removing it from its "natural" context feels strange. Nevertheless, it is essential to do so if the human dignity topic is not to be entangled and obscured in externality and ego.

As a musician, I have spent my life working with cords of every sort that are needed to connect one thing to another, and when it is time to set up for a performance there is nothing more disheartening than opening the cord box to see a tangled mess of wires all intertwined together. One learns early on the beauty and benefit of a properly wrapped and secured cord. Likewise, setting ourselves up for a psychological understanding of human dignity will require us to disentangle many concepts that will, if left as they are in our day-

---

[2] Wolfgang Giegerich, *The Soul's Logical Life: Towards a Rigorous Notion of Psychology* (Frankfurt am Main: Peter Lang, 1998), p. 109.

to-day thinking, make it impossible to make a proper connection to our topic.

A first cord we reach for is the concept "I" in modernity, and perhaps to our consternation, when we pull out our hand we find ourselves holding three "I"s, two of these being objective forms called the "modern I" and the "modern ego" and one of them the subjective "I" that we had expected to be there. To disentangle them we have to ask who or what are these "I"s? In correspondence Giegerich explained:

> The modern I and the modern ego are both objective cultural forms, formations, and must be distinguished from me and you as real people having subjectivity and saying "I" when referring to ourselves. We must distinguish between the objective forms and existing people. These forms are not themselves beings. Just like a democracy or absolute monarchy are forms and not beings or entities. These forms transcend us as people. We are in such forms, and to the extent that we are in them, they define us. I as person am, to the extent that I am a truly post-medieval person, in all essential regards inescapably in the form of "modern I", that is, defined by my being the center of my world, autonomous, self-determined, self-governed, etc. As modern I, *I* (the real me) may, however, also succumb to the form of the modern ego in the narrower sense, which is characterized by a narrow, more or less exclusively practical-technical, utilitarian (and thus "soulless") orientation (whereas the modern I as such is much more open, can have a much wider horizon, multiple perspectives).[3]

For Giegerich the modern I has the potential for a soul perspective of human dignity, that is to say, as a purely negative or conceptual truth, whereas the modern ego, being a form that is " [...] incompatible with soul [...],"[4] can only conceive of human dignity as a positivity that must have empirical consequences. The former is reflected in the first sentence of the German constitution which states: "The dignity of man is inviolable"[5] The latter shows itself in the second sentence of that document, "To respect and protect [...]

---

[3] Personal email, April 18, 2023.

[4] Personal email, April 4, 2023.

[5] German Constitution, Art. 1, Sec. 1.

[human dignity] shall be the duty of all public authority."[6] The first of these reflects the stance of interiority while the second indicates a view rooted in externality.

When human dignity is viewed from a stance of externality instead of interiority, it is conceived as an aspect of man's concrete, positive reality. One may ask, what is wrong with that? In a reality moulded by modern science and thus a positivistic relationship between idea and the "real world," it seems natural, even an obligation, to test any claim against its supporting evidence. But for Giegerich human dignity is an idea, a concept, and as such, not thing-like, but logically negative, and because of this, nothing empirical-practical is to be derived from it.[7] Accordingly, interpreting human dignity in terms of particular human rights, as pleasing as this is to the ego, eclipses the modern I, the objective cultural form that has the capacity to comprehend human dignity in its proper, negative-only sense.

Reaching into our cord box of concepts once again we pull out "human dignity" only to find that it is inextricably fused with another cord, the idea of the finite insignificance of man or, as Giegerich often says quoting Jung, man's being "*only* that!". Returning with *these* "cords" to our concept of "I" we have to say that there are two aspects of being an "I" with human dignity in modernity. On one side there is man as infinite worth and on the other is man as finite and insignificant. The two aspects are equiprimordial in that one does not appear without the other. If one insists only on the worthlessness of man, one is denying human dignity. Likewise, if one insists on human dignity as the only reality, one is in denial of the worthlessness, the contingency, and insignificance of man. If one is seeking to reject the insignificance of man, then it is imperative to prove such an idea wrong by making human dignity real, which is to say, empirically real.[8] From this perspective, that of the modern ego, any empirical evidence of human suffering caused by other humans, or even by humans who

---

[6] *Ibid.*

[7] Personal email, April 4, 2023.

[8] If one possesses human dignity *a priori* with birth, the insistence on proving this to be so is a neurotic project of "carrying coals to Newcastle". This leads one to suggest that the irritation in Giegerich's comments about human dignity come from seeing a neurotic defense portraying itself as the highest good.

suffer at their own hand, as in drug addiction, is interpreted as an intrusion of the unacceptable idea of the worthlessness of man, an intrusion that must be countered with human dignity. But the *idea* of human dignity is not sufficient. The modern ego requires *proof* that the worthlessness of man does not exist and that his dignity does. The means to achieve this and thereby make it real are through rights enforced by laws that in turn produce visible, verifiable proof that human dignity is *not* equiprimordial with human worthlessness. For our task of circumambulating the concept of human dignity to determine how, in it, the soul is talking about *itself*, we will not reject the concept of man as finite and insignificant, as being "*only* that!", but embrace it as an essential aspect of the dialectic within the modern I.

Circumambulation: Approaching the Interpretation of Human Dignity as a *Psychological* Phenomenon

Having taken some steps to work these concepts free from their entanglement in externality and the ego, we can now approach the question of "where" human dignity is in modernity from the standpoint of interiority. A primary task for our method would be to work with an image, the goal being to make explicit the dialectical concept which is imagistically implicit in a dream, myth. or other cultural fragment. But with human dignity we are not working with an image but a *concept*, and furthermore, it is a concept that is one half of the dialectic that makes up the concept of the modern I, the other half being the finiteness or insignificance of man. In *The Soul's Logical Life,* by contrast, it is the *image* of Actaion, the hunter dismembered by his own dogs after seeing the naked goddess Artemis, that is shown to reflect the killing nature of psychological cognition. In describing this movement from the imaginal to thought, Giegerich says, " […] we have to *think* the image, to unfold its inherent complexities and to penetrate into its own logic."[9] In the dialectic depicted in this myth, the encounter with the naked truth is simultaneously the moment of one's current level of understanding being torn to pieces. The old way of thinking has become no more than food for the sustenance of the new. In this way the ancient

---

[9] Giegerich, *The Soul's Logical Life*, p. 125.

myth reveals the true nature of psychology. That is, the nature of soul in modernity as logical life. But there are examples of psychological analysis that has worked the other way around. In his paper "The Burial of the Soul into Technology," for instance, Giegerich takes the most indicative phenomenon of modernity, technology, and reveals it to be the explicit realization of the Christian incarnation, the notion of the union of spirit and flesh having become the union of pure thought and earthly, concrete realness. There is a shining example of this union in the cell phone that is sitting in most everyone's pocket at this moment, the union of "spirit" in its Hegelian sense as thought and "flesh" in the sense of its being empirically real. But interpreting human dignity in modernity in this way, as the explicit realization of an image from the pre-modern era, seems to be a closed door when one considers the recent dispute between Giegerich and Barreto. In this exchange of ideas in *Human Dignity and the Garden of Eden Story*, Barreto's thesis is that human dignity *in modernity* is linked to the *imago Dei* of the Garden of Eden story, where man's dignity was rooted in his being created in God's image. This idea was countered by Giegerich's claim that: "To try to derive the *modern* idea of "human dignity" from the Bible (Gen. 1:26-27) is as illumining as trying to derive the modern physics concept of atoms from the atomic theory of the ancient Greek Presocratics Leucippus and Democritus, or as insightful as explaining modern science psychologically (archetypally) through the Greek mythological figures Apollo and Heracles."[10] With these cautions and concerns in mind, let us nevertheless circumambulate the concept of human dignity in modernity, listening for what it has to say about itself as a psychological concept.

Regarding human dignity strictly as a soul phenomenon, Giegerich writes, "Human dignity is the last retreat or asylum of the *former* 'God' (or 'the Absolute'); it is the result of the Absolute's having been swallowed, incorporated by, or interiorized into, Man (i.e., the *definition* of man, not into man in his positivity). And this definition is what turns man into the modern I."[11] Here is a

---

[10] Marco Heleno Barreto and Wolfgang Giegerich, *Human Dignity and the Garden of Eden Story* (London, ON: Dusk Owl Books, 2024), p. 31.

[11] Personal email, April 4, 2023.

statement that is compelling, and yet, a complete mystery for those of us thinking from an everyday standpoint that is shaped by an empirical, scientific worldview and the ego with its needs and wishes. A first step towards thinking from the soul perspective is to note that the sentence does not talk about the individual person and their dignity, but rather, the dignity of *Man* with a capital "M," indicating thereby that the reverential capital traditionally used for "God" has been transferred to "Man." From this we would conclude that Giegerich's statement is saying that the phenomenon that for millennia gave itself the form of the gods and the Absolute of metaphysics has come down to earth with the result that the human now has the burden and responsibility of *being that* dignity as his innermost essence. If so, one would say that human dignity is the sublation of the notion of God.

This means that human dignity is not just another abstract concept but a true soul phenomenon, differing from past forms, such as the forms of the gods or God, in that it is only negative and conceptual, with no tangible or imagined aspect. For a mythological consciousness the gods were a tangible reality, inhabiting and infusing special places and objects. In the monotheistic religions, God was an intangible reality made real through the efforts of faith. In modernity, human dignity, the sublation or interiorization of God into man, is neither in a tangible object or an intangible image. Rather, it is one instance of what Giegerich calls the Notion, the life of the soul as it is in modernity. The phrase that expresses this "something" that is intangible but also not nothing is "logically negative." Human dignity is more than a simple abstract concept because it is the *sublated* form of the polytheistic gods' tangible presence and the monotheistic God of faith. If we are to speak of a "tangibility" of human dignity, it is in the realness of the feeling in man that emerges when he is faced with its opposite, as Giegerich pointed out in *Human Dignity and the Garden of Eden Story*: "For a fully modern and normal person it is impossible not to *feel*—as ego-personality!—that torture is an outrage, although several hundred years ago people just as honestly really *felt* that torture was legitimate. The real feeling has changed."[12]

---

[12] Barreto and Giegerich, *Human Dignity and the Garden of Eden Story*, p. 58.

From this we can see that while in Christianity God became man, in modernity, man became human dignity. In Christianity, the soul in the form of God begins to come home to itself by becoming man in Christ, whereas in modernity, God evaporates and man becomes, not God, but human dignity. For an analogy we could say that if the concept of God were the Internet, the modern situation is characterized by the entire Internet having been "downloaded" into man in such a way that, through the downloading process, the Internet as a possible concept has disappeared forever.

In Christianity, "infinite worth" and "dignity" were qualities belonging exclusively to God. Man, by contrast, could never claim them as the result of his own efforts. As Giegerich showed in *The Historical Emergence of the I*, Martin Luther proved the impossibility of man achieving sinlessness through exhaustive mental and physical effort.[13] Only through faith in the God who possessed it could man receive sinlessness through redemption and then only as a gift of grace *from* God. In Christianity the gap between man and God was eliminated by the bridge of redemption. This bridge, however, was not expected to produce a utopia of infinite worth and dignity here on earth. It was rather a promise to be fulfilled after death or here on earth only in some far distant future. In our post-religious world today, the modern ego's inability to think the unity of the unity and difference of man's being infinite worth and finite insignificance re-creates a simulation of the gap formerly resolved through grace and attempts to bridge it by making human dignity observably real. This leads us to ask: Is there no relationship between human dignity and "the real world"? As Giegerich explains, the only relation is one of self-relation, taking place purely within the precincts of the individual in their subjectivity.

> I believe that the only possible kind of rightly understood empirical-practical consequences of the transcendental idea of human dignity is the internal and strictly personal question addressed to *myself* as subject, myself as I (not as ego): "Is my intended or already

---

[13] Wolfgang Giegerich, "Young man Luther's terrible spells of religious anguish and the soul's construction of the modern 'I'" in *The Historical Emergence of the I: Essays about One Chapter in the History of the Soul* (London, ON: Dusk Owl Books, 2020), p. 35.

performed behavior in accordance with the infinite core of my being, my own inner infinity called 'human dignity'?" This question and my answer to it stay within my own mind. The question determines the consistency/inconsistency of my *empirical* view or thought of the transcendental idea of my human dignity with my *empirical* thought of a certain possible behavior. Thus no trespassing from the transcendental to the empirical.[14]

In a world "gone wild" with ego demands by individuals who hold others accountable for blocking or denying their full experience of human dignity, it is exceedingly difficult to imagine this self-accountability of the modern I ever becoming the natural state of things, but as Giegerich pointed out in the introduction to *Soul Violence*, such uncertainty seems to be the nature of soul change:

> Just like life in biological evolution, so the soul in its historical movement progresses the hard way, via many errors, losses, victims, much waste and senseless suffering. No easy shortcut, no master plan, not the direct ideal route to the goal, indeed no clear-cut goal at all, but only a restless stirring and rooting of the spirit toward higher levels. What the alchemists called "nature" and we call the soul or the objective psyche is not impressed by what is right or wrong, by what we think is reasonable and just and want to prescribe for its development.[15]

Interiorizing Human Dignity—The Soul's Coming Home to Itself

As we circumambulate our topic, we return afresh to Giegerich's statement: "Human dignity is the last retreat or asylum of the *former* "God" (or "the Absolute"). It is the result of the Absolute's having been swallowed, incorporated by, or interiorized into, Man."[16] The incorporation of the God that man had always beheld or looked upward to *into* man himself recalls the following statement from *What Is Soul?*:

---

[14] Personal email, April 4, 2023.
[15] Giegerich, *CEP* III, p. 19.
[16] Personal email, April 4, 2023.

[...] the soul wants to come home to itself and to human consciousness. It wants to be known as human consciousness itself rather than being only known as and revered as contents of consciousness ('projected' into nature, the cosmos: the polytheistic gods, the demons, and nature spirits; or into transcendence, as in metaphysics).[17]

If one inappropriately literalizes these statements, the idea sounds utopian, a reality where every human lives as the embodiment of, and gives freely to all others, dignity. For psychology, by contrast, "coming home" is always a double move whose other side is ruthless and permanent death or expulsion. This not as a terrible mistake or tragedy of hubris, but simply how the logic of the soul *is* in itself. In Giegerich's interpretation of the myth of Actaion in *The Soul's Logical Life*, for instance, the hunter's encounter with truth in the form of the naked goddess is logically simultaneous with his being attacked and dismembered by his own dogs. Likewise, in *Human Dignity and the Garden of Eden Story* he says that the garden's being a "paradise" arises only as the expulsion *from* it, that only the departure from innocent, unconscious being makes consciousness of that innocence possible and then only as "Paradise Lost." Stating this in a way that shows the simultaneity of this inner logic or dialectic, Giegerich writes: "The strongly felt *loss* of Paradise *is* in itself the childish illusion *and* the awakening from it."[18] Seen from this perspective, the modern ego's project of human rights as the literal abolishment of man's insignificance appears as a hunter who wants to see the naked goddess and escape unscathed or as an Adam and Eve who are determined to somehow stay in the paradise they have been expelled from.

So, we see that human dignity does not arise as a singular phenomenon, but in its unique, modern formulation has a companion. Equiprimordial with the soul coming home to itself as the infinite worth of human dignity, is man's finitude and worthlessness, his being *"only* that!" While the ego is unconsciously compelled to act out and literalize these concepts, the modern I is a stance that reflects humility,

---

[17] Wolfgang Giegerich, *What Is Soul?* (New York: Routledge, 2012), p. 320.

[18] Barreto and Giegerich, *Human Dignity and the Garden of Eden Story*, P. 41.

on the one hand, and an understanding of dignity that is not empirical, but logically negative, on the other hand.

> Through the present-day empirical display of a decided lack of dignity [...] modern man (as ego-personality, as empirical man, civil man) shows himself to be driven to tacitly, unwittingly, unconsciously express his in truth being "only that!", being nothing but human-all-too-human, indeed, his being ultimately worthless (e.g., the fashion of deliberately dressing in torn jeans, of proudly celebrating ragged clothes, dumpiness), while at the same time in his conscious and explicit self-image/self-definition insisting on his literal infinite dignity, his absolute worth. This is to my mind the false way of being modern man and displaying the equiprimordiality of the two sides of the same coin (the merely unwittingly acted out [and thus defended-against] truth of the "only that!", in fact, of one's being worthless AND the conscious but inflated and thus false sense of dignity.) The proper way, I think, would be one's conscious living that truth (the "only that!", etc.) as an attitude of humility on the level of one's self-understanding as empirical man, on the one hand, AND a transcendental and thus legitimate sense or knowledge of infinity, on the other hand. [19]

If the interiorized former God produces man's human dignity, how is it that the same interiorization results in his finite worthlessness or insignificance? Why can man not have his logically negative human dignity and eat it empirically, too? One might say that it seems counterintuitive for such a noble realization to be accompanied by its opposite, like dropping a pail of mud into beautiful crystal-clear water. It is more accurate to say that it is counter-*ego* for both extremes to emerge together as equiprimordial aspects of the I in modernity.

To say that Man is finite and worthless, a human without significance who is "*only* that!," is an anathema to ears steeped in seventy-six years of staunch rejection of such a notion, 1948 being the year of the United Nations "Declaration of Human Rights." How can we hear what man's finite worthlessness has to say, how do we open such a door without succumbing to the idea that doing so is nothing

---

[19] Personal email, April 22, 2023.

but acquiescence to evil deeds without consequence? A first step is to understand that, being dialectical, the modern I's twin aspects of infinite worth and finite worthlessness do not exclude each other but rather *are* each other. One way of saying it: Man's consciousness of his transcendental human dignity is itself the consciousness of his empirical insignificance. To say it yet another way: The modern "I" is the dignity of being, as human-all-too-human without religious or metaphysical "garments" of meaning, the objective, concrete expression of mind in the empirical world.

Core and Nakedness

As Giegerich states in *Human Dignity and the Garden of Eden Story*, within the concept of human dignity we find two images, core and nakedness: " […] [human dignity] is decidedly *born man's* metaphysical core, the *metaphysical* core *of* man in his *metaphysical nakedness*."[20] The adjective "metaphysical" serves to remind us that these definitional qualities of man are logically negative. They are transcendental in the sense that they are not earned or developed but come with birth in modernity. In correspondence, Giegerich further clarifies that " […] [n]akedness means: without cover, coat, external containment, living in an utterly meaningless world. Core means: deepest inner essence."[21] By definition, a core is deep within, "the central, innermost, or most essential part of anything."[22] Human dignity is not just some attribute or mental appendage of modern man, but is the innermost, essential part of him. Without outer layers and skin to surround and protect it, a core cannot survive, and neither can they without it. In a piece of fruit like a peach the core is covered by a layer of flesh and a protective outer skin. Likewise, the concept that is at the core of a way of thinking is covered by the theoretical writings that give it form and is protected by a layer of arguments against those who would reject its validity. The cover or coat that is absent in *man's* core of human dignity is *meaning*, for being metaphysically naked he lives "in an utterly

---

[20] Barreto and Giegerich, *Human Dignity and the Garden of Eden Story*, p. 59.
[21] Personal email, April 4, 2023.
[22] *Dictionary.com*, s. v. "core," accessed June 10, 2024, https://www.dictionary.com/browse/core.

meaningless world."[23] Modern man has no "flesh" or "protective skin" because the former "God" of religion and "Absolute" of metaphysics that he had been contained within have been interiorized into man himself. In the world of nature it is not possible to exist as a naked core, an exposed core cannot support life. But for man, the creature whose very nature is to be *contra naturam*, this is precisely what he is today, a core without any covering, dignity without the meaning formerly supplied by the gods and classical metaphysics. How can this be? Dignity would seem to require a meaningful world. Indeed, one would think that it is dignity that *gives* the world meaning and that a lack of dignity is the sign of a world built on only greed and selfishness, the ego "gone wild," so to speak.

When one considers the etymology of the word dignity, it quickly becomes clear that its contemporary meaning regarding the intrinsic worth of every person is found only in modernity and primarily in the second half of the 20th century.[24] Giegerich states in *Human Dignity and the Garden of Eden Story* that the root of today's conception of dignity lies in Christianity's emphasis on the individual and the concern for the fate of one's soul: " […] we have to see ultimately behind […] [human dignity] the infinite, absolute worth that Christianity gave to the individual soul: Each soul counts; Christians have to be, each individually, vitally concerned about their personal salvation."[25] In ancient Rome, by contrast, the word *dignitas* had the meaning of worth but it was not possessed by everyone. Rather, it was a mark of distinction where those with *dignitas*, whether through personal reputation or by holding an office, such as senator, held a higher rank and authority than their contemporaries.[26] In this context, dignity is a designation that, when given, marks that person as having a certain, special status while the undignified are simply those with no special significance, with nothing that sets them apart. If all people have dignity with birth as they do in modernity, if everyone holds the distinction of infinite worth, dignity ceases to have a meaning, it

---

[23] Personal email, April 4, 2023.

[24] *The Stanford Encyclopedia of Philosophy (Fall 2024 Edition)*, s. v. "Dignity," by Remy Debes, accessed June 12, 2024, https://plato.stanford.edu/archives/fall2024/entries/dignity/.

[25] Barreto and Giegerich, *Human Dignity and the Garden of Eden Story*, p. 60.

[26] Debes, "Dignity."

cancels itself out. If dignity is the core of man, then it is impossible to have a human without dignity. And not only is its worth universal, but it is also *infinite*. Being without a sense of rank or distinction, human dignity finds its Other only in man himself simultaneously being its opposite and not just partially but fully so in his being also finite and insignificant.[27]

Without a metaphysical covering or coat, there is nothing that modern man can point to that would give him significance beyond himself. This is the fallacy aspect of human rights which, seen from this stance, is exactly the task of insisting on man's significance by creating an infinite project of proving this to be so. In light of what we are saying about the images of nakedness and core, human rights is the attempt by a naked, vulnerable core to manufacture a thick skin for protection, but because the attempt is rooted in a neurotic defense against man's being "*only* that!" the "skin" just keeps expanding with more needs for more rights while getting thinner and thinner in the attempt to be infinite. The alternative is modern man's sober self-understanding that equiprimordial with his transcendental infinite worth is his empirical finite insignificance, that is, his being "*only* that!"

---

[27] The correspondence of this to the theological "equation" for the nature of Christ, his being simultaneously one hundred percent human and one hundred percent divine, does not go unnoticed here.

3

The Sky Ladder, Heinrich Schütz, and Searching for the Arcane Substance

PAMELA J. POWER

Part One

In his book *Coniunctio,*[1] Wolfgang Giegerich engaged a key concept in the psychology of C. G. Jung. Giegerich argues that the *coniunctio* is impossible in the logical status of modernity. We live in a "flat earth" status and do not look to the heavens any more except as a destination for rocket ships, telescopes, and further space exploration. "It is impossible today,"[2] writes Giegerich, because soul has moved on, is departed and now manifests in technology, science, commercialization, and profit making. Of course, *coniunctio* is a general term meaning joining together. What Giegerich refers to as impossible is the connection between heaven and earth, between the soul dimension and the earthly dimension, the unbridgeable "psychological difference" between the *Opus Magnum* of soul and the *opus parvum* of ordinary human life.

This idea makes itself visibly clear in the documentary about the firework art of Cai Guo-Qiang who, over 12 years, attempted to make a fireworks Sky Ladder.[3] He tried to pull it off but failed in Bath, England, in 1994, due to rainy weather; in Shanghai, in 2001,

---

[1] Wolfgang Giegerich, *Coniunctio: Reflexions on a Key Concept of C. G. Jung's Psychology* (London, ON: Dusk Owl Books, 2021).

[2] *Ibid.*, p. 129 ff.

[3] Sky Ladder: The Art of Cai Guo-Qiang, Documentary (Netflix, 2016).

because of safety concerns after 9/11; and in Los Angeles, in 2012, because of danger of wildfires. The project was finally successful in his hometown, Quanzhou, in Fujian Province, China, in 2015.

The fireworks Sky Ladder was a dream project for Cai, about which he said, "I realized art could be my space-tunnel connecting me to the universe. But the purpose wouldn't be for me to go to space but to create a back-and-forth dialogue in between."[4] This sounds like he wants to resurrect Jacob's Ladder, that classic image from Genesis 28:11-19 in which Jacob dreams of angels going up *and* down a ladder from heaven to earth. It is the nature of art to attempt to create a connection to something that is beyond the human, personalistic realm, to stir the universal from the personal. But as impressive as the Sky Ladder may be, that's all it is, impressive. It is a fantastic experience that lives in the moment. All we are left with is a smoky sky, an apt image for the departed soul.

I contrast Cai's Sky Ladder with "Saul, Saul, was verfolgst du mich?,"[5] a song written in the mid-17th century by Heinrich Schütz an Italian-influenced German Lutheran, and the most famous Baroque composer before J. S. Bach. One hears a "ladder" of voices climbing from low to high. It is the voice of God confronting Saul on the road to Damascus, "Saul, Saul, why do you persecute me? It is hard for you to kick against the goads" (Acts 26:14, NIV) This powerful music describes the moment, in Acts 9 in the New Testament, that initiated the conversion of Saul, persecutor of the Christians, to St. Paul, the proselytizer for Christianity.

During the time of Heinrich Schütz (1585-1672), Jacob's Ladder was fully functional in the logical status of consciousness. The up and down movement of angels depicting the connection of heaven and earth was where "soul was at." Whereas for Cai, who works in the flat-earth status of today, there is no Jacob's Ladder, no already made connection between heaven and earth. And while there is impressive artistic success in making his sky ladder, it doesn't connect to anything, it is left hanging up there, by an invisible prop, a stand-in for heaven, that eventually fades away. It was a trick, an illusion. We could say, in the strict sense, that there was no *coniunctio* for Cai, but

---

[4] *Ibid.*

[5] Heinrich Schütz, "Saul, Saul, was verfolgst du mich?, " SWV 415, Kantorei Barmen-Gemarke, (Nonesuch Records H-71134, 1960).

yes for Schütz, but only because the connection between heaven and earth was at that earlier time still intact. *Coniunctio* was possible. Seeing the image of the Sky Ladder, even the successful attempt, brought the point Giegerich makes in his book, *Coniunctio*, squarely home.

Music was thought to be given by the gods to humans, who in return created music to honor the gods. Humans sent music back up to the heavens, thus continually maintaining the connection from earth to heaven. Mozart, metaphorically speaking, was a composer who rained out of heaven, producing music of divine beauty. By contrast, Beethoven, an earth-bound composer, labored and struggled with his work. He reached another dimension when he became stone deaf. Only then was he able to write music that was truly divine. Today music is, for the most part, entertainment, emotional manipulation, and a purely horizontal matter. But there is something about music that is more than just a "memory" of previous times, as when we see art and artifacts from previous eras in our museums. Music has a unique ability to create a powerful echo of Jacob's Ladder, a connection to heaven from earth. Sometimes when I listen to that moving piece by Heinrich Schütz, I feel the urge to convert 'on' the spot!

Part Two

In 2020 I read a review[6] in the *New York Times* of a video game called "The Last of Us."[7] My curiosity was sparked, and within a year, that curiosity turned into action. I found a way to play that game on a refurbished game console. Being a complete beginner, I was at first utterly unable to play the game. So, I played easier games to hone my skills, most notably "Stray,"[8] a postapocalyptic video game, where the gamer plays as an orange tabby cat. But it was "The Last of Us"[9] that I fell in love with and eagerly wanted to play. It is

---

[6] M. Isaac and C. Dougherty, "Two Gamers Played 'The Last of Us Part II.' They Were Blown Away," *New York Times*, June 19, 2020.

[7] Naughty Dog, "The Last of Us, Part 2" (Sony Interactive Entertainment, 2020).

[8] Blue Twelve Studio, "Stray Video Game" (Annapurna Interactive, 2022).

[9] Naughty Dog, "The Last of Us, Part 1" (Sony Interactive Entertainment, 2013).

a postapocalyptic game in which the world has been ravaged by a fungus that infects the brain and turns humans into creatures whose only purpose is to infect others. Ellie, an obnoxious, foul-mouthed teenage girl, has become infected with the fungus, but rather than succumbing to the disease, she becomes immune. This is discovered by a survival group in the east of the US, who make it their mission to get Ellie to a group of doctors in the west so they can attempt to make a vaccine from her. That's the whole game. Getting Ellie to the west and making the vaccine, a world-saving substance that will cure humanity of this plague. Joel, a hardened smuggler, is hired to protect Ellie and to escort her across the country, and while doing so, he must contend with groups of the inflected creatures or gangs of violent people trying to survive the chaos into which the country has fallen.

Ellie's infection is an inoculation that has made her immune to further infection. This creates a problem. What remains of the government has made a device that tests to see if someone is infected. If the meter indicates positive, the person is killed on the spot, because quickly they will "turn" and seek to infect others. If Ellie is caught by the authorities, she will test positive and be killed. She must be protected, and her status of immunity kept hidden.

Several things in the game grabbed my attention. Being steeped in alchemical imagery, I immediately thought about *Mercurius duplex* and the poison/panacea paradox of the "arcane substance." I was also reading Wolfgang Giegerich's *Working with Dreams*,[10] in which he described the structure of dreams. Some have a fairytale structure while others have a myth structure. A myth is, in its narrative style, the unfolding of one soul truth, whereas the fairytale structure has a beginning, a journey, and a conclusion.

When thinking about the story of my video game, "The Last of Us," I saw it as having a myth structure, although the action seems like a fairy tale. My initial thought was that it was the unfolding of one soul truth: *soul negating itself*. The cordyceps fungus was soul negating itself. An actual fungus converts something that is already dead or dying and folds it back into the earth to be renewed. It is a

---

[10] Wolfgang Giegerich, *Working with Dreams: Initiation into the Soul's Speaking about Itself* (London and New York: Routledge, 2021), p.138 ff.

compost system, breaking down already dying material so it can rejuvenate life. A myth interpretation of the video game suggests that the current status of consciousness is dead, or dying, and it being sublated to a new one. At the end of the game, Joel successfully brings Ellie to the doctors, but when he discovers that the doctors are going to use Ellie's brain, rather than her blood, to make a vaccine, Joel rescues Ellie from certain death. There was, and continues to be, lively controversy outside the game on various forums as to whether Joel did the right thing. He has been accused by most of being selfish, caring more about his personal feelings for Ellie than about saving humanity.

Ellie's status of being infected by the fungus, but at the same time being immune, made me think that this is the position one is in when one has, so to speak, been infected by soul as we think about soul in psychology as the discipline of interiority. Then one takes in that soul has moved on, that we are left behind to learn from soul in the Real. One must let go of fantasies of progress, betterment of humankind, fantasies of "wholeness" and the idea that personal individuation can save the world or in any way play a role in the soul's *Opus Magnum*. Those ideas are logically dead. But in many Jungian circles, it can be dangerous to speak of soul in such terms. You'll be considered positive for the plague that will destroy Jungian psychology.

And there is no vaccine to cure soul from where it has gone, or what it is about. No cure to bring it back, to restore soothing fantasies of hopeful progress. Considering this idea, the search to make a vaccine was a search for fool's gold, not a search for the true "arcane substance."

If one is infected by soul and develops an "immunity," this means being fully conscious of the soul dimension as definitively separate from the human dimension. This is the recognition of the "psychological difference." One becomes immune to the lure of the archetypes and to seductive ontologies. One can be aware of the soul in the Real without being pulled into all the alluring aspects or idealizations that soul has to offer in technology, science, and AI (artificial intelligence).

The "arcane substance" today is mindedness and thinking that has moved beyond the subject-object split, beyond imagination to thought, to reflection and reflexivity. But here's the thing about the arcane substance. There is no search for it because "it" is already here, not as a positively existing thing, but as methodological possibility. One must, so to speak, acquire the ability to see it, so to speak, hear it, feel it. That's a bit of what Ellie is a personification of. It is what Giegerich calls the "psychological I." And while the arcane substance is already here, it still *always* is and remains the "treasure hard to attain."

Ellie is highly valuable because her immunity is singular. The fungus, as soul, has become incorporated fully into her being. The fungus recognizes her as part of itself. She is a personification of the *coniunctio*, within the mythology of that video game.

I think when you "get it" about the soul as negation (i.e., about soul negating itself, or again, as the internal logic of soul) and it isn't just an interesting set of ideas, then it dawns on you that there is no going back. You can try, but you may bruise yourself kicking against the goads, as in that music piece by Heinrich Schütz. You may suffer, become blind for a while, as happened to Saul on the road to Damascus. You may be disoriented for a long time, then maybe eventually relieved that the soul dimension has reached you. It has opened the eyes to see and the ears to hear. I do not mean soul as in the *Opus Magnum* soul, but the soul way of thinking, that is always there, but difficult to find. We don't make it an ego project; it reaches us. This *coniunctio,* as a process, is possible *within* a person, not as a positivity but as a dialectical process of being negated, of becoming soul stuff, so to speak. It's like being a fish, but knowing one is a fish, knowing water and living in water, and knowing one is a fish living in water.

Something else that impacted me from playing "The Last of Us." Soul is not nice. We already know that soul's progression throughout history has been brutal and violent, but playing the game, even though it is "just" a game, brought this reality closer. Although I understand well why the word "soul" is used, it has a religious and mythological carryover that gives it positive, poetic connotations. Sometimes I prefer "objective psyche," or "autonomous psyche." As such, I can more easily comprehend that it has its own agenda that is expressed in and through the human psyche, through human activities and culture, whether one knows it or not. We are unwittingly caught up in soul's negation of itself, soul's wanting to know itself. "The Last of Us" shows from a strictly human perspective how devastating, cold, and brutal soul can be. The deadly, dangerous, and terrifying agenda of the objective psyche that is negating itself is expressed well in this video game, and the necessity to fight it is completely understandable. Most of the game is fighting against the change that is happening, killing the people who are infected with the fungus and who are increasingly dangerous, the longer they have the infection.

Now, here I need to stress that these ideas about this video game, "The Last of Us," are purely my own, and nothing I have read gives me any indication that any of this was in the minds of the game's creators. It seems to me that they created a dream myth without knowing it. I fell in love with this game, even obsessed with it, feeling something of value in it. I saw it as more than *just* another in the genre of zombie apocalypse movies and video games. But the value was in my own process of thinking that was set in motion by the game. I saw meaning where there was perhaps no significant meaning, certainly no soul meaning, only meaning to me as my ideas about it emerged and developed.[11]

A more likely, and conventional, understanding of this video game is that it is one out of hundreds of movies, stories, or video games in which humans must fight and ward off hordes of zombies, aliens, or other "low life" creatures. Could their popularity mirror the human struggle against its own destructive, anti-human nature, or even represent the state in which people lose their individual minds to a mindless collective emotional functioning? In this sense, those games and movies are a mirror of collective consciousness but unrecognized as such. My "depth" of understanding of "The Last of Us" and the meaning I see in it are a mirror of my interest, love, and devotion to depth psychology and the methodologies of psychology *with* soul.

Part Three

Ten years ago, at the International Society for Psychology as the Discipline of Interiority conference in Berlin, I spoke about Jung's stages of the *coniunctio* as described in *Mysterium Coniunctionis*.[12] Jung

---

[11] See in this volume Wolfgang Giegerich, "Interiority and Accomplished Modernity," pp. 1-11.

[12] C. G. Jung, *CW 14*.

derived them from the works of Gerhard Dorn, an alchemist and philosopher whom Jung understood as one who viewed the "alchemical opus" as being "spiritual and moral as well as physical."[13] Stage One, in Dorn's scheme, is the achievement of the *unio mentalis*, a status of consciousness that is a mental or spiritual counter pole to the purely naturalistic, the *unio naturalis*. Jung wrote that this achievement then creates a dissociation between mind and nature, requiring a second procedure that joins the *unio mentalis* to the body that has been left behind. In that earlier paper, I argued that the second stage, joining the *unio mentalis* back to the body to create the Jungian Self, was a personalistic interpretation that blurred the "psychological difference," i.e., the difference between soul's *Opus Magnum* and the *opus parvum* of the individual. The *unio mentalis*, I wrote, is an ongoing process of overcoming the *unio naturalis* in the logical life of soul's *Opus Magnum*. I suggested that that the second stage really means the achievement of the dialectic that continues to negate and sublate the imaginal, literal or naturalistic rather than creating the ontological Jungian Self.[14]

The *unio mentalis* as mindedness, consciousness, is a union of mind with emotion. Emotions have a natural affinity with the body, but with work they can be compelled to join with the mind. This is no small achievement, as one can easily note how emotion and feeling are conflated and thought to be the same thing, and generally they are lived as the same thing. This suggests that until feeling as a rational function is separated from emotions, there can be no access to feeling as "bridge to the soul," as Giegerich describes it.[15] Emotion doesn't connect to soul because emotions are an ego matter, whereas only feeling can apperceive and connect to soul.

The necessity and importance of the second stage of the *coniunctio*, rejoining the *unio mentalis* to the body, doesn't arise until the dissociation between them has been achieved. This is extremely

---

[13] *Ibid.*, § 118.

[14] Pamela J. Power. "'The Psychological Difference' in Jung's *Mysterium Coniunctionis*," in Jennifer M. Sandoval and John C. Knapp, eds., *Psychology as the Discipline of Interiority: "The Psychological Difference" in the Work of Wolfgang Giegerich* (London and New York: Routledge, 2017).

[15] Wolfgang Giegerich, "Psychologie Larmoyante," *CEP 4*, p. 510 ff.

important because otherwise there is no access to the "truth hidden in the body," as Dorn described it.[16]

The procedure of combining ingredients must be done very meticulously because if the *unio mentalis* is brought too carelessly together with the body, they will simply *smoosh* back together and revert to the *unio naturalis* undifferentiated nature. All the spiritual, i.e., genuine psychological, status accomplished in the *unio mentalis* might be subsumed back into concerns of the body, i.e., the personalistic and literal.

The stages of the *coniunctio* as described by Jung drew my interest once again because of the following question. Given the methodology of soul, for those who value psychology and the psychological, how does one retain the achieved *unio mentalis* when confronted with human issues that threaten to undermine or undo that standpoint? There may be a collapse to the *unio naturalis*, in which the emotions revert to join the body. But if the *unio mentalis* is regained (through negation and sublation), it can create a higher status of itself, further work off the naturalistic understanding, and thereby increase psychological thought. For this situation and its dangers, I could well understand the careful procedure of creating the special "joining substance."

The process of creating the joining substance begins with distilling "a certain heavenly substance hidden in the human body."[17] It is thought to be an imprint of God, "the truth" and "the panacea," to which other ingredients are added. What could this heavenly substance, the *caelum*, be other than the *possibility* of consciousness, mindedness, i.e., the imprint left by *soul*, departed as it may be? This truth is the soul truth, which can be ignored, unknown, or recognized. One can also think of it as the organ of feeling that Wolfgang Giegerich describes as the "bridge to the soul." It can mean, with development of that feeling, the ability to recognize soul in the Real, about which Giegerich writes: "The adaptation of consciousness to the soul (that is, the inner logic) of the Real in its present form is tantamount to the achieving the *coniunctio*."[18]

---

16 Jung, *CW 14*, § 681.

17 *Ibid.*, § 681.

18 Giegerich, *Coniunctio*, p. 127.

I was drawn to play video games during the pandemic. I then found playing helpful when I had to manage difficulties arising in my personal life, particularly my husband's cognitive decline. At first playing my favorite video game, "The Last of Us," provided a helpful dissociation from my awareness of what was happening to him. Later, playing the game helped manage my challenging emotional states. As the video game progresses, the tasks become more arduous and require the player to learn new skills. The parallel in my personal life required me to learn new ways to manage the situation, deal with frustrations, and take on complicated tasks that were new to me. All this along with my work, teaching, writing, and my own aging issues.

The pull to lose my psychological footing had its way many times. When things collapsed into a state of *unio naturalis* during which I might feel a victim of my circumstances or embroiled in emotions of anger, resentment, or helplessness, I worked to recover the *unio mentalis*, rediscover it, allow the negation of purely natural responses, and recover the standpoint of the psychological I. I found that when I could say, paraphrasing Jung, "This situation has everything it needs within itself,"[19] something shifted. I did nothing more than have that thought, which sublated the situation. Then it was not *about* my emotions, the concrete situation, my psychology, my reactions. Those are all sublated by having that thought. It is noticing the logic of the situation that it "has everything that it needs"[20] rather than the logic of self *and* object, of me *and* him, or even me *and* my feelings. The thought is the beginning and the end, the uroboros. That moment of reflexivity, if I can call it that, and other moments like that, are the connection. They are the *coniunctio* that preserves and is the work of the *unio mentalis Then it isn't about the people, the literal situation, it is about the dialectic of consciousness that is at work.*

This thought also includes: "Don't let anything from outside, that does not belong, get into it."[21] This means not to allow facile solutions to be smuggled in. It is not a lateral bringing together of the opposites such as "he deserves compassion, I owe him, he's doing the best he can," as true on one level as they may be. Those

---

[19] Jung, *CW 14*, § 749.
[20] *Ibid.*
[21] *Ibid.*

thoughts make it an ego project. It is as Jung wrote, put the matter into a vessel and then observe it, *on its own terms*. "Give it your special attention, concentrate on it, observe its alterations objectively."[22]

I described the overall myth structure of "The Last of Us" as soul negating itself and from a fairytale structure, it is preventing the fungus creatures from infecting you, as the gamer, and for you to make it to the end of the game. Just as I described the video game as a myth structure of soul negating itself, I felt my internal structures being negated, I was being composted on the inside. I had no choice but to relinquish long-held cherished beliefs and expectations, about how things ought to be, how I ought to be, hopeful fantasies, and instead allow myself to be folded under into a different version of myself. I called it a sublated version of myself. And in this sublated version of myself, the sentence, "I have a spouse with dementia" becomes a speculative sentence in which "the predicate is thrown back on to the subject."[23]

His dementia is a fungus in his brain, composting him, as well. Happy to let go of the demands, ego concerns, and expectations of life, in that way, he is ahead of me, already in another dimension. I try to do things to keep him in my ego dimension, but they are for my ego reasons. I want to find a vaccine to cure his brain, but that wish misses a bigger picture. Being cured is not what he wants. He is already cured. When that thought reaches me, then I, too, am cured.

Playing "The Last of Us" was powerfully protective and probably why I fell in love with the game. It allowed the thinking methodologies of psychology as the discipline of interiority to enter in a deeper way. What was spiritually alive in me was held apart and separate in the proximity of a spiritually dying process as my husband's cognitive decline slipped into dementia. My mental preoccupation with the game, with my thoughts about the game, my thoughts about me as the gamer, protected the life of my spirit.

Not to lose my mind, my spirit, and the methodology of the psychological I, these difficulties require meticulous efforts that Jung

---

[22] *Ibid.*

[23] G. W. F. Hegel, A. V. Miller, trans., *Phenomenology of Spirit* (Oxford: Oxford University Press, 1977), p. 39. See also Greg Mogenson, *Vicarius Animae: Speculative I-Statement in Jungian Psychotherapy* (London, ON: Dusk Owl Books, 2023), p. 80.

described in the second stage of the *coniunctio*. This *coniunctio* is not about creating the ontological Jungian Self, nor what Wolfgang Giegerich describes in his book *Coniunctio*, as connecting heaven and earth, nor any grandiose project of healing the world. It is allowing the ongoing work of the dialectic within the person, working off the personalistic, the personal thoughts, reactions and feelings, making higher statuses of the *unio mentalis*. It is the work of negation that composts the ontological sense of oneself in the *opus parvum*. It releases Mercurius, the "arcane substance," and, notwithstanding the logical status of modernity that precludes such things, it is a kind of miracle.

Consciousness of the inner logic of soul, the soul's logical life, is a possibility in human life, and when it is recognized as "the truth" it can be a sort of "panacea" and is the sought for "arcane substance." This awareness, consciousness of the inner logic of soul, is the necessary beginning and end of the *coniunctio* as it manifests in the human psyche, in the *opus parvum*. It is not the content of my thought but how thought happens. Thus, when I say I treat a situation as a dream or fantasy as Jung described, I allow the alchemical operation to occur without "interfering by conscious caprice."[24]

Within traditional Jungian psychology, much is made of sacrifice or relativization of the ego in the service of "individuation." This is described as making conscious a relationship with the Self, which Jung describes as the God-image or imprint of God within. However, there is no easy exit route for the ego. There must be a structural change that happens, and that is not an "ego project." This is how I understand the stages of the *coniunctio* that Jung described in *Mysterium Coniunctionis*. It amounts to a negation and sublation in which the naturalistic ego is continually changed, narrowed, distilled, and preserved as the Psychological I.

By my thoughts presented here, I do not mean to blur the "psychological difference," rather to preserve it. I answer for myself how being marinated in soul's logic opens a methodology for a person to engage *not* with the Soul's *Opus Magnum*, but via the imprint of soul that is, within the individual, the "arcane substance."

---

24 Jung, *CW 14*, § 749.

4

Modern Technology as Antichrist

JOHN HOEDL

Introduction

Viewed from a psychological perspective, technology can be seen as a reflection of the unfolding of the soul's logical life.[1] In addition to the assistance it provides with respect to the tasks and challenges of practical living, technology "produces," often in a revolutionary manner, new levels of consciousness and is thus a function of the soul's *Opus Magnum*, its great work, in culture and history.[2] From this vantage point, technology is a form of soul-making.

If we begin our examination from the earliest origins of human culture, we can speculate that simultaneous with the primordial appearance of toolmaking (which can already be regarded as a form of technology), the soul gave birth to itself. Assuming that this was indeed the case, then the unprecedented creation of the first veritable tool was also the incisive act wherein consciousness gave rise to itself by opening up for the first time a substantive difference between subject and object, nature and spirit, earth and heaven, and other distinctions of the like.[3]

---

[1] The importance of technology as an essential topic of study for psychology and the soul's movement in culture at large has been demonstrated in the work of Wolfgang Giegerich. See, for example, Wolfgang Giegerich, *Technology and the Soul*, *CEP* II.

[2] In contrast to the *opus parvum* or "small work," which is soul in the realm of individual and personal psychology.

[3] This distinction would eventually be comprehended in Jungian psychology as the difference between consciousness and unconsciousness

In this essay, I will discuss how the consequence of this original Promethean act continues to reverberate even in the technological achievements we live within today and how it laid down a blueprint for successive metaphysical worldviews, culminating in the West with the advent of Christianity. Also to be discussed is how, in a kind of reversal, "the soul" as technology played a significant role in the collapsing of this Christian worldview, clearing the way for the "waking up of the dreaming soul" via the scientific point of view and the Enlightenment. Apperceived by many in terms of such traditional motifs as the Christian apocalypse and the coming of the Antichrist, in these times transpired what Jung called "[...] the splitting of the world and the invalidation of Christ."[4]

The early biblical references to the Antichrist are interpreted here as harbingers of the imminent arrival of a modern, "born" soul and the reformulation of the concept of the divine. This change, already present deep within the soul's logic at the beginning of Christianity, would come to threaten its very core. But ultimately, the demise of the traditional Church was not due to the "Antichrist," i.e., that unfathomable force arriving from the depths of the beyond for the final battle against Christ and the Church. Rather, it was a shift in the logic of the soul and in the minds of Christians themselves, which was brought about by the empirical findings of technology.

Viewed from a psychological standpoint, technology may be understood as a symbol for and "production" of "soul," and as having developed through three stages:

(1) As the means for consciousness's primordial emergence and consolidation in the form of self-reflection and "soul."

(2) As a "tool" for the negation and reformulation of the soul's long-established metaphysical truths, as manifested in Christianity (technology as Antichrist).

---

and by Giegerich as the "psychological difference." For more on the psychological difference, see Greg Mogenson, "*Notional Practice: The Speculative Turn in Analytical Psychology*," (London, ON: Dusk Owl Books, 2024), chapter 2, especially pp. 80-97.

[4] Jung, *Letters 2*, to Father Victor White, 4 November 1953, p. 138.

(3) As a modern expression of the soul's logical depth, as well as a reflection of its desire for, and work towards, a new concept of the divine.

Soul

Soul in the present context is to be understood psychologically, not from a traditional or religious perspective. As I have already alluded to, this conception of soul is a form of consciousness that both preceded and provided the foundation for religious and theological beliefs. It corresponds to Jung's concept of the "objective psyche," which is the foundational basis for the human psyche and personal subjectivity. When describing the objective nature of this level of consciousness, Jung stated that, different from Descartes's famous starting point, "I think, therefore I am" (i.e., I give myself my sense of being through my own thinking), in his view it is rather a matter of: "I am subject to thought, therefore I am" (i.e., I receive my sense of being from an objective thinking that has no thinker). In other words, this is a non-human, objective thinking within which I am contained and have my sense of being.[5] This is one way to grasp what is meant here by "soul."

In other contexts, and in previous times the soul was thought of as a real substance, an existing "thing" or entity. The modern psychological concept of soul, by contrast, contains the essence and spirit of these previous expressions, but in a sublated and interiorized form. Within the discipline of psychology, even though the soul can figuratively appear in dreams, visions, symptoms, and feelings, etc., in its essence it is not conceived of as noun-like or thing-like, but as having the adjectival and verb-like character of a living dynamic, a kind of thinking. Therefore, the word "soul" does not mean our personal, egoic thinking, but an objective, transpersonal thinking that we find ourselves contained within.

Psychological thinking is then the discipline of interiorizing substantive phenomena (i.e., matters referred to with nouns) into the fluidity of a thinking (as processes and dynamics referred to with

---

[5] C. G. Jung, *Consciousness and Unconscious, Lectures Delivered at ETH Zurich*, Vol. 2, 1934 (New Jersey: Philemon Series, Princeton University Press, 2022), p. 24.

verbs), revealing, thereby, their existence as consciousness, which is also to say, as soul. This is what we will endeavour to do with technology as our *prima materia*. In other words, we will look at technology not as a thing in the world invented by and existing for the use of humans, but rather as a "tool" used by "the soul" for its own logical development and self-unfolding.

Technology

The Merriam-Webster dictionary defines technology as: the practical application of knowledge in a particular area. What is interesting for our discussion is the amalgamation of thought (i.e. "knowledge") with something "practical" (i.e., in the empirical world). The unifying of these is a clue that technology should be psychologically interesting. We must keep in mind, however, that psychology is not interested in the literal application of knowledge in factual reality *per se* or how physical tools work in the world. Technology is relevant for psychology only to the extent that it is conceived of as the reflection and location of soul.

Technology is obviously a very broad term and can mean different things in different contexts. The appearance of a single tool, for example, if replicated and dispersed throughout a culture over a long enough time, can become a full-fledged technology and have deep implications for that culture. Just as there are so-called "big dreams" in psychology, there are "big inventions" that have much more impact on society and indicate a larger shift in its culture. Examples include the hand axe, the spear, smelting, the wheel, the printing press, paper, glass, the telescope, the airplane, the Internet, etc. We can also think of technology in a more comprehensive sense, i.e., as the so-called "technium,"[6] defined as: the greater, global, massively interconnected system of technology.

Technology has become so common in our world today and we are in such a symbiotic relationship with it that we usually do not even notice or see it. The perennial worry that technology will one day become too dominant should thus be a moot point by now, because in fact it has long ago "taken over the world." In fact, technology did not have to take over the world because it is due to certain

---

[6] Kevin Kelly, *What Technology Wants* (New York: Viking Press, 2010).

technologies that we experience the world the way we do. As we will observe below, without technology we would not really have a "world," since it was through the invention of a specific tool and its subsequent development into a technology that the soul came to be.

While we have grown so accustomed to the technology around us that we no longer see it, what we do notice is new and developing technology. Arthur C. Clark, author of *2001: A Space Odyssey*, stated that if cutting-edge technology is sufficiently advanced, it cannot be distinguished from magic. If we extend this idea, we could say that technologies that were once state-of-the-art and have now become part of our practical life, have lost their "magic" and become the equivalent of the "dead letters." Psychologically speaking, these older technologies are the former "footholds" of where soul was at one time. Then, after the consolidation and integration of what it wanted to achieve through these particular technologies was complete, the soul used this newly established level as a base from which to move on to something more complex. We will come to an important example of this in a moment, but in any case, we can think of the "magic" of cutting-edge technology as where the soul is active today.[7]

Psychological Necessity

The special relationship that exists between technology and the soul was highlighted by Jung on one occasion in terms of what he called a psychological necessity. The notion came up when someone was showing Jung an ancient Roman toy at a dinner party. After it was agreed that the toy, ascribed to Hero of Alexandria, was basically the combustion engine in miniature, the conversation went to the question of why, if the Romans had the materials and ingenuity to make this engine as a toy, did they not invent a larger and more useful version of it, even a full-blown steam-powered locomotive. Jung's reply was that the development of the toy did not advance further because there was no psychological necessity at that time. The invention of the steam powered locomotive would have to wait until conditions in the Western cultural soul were such that it could exist.

---

[7] The most obvious example of this today is, of course, Artificial Intelligence.

From Jung's example we can surmise that the state of the soul in a culture has a determining effect on the creation and appearance of a technology. In other words, from a psychological perspective, the emergence and development of some technologies are dependent upon and reflective of unconscious variables that may or may not be present in the culture at a given time.

Keeping the psychological dimension of technology in mind helps us not to fall into the trap of thinking that technology is developed only for our own purposes and benefits. In fact, we can perceive technology as having its own trajectory or goals, which it uses us to reach. This view, that technology seems to have an autonomous nature, has been put forward by others, including Kevin Kelly, who has written that technology wants the same thing that life wants, i.e., increasing diversity, sentience, and the ability to generate new versions of itself. "Technology," he continues, "amplifies the mind's urge toward the unity of all thought, it accelerates the connections among all people, and it will populate the world with all conceivable ways of comprehending the infinite."[8]

At the inaugural ISPDI conference in Berlin in 2012, I spoke about the American space program in the late 1950s and how the astronauts, all of them former pilots, started to complain that the rockets they were operating were becoming so advanced that there was not much "flying" left personally up to them to do. The spaceship, they said, basically flew itself. The process was so automated that the flight engineers used to boast, to the astronauts' annoyance, that if given a year they could instruct anyone off the street on how to fly a rocket to the moon. The human element was being reduced, or sublimated, almost to the point that it was the machines and the computers that were flying humans into outer space, and not the other way around.[9]

Also, in that earlier talk, I quoted Norman Mailer who had been hired by *Life Magazine* and embedded in NASA's Apollo 11 project:

---

[8] Kelly, *What Technology Wants*, p. 359.

[9] John Hoedl, "One Small Step for a Man …," in: Jennifer M. Sandoval and John C. Knapp, eds., *Psychology as the Discipline of Interiority: "The Psychological Difference" in the Work of Wolfgang Giegerich* (London and New York: Routledge, 2017), p. 170.

...[I]n NASA-land, the only thing [of real importance] was the technology—the participants were so overcome by the magnitude of their venture they seemed to consider personal motivation as somewhat obscene. [I] had never before encountered as many people whose modest purr of efficiency apparently derived from being cogs in a machine.[10]

Turning to our own time, we can give thought to the psychological necessity prevalent today for humans and technology to have increasingly personal and intimate relationships. Wearable devices continually monitor private data like heart rate, blood oxygen levels, heart rhythms, sleep patterns, steps per day, location, and so on. We think of these new instruments, along with their necessary attachment to the global Internet, as tools that help us maintain better health, be better organized, catch buses and trains on time, get orientated in a new city, and so on. More and more we rely on the "benefits" these technologies have to offer, but increasingly we defer to them. It is no wonder that many of us have become reliant or, in some cases, identified with our smart phones.

Some of us are beginning to feel a bit lost or handicapped without our devices. Ordinary wallets, when they are still used, contain examples of "low-tech" items such as physical cash, credit cards, and identification. These "crude non-technological throwbacks" have now been sublated by the smartphone, which is not only used for identification, but can master a growing number of functions that would have been inconceivable just a few years ago. What the psychological necessity was that precipitated these whirlwind developments, and why it seems important for ordinary people today to carry around a device that has exponentially more processing power than the computers needed to land a spaceship on the moon in 1969, are of course interesting and important.[11] Unlike the spaceship that ferried the astronauts to the moon, we may not be literally carried by

---

[10] Norman Mailer, *Moonfire: The Epic Journey of Apollo 11* (Cologne: Taschen, 1969/2010), p. 220.

[11] According to RealClearScience, the latest iPhone has 100,000 times more processing power than the computer that landed Apollo 11 on the moon: https://www.realclearscience.com/articles/2019/07/02/your_mobile_phone_vs_apollo_11s_guidance_computer_111026.html.

this technology, but we may likely be transported to some as yet unknown psychological destination. In any case, to approach this and other questions in depth, we need to look closely at the beginning of technology and soul, from a psychological viewpoint.

The Primordial Birth of Technology and Soul

We know that objects have been used as tools for eons by animals such as chimpanzees and orangutans and even some birds. A stick could be used, for example, as a weapon or to reach ants or termites to eat, or a rock could serve to crack open a nut for food. Then, at some point in the evolution of humans, our ancestors began altering stones to make them more effective implements. But these actions were still more or less instinctual and therefore cannot be considered within the realm of real tool-making and technology. Eventually, about 1.7 million years ago, there occurred a somewhat miraculous Promethean moment that resulted in the appearance of the revolutionary hand axe. At this moment in history, the first post-instinctual tool was created, and along with it, a new kind of consciousness.

Officially called the Acheulean hand axe, this primordial tool was crafted by carefully and skillfully hitting one stone with a second, knocking off chips and flakes until the desired form emerged, which was at once both fit to its practical purpose and to the hand of its owner. The importance of this tool for the emergence and consolidation of consciousness is shown by the vast amount of time over which it was manufactured. One production site near Saint-Achel in France (the town from which it received its name) was still being used until 100,000 years ago. This would make it not only the first, but by far the most long-lasting technology in history.

Like all technologies, this hand axe had practical uses such as cutting up and filleting raw meat, crushing bones, etc., but importantly, it also had an aesthetic element, highlighted by its being crafted to have a beautifully balanced and symmetrical shape. Surprisingly, with many of these axes, the ratio between their length and breadth corresponded exactly to the so-called "golden ratio."[12] One might

---

[12] The golden ratio, also known as the divine proportion, the golden mean, and the golden section, is approximately equal to 1: 618. It can be found in nature, for example, in the shape of pinecones, certain flower petals,

assume that the shape, harmony, and stability achieved in the physical stone was also simultaneously desired by and produced within consciousness itself.

Looked at from a strictly pragmatic perspective, this axe was quite primitive, but from the point of view of consciousness and the soul, this tool was a game-changer. Practically speaking, new levels of thinking would have been required to create this tool. Not only would higher levels of patience, skill, and focus have been needed, but a new kind of forethought. We can even surmise that some insight into cause and effect, "before and after," would have had to be attained at the same time. Indeed, recent speculations have placed the appearance of verbalization in our ancestors at around the

Acheulean hand axe discovered in Kent, UK

Source: William Page, ed., *The Victoria History of the County of Kent*, Vol. 1 (London: Archibald Constable and Company Limited, 1908), p. 312.

same time. The appearance and development of language here would be a clear indicator of the beginning of a shift, or extension from basic instinctual awareness, towards conceptual consciousness.

One must be careful not to assume that we can faithfully imagine what kind of consciousness was active in whoever made these tools. In fact, we are not even talking about the same species as us; it was our distant hominin cousin, *Homo erectus*, who first mastered this skill. But nonetheless we can speculate, from a psychological viewpoint, that this technology was the implicit soul finding its "edge," so to speak, even as it chipped itself forth from its *prima materia*, or instinctual "mater," creating, thereby, a new reflective dimension and

---

Nautilus shells, parts of the human body, DNA, etc. https://www.math nasium.com/blog/golden-ratio-in-nature. The Acheulean Hand Axe would, of course, be the first time in history that an object following the golden ratio was artificially created.

distinction within itself. In other words, the making of this first tool was the soul's self-generation out of basic biological and instinctual awareness, to a level of self-consciousness that would be the foundation for all subsequent technology and human culture.

When crafted, these tools were seen by the group as being animated with a special power. The material from which they were formed, previously just regular and innocuous stone on the ground, was now imbued with an extramundane spirit or magic. Many axes were found that were too large to have been of practical use, giving the impression that they could have had symbolic or proto-religious functions. It is assumed that just having these out-sized axes around had an enduring effect. Psychologically, they were likely mental prompts for commemorating and consolidating the new level of consciousness that emerged with the revolutionary creation of the smaller, usable ones.

Technology and Myth

As we continue to deepen our understanding of the link between technology and soul, we must now fast-forward many millennia to the age of myth, when a founding story needed to be known about the origin of technology and human culture. We find a beautiful accounting of this in the Greek myth concerning Prometheus. In the beginning of the myth, it is told that Prometheus wanted to help humans. He observed that the animals had their own ways of looking after themselves, but humans were kept in a position of underdevelopment by jealous Zeus. To help, Prometheus stole fire from the gods and brought it to earth. In one version, the fire comes from the sun, giving humans the ability to think in a new, enlightened way. In the second version, which for us is the relevant one, the fire is taken from the workshop of Hephaestus, the god and patron of artisans and craftsmen. The reason for this is that for the early Greeks there was no difference between thinking, *epistêmê*, and making, *technê* (the root of the word technology). It was not until after Aristotle that these two activities or concepts began to separate,[13] but for psychological thinking, they remain a unity:

---

[13] *Stanford Encyclopedia of Philosophy*, https://plato.stanford.edu/entries/episteme-techne/.

thinking is a kind of making, and making is a kind of thinking. Understanding this is important for comprehending technology as the work of the soul.

Martin Heidegger revisited in his writings the ancient interconnectedness between *techné* and *epistémé* and described how they played a fundamental part in defining what it means to be human. He wrote: "Being-human, as the need for apprehension and collection, is a being-driven, into the freedom of undertaking techne, the sapient body of being."[14] Here Heidegger claims that inherent in the nature of being human is the need and freedom to create, which is also to say, of "undertaking techne" or technology. This innate drivenness-to-create, which is part of our human inheritance, results in a technology that is not only technical and practical but exists in the world as a kind of wisdom, or as the "sapient body of being."

Heidegger also looked into the deep and syntactical meaning of technology, past the obvious and superficial advantage it might bring: "Technology is a mode of revealing. Technology comes to presence in the realm where revealing and unconcealment take place, where aletheia, truth, happens."[15]

The Incarnation

What technology reveals, psychologically speaking, is the state of the soul's *Opus Magnum* at any given time in history. For many millennia, the story of tools and technology fit comfortably within the mythological, spiritual, and successive metaphysical worldviews that their original invention helped bring about. The plow, for example, was a gift from Demeter; spears, axes, and other weapons carried the spirit and essence of their owners and their makers. One can think here, for example, of the divine power of Excalibur, King Arthur's sword, or Thor's hammer. Even up to 700 C.E., a warrior, when asked what he worshiped, replied, "Wind, fire, and my

---

[14] Martin Heidegger, *An Introduction to Metaphysics* (Dunmore, PA: Yale University Press, 1959), p. 170.

[15] Martin Heidegger, *The Question Concerning Technology* in: *Basic Writings* (New York: Harper Perennial, 2008) p. 319.

sword."[16] However, a new and powerful necessity was rising up in consciousness that would fundamentally alter technology, religion, and all of Western culture.

From time immemorial, the soul had displayed and celebrated its depth in the rituals and traditions that honoured an immortal and powerful God or gods ruling in an eternal, unending cosmic expanse. This meant that the orientation of the realm of the soul was mostly vertical and celestial; however, because of a radical change that began deep in the soul, this was later to change fundamentally. The advent of a new logic and renewed understanding of the spiritual and divine would have the effect of reversing the previous orientation and would force God to come down to earth and incarnate as a human being. The manifest result of this shift was the Christian doctrine of the Incarnation.

The Incarnation was and remains a radical idea. Not unexpectedly, many Greek philosophers at the time found it absurd. The idea that the divine God himself, who was master of all beings as well as the entire universe, could literally incarnate in one limited human being was anathema to them and their philosophy, and they dismissed the idea as ridiculous. But as it turned out, the doctrine proved to be a powerful and consequential notion. As we know, most of Europe eventually converted, and the Christian notion of the Incarnation took root and flowered over the course of almost two millennia.

One of the consequences of the unfolding and maturation of the concept of the Incarnation was a burgeoning interest in nature and the physical world. After all, if God had lowered himself to the point of taking on corporeal form, then it must be good to appreciate and study the material world around us. This led to improved measurement and analysis of nature and the subsequent invention of tools and technology to support this.

But the interest in and closer examination of the physical world, aided by technological advances, eventually yielded unexpected

---

[16] The belief in technology's divine provenance was still held by one of the most well-known modern physicists, Freeman Dyson, who wrote: "Technology is a gift of God. After the gift of life it is perhaps the greatest of God's gifts. It is the mother of civilizations, of arts and of sciences." In: Erik Brynjolfsson and Andrew McAfee, *The Second Machine Age* (New York: W. W. Norton, 2016), p. 1.

consequences. At some point in time, a perception of reality that adhered to the biblical account of heaven and earth became untenable. This was an unexpected shadow element hidden in the Incarnation, namely, a turn away from the divine element that was supposed to be incarnated into the "flesh" or matter, toward a newfound interest in the physical world. In other words, the "physical" became more compelling than the meta-physical. This shift was initially not exactly anti-Christian, but it would eventually be anti-metaphysical and anti-Christ, especially with regard to Christ as a specially anointed divine figure with otherworldly status and power.

The Antichrist

Here we are concerned with a psychological understanding of the Antichrist and not with what it may symbolize within its original theological and eschatological context. Historically, the image of the Antichrist first appeared in the First and Second Letters of John and in The Book Revelation, all probably written before 100 B.C. It reappeared in the writings of various Christian leaders and theologians over the centuries to describe either a powerful force whose arrival signaled the end of times, or to characterize people and influences deemed a threat to Christianity.

For Jung, the figure of the Antichrist was a compensatory reaction to the overly positive one-sided nature of Christ. He interpreted Christ as a symbol and personification of the *summum bonum*, or highest good, but thought that this represented only one part of the Self and psychological wholeness.[17] This one-sided image of God accentuated all that was righteous and virtuous, but had the effect of creating an imbalance in the Western soul, generating the need for a counterpoint which appeared in the form of the Antichrist.

The image of the Antichrist in this essay is broader in scope in that it is understood not only as the "shadow side" of Christ, as Jung thought, but as an impulse in consciousness towards a reformulation of the entire expression and conceptualization of the divine. It is a

---

[17] Jung thought that the Antichrist was just as much a manifestation of the Self as was Christ. He wrote, "[Christ] corresponds to only one half of the archetype. The other half appears in the Antichrist." (Jung, *CW* 9 ii, § 79).

necessity in the soul to sublate longstanding religious and metaphysical notions in order to restore them with new and relevant living forms.

The biblical figure of the Antichrist is characterized by astonishing and almost inconceivable imagery. These shocking descriptions show the scale of what was at stake for the soul, and one has only to read descriptions of the visions in the New Testament to glimpse the forcefulness of this change and appreciate the validness of Jung's earlier mentioned comment about the "splitting of the world and the invalidation of Christ."

But to perceive the deeper syntactical meaning within these images of the Antichrist, we must see through them to the underlying logic and psychological meaning that they reveal. It is perhaps helpful to remember that on the level of the *opus parvum*, the smaller work of personal psychology, we often see the appearance in dreams of a balancing "shadow" element in the form of disturbing, frightening, or even demonic figures and events. This is how a difficult progressive shift in consciousness can appear to an ego invested in continuing its established and perhaps entrenched mode of thinking. The arrival of a more developed and advanced viewpoint, especially one of significant value, can be accompanied by exaggerated imagery portraying, for example, death, dismemberment, or some kind of apocalypse.[18] Consciousness will then naturally be invested in avoiding or sabotaging its inevitable "going under" which has the effect of increasing the intensity and urgency of the yet-to-be-fulfilled position.

In the scriptural narrative, the Antichrist denies and rejects the divine aspect of Jesus as the Christ, the anointed and incarnated Son of God. This is a challenge to the soul's established and long-held position as well as an indication of the upcoming birth of a new conception of the divine. We read in 1 John 4:2-3: "By this you know the spirit of God: every spirit that acknowledges that Yeshua Mashiah [Jesus Christ] has come in flesh, it is from God: and every spirit that fails to recognize Yeshua, it is not from God. This is the spirit of the antichrist, of which you have heard that he was coming. He has come, he is already in the world."[19] The fact that the "spirit

---

[18] "Apocalypse" comes from the Greek *apokalyptein*, "to uncover and reveal."

[19] *Restored New Testament* (New York: W. W. Norton and Company, 2009), p. 1036.

of the Antichrist" is already in the world shows that the upcoming rupture is already in the logic of the soul, but only as impulse and necessity, not yet in lived reality. Over the centuries, many entities had been charged with being the Antichrist including the Roman Empire, Nero, false messiahs, false prophets, even some popes, but Christianity survived them all. What it could not survive, at least in its traditional form, was the transformation of perspective brought about by the development of technology.[20]

If we remember Heidegger's comment about technology being a "revealing" and a place "where truth happens" and apply it to this point in the history of consciousness, we can consider what was being revealed was twofold. What the telescope revealed was that theological principles and religious teachings were not empirical realities and had to be either left behind or conceived of in an entirely new way. What the printing press revealed was that the eternal truths described in the Bible were ultimately speculative, theoretical, and symbolic.

But in what way are they to be understood? From the perspective of psychology as the discipline of interiority, the concept of the Antichrist is not a desire on the part of the soul to simply cancel or negate Christ once and for all, but rather to move towards the interiorization of the entire understanding and notion of God. It is the negation of the simple negation, an anti-antichrist, if you will, that is, for the soul, a fulfilled or absolute Christ. This is a restructuring in the soul of the vertical theological difference, the difference between heaven and earth, into a logical concept that is down to "earth," in consciousness and in thought. Also, because we are dealing with the concept of an Incarnated God, the interiorization brings about two aspects of the concept of the divine: the divine incarnated *in* thought and the divine *as* thought incarnated.

---

[20] Two important inventions that are pertinent here are the printing press and the telescope. In the case of the former, the availability of bibles for ordinary people resulted in the possibility of multiple interpretations of holy scripture. This set the stage for a consciousness that was open to questioning authoritative versions and traditional principles. The telescope, in turn, facilitated unprecedented images of the sun, moon, and planets which led to a questioning of the fundamental structure of the cosmos and to a noticing of how these discoveries differed from Church doctrine.

Bringing Heaven to Earth

It would be too much to call them the "four horsemen of the Apocalypse," but a case could be made for ascribing at least some part of the reshaping of Western consciousness to the scientific work of Copernicus, Brahe, Kepler, and Galileo. These men, good Christians every one, were fixing their minds and their instruments on the heavens and measuring the movements of the moon and planets with the intention of glorifying God and deepening faith in the Church. Instead, their work had the effect of eventually bringing heaven down to earth and making it factual and empirical, upsetting the very foundations of the Church.

If we focus on just one of these men, Tycho Brahe, the Danish mathematician and astronomer, we know that something important happened to him on November 11, 1572. He observed with his naked eye what he thought was the birth of a star.[21] The problem was that according to the biblical account of a fixed and eternal heaven, this was not supposed to happen; a new "star" was not supposed to be there. This compelled Brahe to begin developing a more systematic observation of the heavens. He invented new and exacting ways to measure the movement of stars and planets with, for example, quadrants, sextants, and armillary spheres. He also devised an unprecedented way of collecting and cataloging empirical data that proved useful to subsequent scientists and researchers.[22]

He was astonished to discover that many of the astronomers he had read and learned from had never actually observed what they were writing about. Instead, they had arrived at their conclusions mathematically, theoretically, and often gerrymandering it to fit within the context of Church doctrine. For him, this was a problem that needed to be rectified with empirical data and direct scientific observation, i.e., looking up into the sky with his own eyes and with

---

[21] In fact, it was a supernova, the beginning of the "death" of a star. It is now known as the Tycho Supernova.

[22] Brahe's measurements were essential to his onetime assistant, Johannes Kepler, in consolidating his own theories, including, for example, the elliptical orbits of the planets. See: John Robert Christianson, *Tycho Brahe and the Measure of the Heavens* (London: Reaction Books Ltd., 2020), pp. 198ff.

his own instruments. This is a concrete example and result of the cultural soul's shift away from its own established logical position. Brahe was not the first person to empirically formulate a map of the heavens, but as we have seen, if there is a necessity in the soul, something that might not have made a difference before can have profound implications at a different time.

Brahe's work sits perfectly on the divide between two logical worldviews. Despite the fact that his work was rigorous and challenged long-established precedents set down by Church dogma, a number of factors showed how the pre-scientific logic continued to be operative in him: First, he named his extensive and famous observatory Uraniborg after the goddess Urania, the daughter of Zeus and Mnemosyne. Second, it was important to him that the buildings and the surrounding landscape be set up in symmetrical and mathematical harmony. This, he believed, would support and validate his measurements of the heavens. Third, the instruments he developed and used for tracking stars, planets, and comets, along with being able to record the most precise astrological observations ever taken in Europe, were decorated with esoteric symbolic images, not simply for aesthetic reasons, but to enhance their effectiveness, and last, there was a functioning alchemical stove in the basement of the observatory.

Despite his empiricism, Brahe was also unable to get on board with the, at the time, radical Copernican idea of a heliocentric solar system. For him, it went too much against Holy Scripture to have anything but God's earth at the center of the universe. After his death, however, came the invention of a tool that would pull out the last stop of the old worldview and would have convinced even Brahe: the telescope.

When the telescope allowed Galileo to see with his own eyes Jupiter's orbiting moons and the mountains on our moon, the bubble of metaphysical meaning and divinity was punctured. It became clear that the preordained understanding of the workings of the universe taught by the Church and the Bible was in peril. It was as if peering into the heavens with the new tools of technology forced the acknowledgment that previous belief systems had been nothing but psychological "projections." If the celestial bodies were composed of the same material as the earth and were under the same physical laws, then the traditional understanding of the theological difference, the difference between divine and the earthly realms, must either collapse or be expressed in a radically different way.

A Technological-Psychological Future

To summarize: The Antichrist is the negation of Christianity and traditional metaphysics as personified in biblical and theological writings. In addition, it is the first representation of the dawning of a restored concept of the "divine." Psychologically conceived, it was by means of the Christ/Anti-Christ dialectic that the soul moved from one manner of living out its inner depth (mythological, dogmatic) to another (modern, conceptual). This shift in consciousness was initiated by and reflected in technological developments and inventions. The arrival of these revolutionary tools helped confirm the truth and reality of an empirical universe that undermined unquestioned adherence to Church authority and established a new paradigm within which to think about religious and spiritual truths.

This shift also brings about the possibility of a technological fulfillment of the concept of the Incarnation, the "Logos become flesh."[23] It is Logos, the "Word," or "principle of the divine," fully in the world as it is, i.e., limited, finite, and contingent; needing no faith, no dogma, no meaning or metaphysics. On this theme Giegerich writes:

> What else could one expect technological reality to be but the Logos become flesh? And how else could one conversely imagine a Logos become flesh than in the style of technological reality? […] Technology is Logos because it is what has its origin in reason, a product of the mind, idea. It is flesh because it is material reality and does not simply remain an idea. […] This is not only true for technical apparatuses, but also for the explanation of the world by the sciences.[24]

From the Christian perspective, this certainly marks the end of times and the apocalypse, but from a modern vantage point, it reveals a new world of possibility. For example, in Giegerich we read that just

---

[23] John 1:14.
[24] Wolfgang Giegerich, *CEP* II, p. 178.

as the Church provided meaning and context for humans in the past, now technology has taken over that role. It has, for example, even created a new form of God which is, surprisingly, the nuclear bomb. But why not? The bomb has the power to destroy everything, just as God did. It has a power greater than that of the sun, and we all fear it. But this god manifests in a way that is commensurate with our time, i.e., it is physically and empirically "real," a truly incarnated God, a technologically fabricated Incarnation of the "divine."[25] With this example, we can see that in the modern world the divine is now "produced," it does not create tools any more and give them as gifts to humanity, it is itself created by these tools.

Another example is the technology that has made movies possible. Since the time of the cave paintings of Lascaux, aesthetic images have been appreciated and valued within the fixed and constant reality in which they were created. That changed with the arrival of "moving images," which came alive when projected onto a screen as silent movies in cinemas. This was cutting edge technology in the late 1800s, and it caused a huge fascination in the general public. People were so captivated by this new phenomenon that when the technology advanced to the point that the movies had sound (the so-called "talkies"), a psychologist at the time wrote that it was: "The nearest thing to a resurrection!"[26]

Today we carry the ability to watch a movie in private anytime we like on the smartphones we carry in our pockets. However, the statement from the psychologist about the "resurrection," despite its coming from one person responding to one particular technology, hits the mark and could apply to modern technology in general. In other words, technology today, from a psychological viewpoint, is the soul's work of "resurrecting" a new concept of the divine, which has been lost since the "splitting of the world" and the beginning of modernity.

Recalling the title of Jung's last major work, *Mysterium Coniunctionis: The Separation and Synthesis of Psychic Opposites in Alchemy,* we know that consciousness's "splitting" can be the first step in the process of uniting on a more complex and differentiated level. I previously

---

[25] Giegerich, *"The Nuclear Bomb and the Fate of God,"* CEP II, pp. 69 ff.

[26] Fitzhugh Green, *The Film Finds its Tongue* (New York: The Knickerbocker Press, G. P. Putnam's Sons, 1926), p. 12.

described how the soul's (and technology's) primordial birth necessitated a bifurcation in consciousness, i.e., between subject and object, the natural and spiritual world, earth and heaven, and so on. This was the original "separation" which generated the various metaphysical systems, the "synthesis" that maintained a sense of balance and meaning for consciousness and culture for most of human history.

Now, after perhaps the most consequential rupture in the soul's history, modern technology is the location for soul's work towards a new synthesis: Logos (soul) and flesh ("matter") in a new post-metaphysical dialectical unity. A modern "Mysterium Coniunctionis," the separation and synthesis of opposites culminating in a more complex level of the soul's logic, revealed in and through technology.

However, to comprehend the modern soul's search for this synthesis, it is important to see through the surface or semantic level to the logic of what is happening in technology. For otherwise, our vision stays on the literal level and reacts only to, for example, the fearful power of destruction, in the case of the bomb, or is captivated and numbed by pointless entertainment and distractions, as in the case of movies and smartphones.

A more psychologically informed consciousness sees through to the syntactical life and logic of modern technology. With its work of interiorization, psychological thinking brings the insight of the animus, or "Antichrist" if you will, to the one-dimensional anima level of ego-consciousness. If we can include this kind of thinking in our appreciation of modern life today, we might then catch sight of the soul's self-unfolding in technology. In any case, the work of the soul as technology continues; it was with us there at the beginning and will no doubt be with us at the end.

5

Consciousness, Entropy, and the Edge of the Psychological

PHILIP KIME

The starting place for what follows is that reflexivity of consciousness stands out in the history of the world as a phenomenon that marks the edge of the psychological. This is due to the logical form of reflexivity, which breaks the structural requirements for psychology proper to fall under the explanatory framework of evolutionary theory. The idea is that reflexivity constitutes a logical situation, in which the subject and object are the same and this falls outside of the logic of evolutionary science, in which there needs to be a real, separate "other" to act as the environment in order to exert meaningful differential selection pressure. One cannot talk of differential selection pressure when the environment *is* the thing that is being acted on by the environment, as we have in a situation of reflexivity. No multiplicity of things shares such an environment and so the notion of differential selection does not apply. This is, I think, related to the great distinction Hegel makes between the logical and temporal order in that, as soon as reflexive consciousness is extant in time, theories which fundamentally depend on time, such as evolutionary theory, cease to be an appropriate explanatory framework. This is because the logical structure of the explanandum is now separate from temporal measurement and effects. When the subject and object are the same, when the organism and its environment are in a sense one, there is no movement of information in time between the two, since there are not two things any more but only perhaps two aspects of a single entity and it is a logical structure that differentiates these, not a temporal one.

Since this is, I fear, a difficult and somewhat controversial position, I thought it useful, at least for me, to try to come at it from a different side. This turns on an idea which might be described as a kind of logical "isolation" of the psychological from the empirical world and so I would like to try to approach the topic again from this concept. There is a naïve empiricism, which aims to exhaustively explain psychology and the intention here is to motivate a principled objection to any purely empirical account of psychology proper. Mainstream psychology, and not a little mainstream Jungian psychology, is rife with such in-principle assumptions regarding the explanatory framework adequate for psychology, and I have argued elsewhere that this is blindly leading modern psychology into a situation where it will be irrelevant and consumed by biology and evolutionary theory.[1] This is in my view no bad outcome as, I think all here would agree, most of what passes for psychology these days has very little of the psychological about it. Evolutionary theory is a fundamentally *temporal* theory concerned with the structures which establish over time and so if we are to find out where such a theory fails to capture the essence of the psychological, it will be where the notion of time required by evolutionary theory fails us, and the point of this paper is to try to say something more definite about this very topic. I hope then, you will allow a very brief *excursus* into areas that have, of necessity, already developed distinctions that we might use.

Giegerich says, right at the beginning of *The Soul's Logical Life: Towards a Rigorous Notion of Psychology*, "Psychology proper is *only* about those things that one cannot talk about."[2] When subject and object are the same, you are only talking to yourself and that is, as Wittgenstein was wont to stress, not really talking in any meaningful sense. Psychology proper means a "being alone with" in some fundamental way, that is, it means isolation, but we have to try to

---

[1] Philip Kime, *Consciousness, Reflexivity and Evolution*, in: Jennifer M. Sandoval, Colleen El-Bejjani, and Pamela J. Power, eds., *Essays on "The Soul's Logical Life" in the Work of Wolfgang Giegerich* (London and New York: Routledge, 2023), pp. 131-144.

[2] Wolfgang Giegerich, *The Soul's Logical Life: Towards a Rigorous Notion of Psychology* (Frankfurt am Main: Peter Lang, 1998), p. 32.

tease out what the nature of this isolation is by talking around it, since we cannot talk about it. However, *ex hypothesi*, it must be something to do with isolation from an inappropriate notion of time.

I would like to introduce here the distinction between the ordinal and cardinal notions of time,[3] which are, it seems to me, a useful way of framing the discussion of time in relation to our topic of the limits of the properly psychological. There is a distinction between Time in the ordinal sense and time in the cardinal sense. In its ordinal sense, time is taken as being ordered in the sense required by the question "when did that happen?" The assumption here is of an absolute ordering of an ordinal line wherein we can locate events. When we are presented with a picture of a dinosaur, we know that this depicts something absolutely earlier in ordinal Time than what is depicted by a picture of, say, a bicycle. However, we can also be concerned with time as a cardinal concept when we talk of time intervals and ask about "how much time" something took. This doesn't say anything about when in ordinal time something occurred, only something about the size (i.e., cardinality) of the time interval.

It is a significant and interesting fact that in physics only thermodynamics concerns itself with ordinal Time, while most physical laws are defined in terms of time intervals, that is, in terms of cardinal time. It is this that leads to the famous in-principle reversibility of most physical laws and to the equally famous "arrow of time" discussions. In the modern world, the discussions about ordinal Time and thermodynamics are usually cast in terms of the concept of "entropy," which is a difficult concept to really pin down but is often spoken of in terms of a measure of disorder. The laws of thermodynamics dictate that entropy always monotonically, globally increases towards a state of maximum structureless disorder, a state known colloquially as the "heat death" of the universe, where there are no structures, no local order anywhere, and the universe consists of a statistically uniform background of particles at a temperature close to absolute zero. Thermodynamics, having a notion of ordinal

---

[3] I am grateful to Nicholas Georgescu-Roegen, *The Entropy Law and the Economic Process* (Cambridge, MA: Havard University Press, 1971) for a clear introduction to and use of this distinction, albeit in a somewhat different context.

Time, can in principle locate any state of the universe in ordinal time by the measure of its entropy. No global state of lower entropy may succeed another global state of higher entropy and so every state of the universe is located in ordinal time, by its entropy measure.

It is important to note that these remarks were about the global entropy of the universe and for a good reason; locally, entropy may well decrease. The entropy of the surface of the Earth has decreased dramatically as humans have built complex, organised structures over millennia, for example. This is a local decrease in the context of a relatively global increase in, for example, the solar system as the sun eventually burns out in its inevitable entropic death. Organic life is effectively a locally negative entropic system that structures and organises on a cosmically small scale, providing a short-term reversal of the global monotonic increase in entropy. Now, let us take an individual person. Their life is one of a negative entropic contribution to their local environment. We build and arrange homes, organise our lives, structure our time until we die and our bodies decay into the ground in a grand release of the negative entropy we have accumulated.

The idea here is that since the essence of psychology proper is the break in the natural confluence of the logical/temporal order, perhaps then we can frame our notion of psychology in terms of entropy and its associated notion of ordinal Time. The idea of a temporal "order" is plainly Time in the ordinal sense, that is, in the sense relevant to thermodynamics and therefore the notion of entropy. If we speak of a break in that order, the Hegelian bifurcation that is so important for psychology, we are therefore led to conclude that psychology proper must have something to do with time in the cardinal sense and not the ordinal sense. This is precisely how the non-thermodynamic laws of physics are said to be "timeless"—they involve only cardinal notions of time and so psychology proper would also be timeless by the same criteria. So, I suggest, the notion of locally isolated negative entropy is a way of looking at Giegerich's "psychological difference." However, it must be a very particular type of negative entropic system since otherwise it would fall under the same rubric of any locally negatively entropic system and therefore would be equivalent to most empirical phenomena. As mentioned earlier, we do not believe that a purely empirical approach is a credible position and looking at the issue in this way may help us to see more clearly why the credibility is lacking.

So, why does psychology proper take the special form of negative entropy? Once reflexive consciousness exists, that is, appears at a point in ordinal Time, it represents a novel structure that splits the logical/temporal order and therefore is characterisable only in terms of cardinal time and this means that it is, in ordinal terms, as atemporal as the laws of physics, which also arose in ordinal Time. This is a way of framing the postmodern insight that Giegerich often mentions that after the advent of language, there is no going back "before" language any more. It has now "always already" existed. This means that it has no place any more in the history of the world, in the ordinal sense of Time. Once language exists there is now no sense to the very idea of the "time before language" because its structure (the fact that it makes reflexivity possible) means that only the cardinal sense of time can be meaningfully applied to it.

We still have not really addressed the question of why such a structure as reflexivity performs such a miracle and takes us, so to speak, out of time, out of ordinal history, out of the global march of entropy and into the realm of psychology. It is in order to look into this that I find the notion of entropy useful; however, the colloquial framing using the concept of "disorder" is quite hard to spell out in detail. A more useful and less vague formulation of entropy is in terms of "multiplicity," which helps to connect to our topic of logical "isolation" and thereby to our psychological concerns in a more obvious fashion. A state that can be realised in multiple ways is more probable than one that can be realised in only a few ways and probability is connected to entropy in quite a deep way. A state of low entropy is less probable because there are fewer ways of configuring things to achieve the state. An example might roughly be that the probability of finding civilisation on a random planet is very low and therefore any civilisation is an event of low entropy. The reason that it is a low probability is that there are many ways for a planet to be barren, many physical configurations which are consistent with a barren planet. The number of ways a planet can be barren and lifeless are multiplicitous compared with the number of ways a planet can bear life. Therefore, life is a condition of lower entropy. Another example: If you roll two dice, there are six ways of generating the number seven. There is only one way of generating the number twelve. The configurations of the dice that result in the number seven are more multiplicitous than the configurations that result in the number twelve. Therefore, the result of obtaining a seven is a state of higher entropy than the result of obtaining the number twelve. This accords with our notions of probability, since we think we are more likely to roll seven than to roll twelve. This is a common way of defining entropy—it is a measure of the multiplicity of ways in which the state can exist.

Let us now try to move things into a vocabulary closer to our target topic. Let us take three states that a person might be in:

(1) The state of having a thought
(2) The state of having a thought about a dog
(3) The state of having a thought about a dog chasing a ball

Some things are, I suppose, obvious about these three states. First, there are many more events that satisfy State 1 than State 3. For a random individual, State 1 is more likely than State 3. State 3 is more structured and has more information in it than State 1. State 1 is more multiplicitous than State 3. So, these states are ordered 1 to 3 by decreasing entropy. A simple way of putting this is that general thoughts are likely than specific thoughts. Notice that these conclusions have nothing whatever to do with the content of the thoughts. Indeed, they have nothing to do with thoughts; this is just an example to show that any event at all, even those events that we take to be, say, mental states, are frameable by the notion of entropy seen as a measure of multiplicity.

Multiplicity is a measure of the ways in which a state can vary but still be classed as the same state in some sense. Let us take this a step further towards our goal. A conscious state, I argue, is less multiplicitous than an unconscious state. There are fewer ways for an event to be conscious than for an event to be unconscious, however you define unconsciousness. Consciousness is less likely. Therefore, again, consciousness is a lower entropy state than unconsciousness. It is more structured; there is less disorder.

An Aside on Disorder

There is a disadvantage in casting entropy in terms of order and disorder since we might try to argue that unconscious states, as in animals, are more ordered, simple, less chaotic compared with the messy disorder we see in some conscious states. This is not correct, however, as the messy conscious states, which we all know and perhaps love, are far more structured, ordered, and rare than any unconscious state, for the simple reason that there are more variables involved, and disorder is a function of the structure exhibited by a given number of variables.

Our instinctive and natural sense of structure and order is quite primitive, and I believe that this is one of the reasons why mainstream psychology remains in such an unsophisticated state. Our default perception is essentially that structure is defined by things and their relations, but there are, for example, what in formal logic are called "second order" relations, which are relations between relations. We engage in such second-order aspects constantly in therapeutic work as we notice and track, for example, the tendency for the formation of certain *types* of relation. Perhaps a patient sees everyone with whom they have a relation of authority in a certain way. This is a second-order structure *about* relations and a simple example of the more complex structural forms that exist.

For a much more comprehensive attempt to trace the development of structure from the most simple to the most complex, one can with great profit read Hegel's Greater and Lesser Logics, which, regardless of how one sees the legitimacy of every individual step on the way, are a unique and magnificent labour of laying bare structural bones piece by piece. In following this enormous and dense undertaking, it is inevitable that one sees repeatedly how complex and intricate the structure of the concepts we take for granted are, leading to the realisation that our pre-dialectical intuitions regarding order and disorder are not remotely adequate. Very often, a primitive perception of disorder is simple due to an unsophisticated notion of order.

Consciousness and Entropy

So, consciousness has lower entropy and the next and final step will be apparent. Reflexive consciousness has the lowest entropy of all putatively psychological states, and so I would like to suggest that the psychological difference is a way of looking at the radical logical change brought about by the lowest entropy forms of certain states.

There is a longstanding idea that human beings are the most evolved low-entropy generating machines on the planet. They are locations where high entropy is converted into low entropy in a localised manner—disparate resources become dwellings, random ideas become products—and this accounts for their position as the dominant species. Life is, in this view, a fight against the inevitable march of entropy, and it succeeds as long at the power to locally reduce or stay an increase in entropy continues. Consciousness is fairly obviously an enormous contributing factor to the ability to perform this entropy-reducing function, but it is reflexive consciousness, that is, the truly psychological, which splits completely from the ordinal Time behind the march of entropy.

Now we need to ask: Why is reflexive consciousness such a unique source of low entropy? I think that this is due to the fact that reflexivity is characterised by the subject and object being the same thing and this enormously reduces the multiplicity of reflexive states, thereby enormously reducing the entropy of such states. For example, if I am thinking non-reflexively, roughly speaking, I am thinking about something other than myself, and the greater frequency of this follows from there being far more ways to be in a state of thinking about things other than myself, simply because there are far more things that are not me. States of thinking about an object that is not the subject are far more multiplicitous. Reflexive consciousness
is a much less multiplicitous state than any non-reflexive state and therefore by its very form represents a uniquely low-entropy state.

To relate this to isolation, let us consider a rough example. Take the event of "food being thought about." How many ways are there for this event to occur? It is at the very least as multiplicitous as the number of people on earth. What about the ways of me alone thinking about food? Clearly less multiplicitous. What about me reflexively thinking about my process of having food-related thoughts? This seems to me to be a limit to multiplicity, since the count of possible subjects and objects is the same in being simply one. Reflexive consciousness marks a line in the sand of multiplicity and therefore entropy, which takes reflexively conscious events out of ordinal Time, even though they may last for some time in the cardinal sense. This is just another way of looking at the Hegelian time/logic split. Once ordinal, historical time is no longer applicable, one is left with a so-called "timeless" event (which means it can still take some time, but it is no longer possible to speak of it coherently in terms of existing in ordinal Time). Such an event is isolated and has to be considered in terms of itself, which is the demand of real psychology. Giegerich makes a great deal out of Jung's statement that the dream has "everything it needs within itself," that is, the dream is to be taken as an isolated phenomenon because this is the only truly psychological way of taking phenomena related to a creature capable of reflexive consciousness. Note that this is a *decision*, since it is not dictated by any empirical fact, because we are *ex hypothesi* outside of that realm entirely. Animals may well dream, but their dreams do not have everything they need within themselves because the lack of reflexive consciousness means that such phenomena are not isolated, not outside of ordinal Time, and have relatively high entropy.

Real psychology is timeless in that it is only a logical, not temporal structure and is therefore outside of the remit of empirical science which has ordinal Time at its core, such as evolutionary theory. The march of increasing entropy is the march of ordinal Time and therefore a decrease in entropy is eventually a step outside of ordinal Time and, when this step *has* happened, there is no more any sense in asking *when* it happened. This is why we say that great art and ideas "live forever," because there is a sense in which they do not become irrelevant in the ordinal time sense as do less structured events such as the growth of organic life. A plant, an animal, a physical object does not "live forever" but ideas and art may, as these are intimately related to the phenomenon of reflexive consciousness.

A last comment now on the normative aspect of all of this. To say that real psychology exists outside of ordinal Time is not to celebrate this fact and to advocate for it. In Giegerich's early work, he talks about a problem of our age being that the fascination with atemporal, magnificent images keeps us in a state of fake, regressive bliss, in which we can escape the supposed banality and misery of the world and its entropic decay. Psychology as reflexive consciousness allows us to step outside and preserve, but it also allows us to regress and escape. We sometimes call this in English "navel-gazing," or being in an "ivory tower"—all such metaphors are metaphors of what I have called "isolation." It is the task of thought to keep psyche relevant to ordinal Time so that it is relevant to actual humans in an actual physical universe with its unidirectional arrow of Time, defined by increasing entropy. We see this also in the related geometrical problem in physics, where the reversibility of many physical laws requires thermodynamics to force them back into ordinal Time and into engagement with entropy, thus making them in principle relevant to our actual, material universe. It is our job as psychologists to manage the phenomenon of the logical/temporal break as best we can, allowing it to further develop while not allowing it to drift so far into a polarisation that it is no longer relevant to actual humans and their temporal history. A great difference appearing in ordinal Time can perhaps allow the suspension of ordinal Time forever, but this is an illness rather than a virtue in an animal that must exist in ordinal Time. Maybe our psychotics can step across the break and by tremendous and destructive force remain outside of ordinal Time, but this is not a desirable state for a human being who is defined as an event forever within the grand march of entropy.

Negative entropy is temporary, a relative isolation from the long-term energy gradient of the environment. Reflexive consciousness *is its own environmen*t and so is absolutely, logically isolated and therefore represents the edge of psychology proper. I would like to emphasise, however, that this *is* so; it is a descriptive fact, not a normative desire. Framing it as a normative desire and acting it out with specific contents is what leads to the embarrassing and profoundly unpsychological excesses of much of the New Age phenomenon. Psychology proper is a formal, structural fact, which can be seen in, reflected in, other congruent formal structures, such as entropy and reflexivity. The contents are as irrelevant to psychology as the things subject to entropic decay are to entropy, and this ensures that psychology exists, as does entropy, even in the absence—in a sense *only* in the absence—of anything to experience the process.

As what I suppose could be termed a "bonus," this way of characterising the split of logic and time underlying psychology proper by using ordinal Time as the marker of the empirical, allows a principled objection to various forms of modern theory appropriating the term "psychology." Cognitive Psychology is barely worth mentioning here, since it is positively *trying* to turn itself into biology or neuroscience, and it makes no pretense of supposing a realm of the psychological in anything but name. Developmental psychology and the related psychoanalytic object-relations models are clearly inextricably linked to ordinal Time in that they describe and explain in terms of an order of successive and monotonic stages. Interesting though this might be as a study of the biological structures of a certain species, it cannot, in the sense we have described, be psychological because this requires a structure in which time is at best cardinal, or perhaps reversible or just irrelevant. The development of things in the world, in ordinal Time are so well accounted for by empirical science that having a supposedly psychological theory that recognises such development as being the target of explanations will always ultimately look, and I argue, *be* redundant. The empirical view comes with an ontology and an epistemology that cannot be treated as optional by those wishing to perhaps retain the status of the empirical whilst simultaneously holding theories that no empirical view would recognise as legitimate. The *phenomena* of empirical psychology have also to be given up, and not merely the theoretical layer on top of an unabashed and naïve empiricism. It is not that there is a problem with, say, object-relations theory *per se*; it is that its phenomena are not at all psychological, given that they are so easily cast in better terms by powerful and purely biological or evolutionary theories, which are unashamedly cast in terms of ordinal Time.

In this sense, goal-directed therapy is also nothing really to do with psychology proper, helpful and indeed perhaps essential though it might often be. A goal is a future point in ordinal Time, the therapy precedes it, facilitates it. Therefore goal-directed therapy in general is perfectly at home in the empirical framing of cognitive models or behaviourism and the perfectly respectable but psychologically irrelevant practice of deciding to do something and then doing it. Psychology proper is a phenomenon that might perhaps manifest over a period of time; it will often manifest as having a *duration,* but this is cardinal time. Its moments are isolated in this sense from the order of things in time, though they may take time. They occupy a geometrical or logical structure, not an ordered temporal structure, and cannot simply pass away into the past, for they constitute a redefinition of what *is* rather than a moment in an ordered, developing definition outside of themselves. Naturally, this makes such moments very rare; we are not "psychological" very often, which is why they are low-entropy states, since there are very few ways of being psychology compared with the countless ways of being in an empirical state. The notion of entropy perhaps captures this aspect of the psychological and helps us to sharpen our instincts about what really counts. It is sometimes said that everything is psychology, but I rather think *almost* nothing is; diamonds are valuable because in the mass of the Earth there are *almost* none.

6

Where is the Love (with a Capital L)?

CARMEN KOBOR

> You may have read facts and figures and documentary narratives
> and autobiographies or autobiographical novels; you may have
> seen pictures and even visited the sites. All this will not have
> brought you closer to the experience. For the ultimate mystery
> of the Holocaust is that whatever happened took place in the
> soul. All the rest is commentary.
>
> —Elie Wiesel[1]

My interest in this topic was sparked a few years ago while reading an interview Wolfgang Giegerich gave for *Living with Jung*. During the interview, in the course of responding to a series of questions on the soul, Giegerich was asked, "From the standpoint of 'the soul,' what would be some ways to understand the Holocaust?"[2] The question seemed to come out of the blue, without precedent in the foregoing discussions, and my attention was captured. This was, I must confess, because I am a second generation descendent of Holocaust survivors and have been marred by the mechanisms of the transposition of trauma, "a process by which members of the second-generation live aspects

---

[1] Irving Abrahamson, ed. *Against Silence: The Voice and Vision of Elie Wiesel*, Vol. 1 (New York, NY: Holocaust Library, 1985). p. 30.

[2] Robert and Janis Henderson, *Living with Jung: "Enterviews" with Jungian Analysts*, Vol. 3 (New Orleans, LA: Spring Journal Books, 2010), p. 270.

of their parents' trauma as if they were their own."[3] Giegerich first
observed that the Holocaust has been extensively documented
from an ego perspective through numerous personal and historical
accounts, distinguishing this approach from the soul's perspective.
He then introduced his thoughts on the Holocaust from the
standpoint of the soul with the following remarks:

> I think, the soul is still dazed by the enormous trauma caused to it
> by the Holocaust. It will probably take several more decades, if not
> centuries, before it can truly open itself to the full reality of what
> happened. For the time being, the soul is still completely enveloped
> in and deafened by the buzzing noise of our ego emotions around
> the topic of the Holocaust. And anyway, whatever one can say
> about an event of such unheard-of dimensions is probably at the
> same time too little or too much.[4]

Following upon these words, Giegerich concludes with two
far- reaching ideas. First, "that the Holocaust could be seen as that
event in which the soul attacked and ruined for good its own
innocent belief in 'The Good.'"[5] And second, like a Zen koan "that
the Holocaust is the soul's initiation into Love."[6] Beyond that,
Giegerich would not elaborate further except to say that there are
times when the ego has to remain silent, and instead of turning to
others for an explanation, "one has to turn to nothing else but the
bewildering notion itself, here the notion of Love (with a capital L)
in connection with the Holocaust, and turn to it in the quiet
loneliness of thought, the thought of the heart, with the patience
of being able to wait."[7]

Giegerich's words stayed in my heart like a rose with thorns,
echoing the feeling captured by the 16th-century German scholar,
Georgius Camerarius, in these words: "Like the rose that blooms in the
midst of the thorns that enclose it. So are the pleasures of love never

---

[3] M. Weiss and S Weiss, "Second Generation to Holocaust Survivors:
Enhanced Differentiation of Trauma Transmission," *American Journal of
Psychotherapy*, 54, no. 3 (Summer 2000): 372.

[4] Henderson and Henderson, p. 270.

[5] *Ibid.*, p. 271.

[6] *Ibid.*

[7] *Ibid.*

unshared with its gall."[8] On the one hand, I felt the burgeoning truth in Giegerich's dictum; on the other, the shocking character and killing edge of that truth. But, that said, and bearing in mind the significance that *killing* has to the soul generating itself,[9] the encroachment of personal convictions on the soul's perspective must be set aside if—as Greg Mogenson conveyed to me—one is to examine the Holocaust "as an experience that the soul visited upon itself achieving some kind of form change in the logic of our being-in-the-world."[10]

This shift in consciousness (wherein the logic of soul is independent of ego construal) involves the difference between the soul standpoint and the ego perspective. Giegerich differentiates the two positions thus: the ego perceives things, "in an external, clear-cut division of doer and victim, cause and effect, subject and object, whereas the soul—the methodological principle of inwardness and absolute-negative interiorization—understands what happens to it 'uroborically' in terms of its own self relation."[11]

Outer empirical phenomena in the field of ego-consciousness have within themselves the essence of the soul's internal infinity. Said another way, in Michael Whan's words, "we see then that in the psychological difference the soul's dialectical movement pushes off from the psychic, the ego personality, not outwardly but further *inwardly*."[12] However, this inward movement, which goes against the natural empirical-positivistic literal mode of consciousness in the manner of a contradiction, is far from being nice and harmless. The soul, says Giegerich, "turns against itself, cuts into its own flesh, and destroys and overcomes its own initial innocence"[13] with the aim of evolving to a higher logical status of itself.

---

[8] Jung, *CW 14*, p. 306, fn. 219.

[9] For a fuller discussion on the relevance killing has to the soul generating itself, see: "Killings" in Giegerich, *CEP* III, pp. 189-265.

[10] Greg Mogenson, private communication, dated May 17, 2024.

[11] Henderson and Henderson, p. 270.

[12] Michael Whan, "The Uroboric Logic of Anxiety: 'Not out, but Through,'" in: Jennifer M. Sandoval, Coleen El-Bejjani, and Pamela Power, eds., *Essays on "The Soul's Logical Life" in the Work of Wolfgang Giegerich* (London and New York: Routledge, 2024), pp. 34-48 (here p. 35).

[13] Henderson and Henderson, p. 270.

This objective development, in which a new level of reality is reached by the soul, is the breaking out into the open of a new *logic* of reality that had been gestating for decades and centuries before its history-making manifestation in practical reality. This constitutes what Giegerich calls, "the historically developing logical life of the soul."[14] The soul's own history, in the psychological sense, is comprised of changes in the logic of human being-in-the-world as these transpire concealed in the visible events of history as its inner essence and spirit. By *spirit* is meant, in Jung's words, "all the higher mental faculties, such as reason, insight, and moral discrimination."[15] Not only that, but "insofar as the spirit is also a 'window into eternity' and, as the *anima rationalis,* immortal, it conveys to the soul a certain 'divine influx' and the knowledge of higher things, wherein consists precisely its supposed animation of the soul."[16] Also to be noted is that as a synonym for spirit, *essence* is equivalent to what Hegel has in mind when he declares that "things are not supposed to be left in their immediacy but instead demonstrated to be mediated or justified by something else."[17] In other words, in Hegel's parlance things in their immediacy are like "a curtain behind which the essence is hidden,"[18] for the simple reason that, "there is something enduring in things and this primarily is the essence."[19]

What I am attempting to highlight here is the essence of the *Real I*, the existing concept, the concept as the syntax of consciousness, and not the semantics of the ego. This jointly held entanglement of the empirical-factual historical event and the historical development of the logical life of the soul, yields a new logical status that in essence is a *truth* already reached by the soul, but which is simultaneously obscured in the chaos of the visible historical occurrence. This, Giegerich affirms, is a difference that is "*within* one and the same motif and consists in the

---

[14] Wolfgang Giegerich, *Pitfalls in Comparing Buddhist and Western Psychology: A Contribution to Psychology's Self-Clarification* (London, ON: Dusk Owl Books, 2018), p. 19.

[15] Jung, *CW 14* § 473.

[16] *Ibid..*

[17] G. W. F. Hegel, *Encyclopedia of the Philosophical Sciences in Basic Outline, Part I: Science of Logic* (Cambridge, UK: Cambridge University Press., 2010), p. 174.

[18] *Ibid.*

[19] *Ibid.*

fact that it can come with two conflicting meanings, one manifest and one latent."[20] This asynchronous relationship between history's factual development and the historical development of the logical life of the soul is an entanglement with similitude to quantum entanglement, in which when two subatomic particles become entangled they remain connected even when separated by vast distances. The strange thing about quantum entanglement is that when scientists measure something about one particle in an entangled pair, they immediately know something about the other particle, even if the two particles are millions of light years apart.[21]

The notion that the soul works upon itself to refine and improve itself through a series of self-negations to arrive at a higher truth asynchronous to the factual historical event, yet impossible to disentangle, is also appreciable from the perspective of alchemy. This holds true because the alchemical method consists of a series of operations in which the soul, inextricably bound with matter in a dark unity, is eventually distilled and separated from it, thus extracting the *essence* and *spirit* of its highest *truth*. Alchemically speaking, this process is threefold. The first stage consists of the soul's primordial oneness with itself, the *unio naturalis*. The second has to do with the soul's self-negation and self-overcoming, the opus *contra naturam*. The third stage brings about the soul's harmonious unification with itself on the higher level, even as, on this new level of unity and integration with itself a new level of the *unio naturalis* is established to be pushed off from again at some subsequent historical juncture. Giegerich boils it down to the soul wanting "to free the inner 'mercurial' essence from its imprisonment in the material form of the 'matter'"[22] through a process of "self-unfolding and further development of its own nuclear substance with the purpose for the

---

[20] Wolfgang Giegerich, *The Soul's Logical Life* (Frankfurt am Main: Peter Lang., 1998), p. 248.

[21] Andreas Muller, "What is quantum entanglement? A physicist explains Einstein's 'spooky action at a distance'," Astronomy, last updated May 18, 2023, https://www.astronomy.com/science/what-is-quantum-entanglement -a-physicist-explains-einsteins-spooky-action-at-a-distance/.

[22] Giegerich, *Pitfalls*, p. 20.

soul to reveal itself explicitly as what implicitly it has been all along: Geist (Spirit) Self/objective Subjectivity."[23]

Jung said that in order to come to a right understanding of a contemporary psychological problem, we need to be able to reach a point outside our own time. This point he says, "can only be some epoch that was concerned with the same problems, although under different conditions and in other forms,"[24] because for Jung the soul was "a vast historical storehouse."[25] Elaborating further on history providing points of reference and comparison for psychology, Giegerich emphasizes that while historical epochs are separated from our times by many ruptures and changes, the two are also connected and even identical, "inasmuch as it is the same soul that dealt with the same topics and with the same inner necessities of its own, merely under the conditions of former statuses of consciousness, former modes of being-in-the-world."[26]

Animus-Psychologie Revisited

A considerable amount of time passed after I read the interview with Giegerich, during which I did not consciously engage with the topic of the soul's perspective on the Holocaust. It was not until the ISPDI Conference in the fall of 2023, when Ulrich Stuck presented excerpts from Giegerich's *Animus-Psychologie*, which he had translated from German into English, that I was inspired to think about it again. One of the first writings by Giegerich that I read early on was "Animus as Negation." The essay made a significant impression on me, particularly because Jung's characterization of the syzygy as a "field of personal experience which leads directly to the experience of individuation"[27] was never true for me. I saw the syzygy as the objective soul's inalienable dimension, and Giegerich widened the horizon of that perspective for me. Stuck's roughly translated passages of the German edition of *Animus-Psychologie* had a primal and fundamental feel that drew me in, offering a way to approach

---

[23] *Ibid.*, p. 49.
[24] Jung, *CW 16*, Foreword, p.166.
[25] Jung, *CW 18*, § 280.
[26] Giegerich, *CEP* III, p. 30.
[27] Jung, *CW 9*i, § 194.

the "bewildering notion" of Love in connection with the Holocaust from a soul-internal perspective.

In his book *Animus-Psychologie*, Giegerich emphasizes the posited character of the animus as an immanently self-critical cognitive experience that is suffering through one's own consciousness. "The animus depends on our own thinking for its foundation,"[28] he writes. "I myself must have understood the meaning of 'animus' and the difference between anima and animus."[29] In other words, the animus can only be reached logically, because, having no empirical basis and being nothing thing-like, it is, "ultimately based on its own thinking, on its own concept of itself."[30] The syzygy, it follows, is tantamount to the sphere of reflexivity, which is also to say, to that dimension of inwardness that is opened up by the relating of something to itself. By contrast, the syzygy as reflexive logical movement was theorized in a dialectically undetermined manner by Jung in his contrasexual doctrine of the syzygy. Distributed between the sexes as counter-gendered personality traits, women were said by him to have an animus, men an anima.

Eschewing this positivizing and ontologizing of the internal structure of the syzygy, Giegerich stipulates that in a truly psychological conception of the syzygy, the animus is "a thinking approach, not an entity, not an existing phenomenon,"[31] even as the anima, as image or emotion, is an anticipatory form of implicit thinking. In addition, another salient aspect of the logical movement and syzygial phenomenology of the animus is that "[i]n himself the animus is nothing. As pure spirit, pure negation, he is, in order to be something in his own right, dependent on there being something that can be negated. This dependency is the ground of the syzygy"[32] in which "the syzygial union with the anima is inherent in the notion of the animus, inasmuch as he is nothing but her own Other, her negation."[33] Accordingly, the animus is not viewed in isolation, but as the further

---

[28] Ulrich Stuck, "Exzerpt zu Wolfgang Giegerich: *Animus-Psychologie*," unpublished paper presented at the ISPDI Conference, 2023, p. 12-13.

[29] *Ibid.*, p. 6.

[30] *Ibid.*, p. 19.

[31] *Ibid.*, p. 7.

[32] Giegerich, *CEP* III, p. 112.

[33] *Ibid.*, p. 113.

determination of the anima, inasmuch as what was implicit and only imagined in her becomes explicit and thought in him. Our task, says Giegerich, "is to focus on the whole interplay between the anima and the animus or on the relation of the soul (as animus or killer) to itself (as anima or victim), including all variations of this relation."[34]

The animus and anima undergo a threefold dynamic process towards the experience of the other, in which the soul exhausts different phases and variations of the syzygial relationship, ultimately resulting in the anima and animus going under into each other, no longer substantiated by the imagination as separate figures, but as the reflexive reality of the syzygy itself as spirit, mindedness, and thought.[35] This stage, which Giegerich calls the Fourth Stance, "goes beyond the animus as the experience of the other, and beyond the animus as negation and forms the transition to a new topic, 'The Animus as Spirit and Love.'"[36] Having gone under, the animus lives on in the anima herself, but now as the spirit of a new stage. Having fully integrated into the anima's virginal consciousness, and no longer the alien vis-à-vis that perpetrates aggression within the anima against the alien vis-à-vis he once was, he becomes "the life of the spirit in the soul itself."[37] And with this, the animus's having gone under to become the living spirit within the anima, she too goes under and reveals herself to be the syzygial soul. In Giegerich's words,

> The soul has caught up with its own syzygial uroboric nature, it has become pure self-relation. This, its being self-relation, has now become completely transparent to itself. It must no longer act it out, no longer present it to itself as a play in which the different roles are allotted to different figures. The relation between the soul and its other is no longer a vis-a-vis "in space." It has itself entered the medium of the mental and logical, where nothing can be pictorially represented any longer, but where it now must be thought. And only when this is the case does the animus become realized. For what does it mean to say that "the

---

[34] *Ibid.*

[35] For a thoroughgoing discussion of this dialectic see: Wolfgang Giegerich, "The Animus as Negation and as the Soul's Own Other, The Soul's Threefold Stance toward Its Experience of Its Other," *CEP* III, pp. 111-161.

[36] *Ibid,*, p. 161.

[37] *Ibid.*, p. 163.

animus has become realized"? It means that he as spirit (mindedness) no longer stands, as a demon, face to face with the soul, but that the soul itself has seen through itself in its own mind-nature and knows itself as the life of the mind, as logical movement. Jung once called this the "pneumatic state."[38]

In becoming realized, the animus emancipates itself from having appeared as spirit in a demonic guise. His spirit as demon is sublimated, so as to be spirit in the sense of mindedness, as the logical movement of the soul. The animus wants, writes Giegerich, "the spirit in the sense of mindedness to reveal itself as the spirit of the soul itself or of man's whole being-in-the-world."[39] In essence the syzygy stage is the fulfillment of the animus via a consummate act of negation, the disappearance of himself into himself as the mindedness of the soul. And as Giegerich attests, "Spirit as mindedness is not reached by going up, but by going under. Negativity! It's the only way."[40]

Insofar as syzygial consciousness is concerned, it is not yet in our time a fulfilled historical reality. Although we are on the verge of entering into it, nothing can be anticipated before the progressive stages that preside over its gradual realization actualize. It is the soul's way to be ahead of the factual status of consciousness that lags behind in the old logic of an age that walls off the truth already achieved by the soul.

This brings to mind a dream I had in the throes of writing this talk, in which I (the dream I) had a powerful desire to dive off a diving board into a body of water. Suddenly, I found myself on a concrete sidewalk which was at one and the same time both the diving board from which I jumped and the supple entrance into the water. As I assumed the diving position with my forehead nearly touching the pavement, I knew full well that the concrete, as hard as it was, would at the same time have the buoyant, giving character of water, and vice versa. Yet, I thought, if it doesn't, it will split my head open. Prior to the dive, I had given my purse and money to a stranger for safekeeping, uncertain of his trustworthiness. That evening, soaked and refreshed after the dive, I returned to claim my purse and found

---

[38] *Ibid.*, p. 164
[39] *Ibid.*
[40] *Ibid.*, p.165, fn. 22.

that the stranger had indeed safeguarded my purse and money, and even displayed his own large wad of cash. (Previous dreams of mine had featured the recurring motif of my purse with money in it being invariably forgotten, mislaid, lost, stolen, or found empty, causing utter disillusionment from the ordeal.)

Giegerich talks about the fact that "[w]hen the soul is interested in portraying its own interiority, it uses the image of a stone or a wall of rock."[41] This image helps us differentiate true interiority from what goes on in the ego, or in the interiority of esoteric spirituality. The rock, he says, "saves us from both. True interiority is not in us and is not anything esoteric. It is in the rock. And the rock is out there in reality."[42] He goes on, "It is very concrete, the experience of 'no exit,' of absolute futility,"[43] which opens our eyes provided we "hold our place in the absolute contradiction of a dead end and the continued faithfulness to our purpose. Because then the experienced stone wall interiorizes our progressive movement into itself so that it becomes in itself recursive progression."[44]

Love with a Capital L

As mentioned earlier, it was at the 2023 ISPDI Conference that the link between *Animus-Psychologie* and the notion of Love in connection with the Holocaust became visible to me. At the time, due to time constraints, Ulrich Stuck had to bring his talk to an end without finishing the last part on the syzygy. During the break, I read the last part of his translated version of Giegerich's written work on the syzygy. The literal translation was difficult to understand. I struggled without the benefit of the clarity found in Giegerich's writings in English. It inverted my world because at times the English text did not make sense, yet it felt seminal and inceptive, and I wanted to understand it. As I continued reading the last pages of Stuck's paper, I sensed something important was about to be revealed. From the moment I read Giegerich's response in the interview, I took seriously the advice he gave not to turn to him, but to the bewildering notion itself, the notion

---

[41] Giegerich, *CEP* IV, p. 171.
[42] *Ibid.*, p. 172.
[43] *Ibid.*
[44] *Ibid.*, pp. 171-172.

of Love (with a capital L) in connection with the Holocaust, and to turn to it in the quiet loneliness of thought, the thought of the heart, with the patience of being able to wait. This was especially appropriate, because the Love in question is not conferrable, cannot be conjured up with the consciousness of the past, or understood with the naturalistic subjective feelings of love that a person shows or feels. This is an initiation into logical Love, the consciousness of Love itself. The not-yet-known, unrevealed objective logical status of Love that, as Giegerich explains, is a "particular form of the soul's world-relation and world apperception in which people may find themselves. It is a relation without beings who relate."[45] When I encountered Section IV in Stuck's English translation of *Animus-Psychologie*, "The Spirit as Love," and read this first line, "We stand at the gateway to the stage in which the spirit of Love can reign,"[46] I had a whispery thought of what the Holocaust as an initiation into Love could be. As I continued reading, the eyes of my heart opened wide, and here is what it said:

> Love means purely negatively our grasping it, which always includes our being grasped by it. It means ourselves growing in the consciousness of love, and thus, acquiring a more loving consciousness (a consciousness that looks more lovingly into the distressed world) [...] Love means comprehending: even Auschwitz and the atomic bomb have a place in love," [...]. Herein lies [Love's] uncanniness and [...] terror, that which produces the panic and fear of her. [...] Love is deadly! But not through violence, but through its negativity, its allowing. It undermines the positivity and with it the security guaranteed by boundaries and clear separations of the opposites."[47]

That's it! Everything goes under in the absolute logical negativity of Spirit as Love, because it *is* the *via negativa* itself, "the absolute negative inwardization of positive reality into itself."[48] And, the terrifying thing about it is *its allowing!* It is the ultimate objective logical reality that bears all without interfering. What on earth is this consciousness really like? Even Jung admits in his "Late Thoughts"

---

[45] Giegerich, *CEP* VI, p. 43.
[46] Stuck, p. 49.
[47] *Ibid.*, p. 50.
[48] Giegerich, *CEP* VI, p. 41.

to "faltering before the task of finding the language which might adequately express the incalculable paradoxes of love,"[49] and, when faced with the mystery of love, admits to never being "able to explain what it is." This Love, Giegerich does explain, as follows:

> Is a real power, the ultimate objective reality. *But* it is only really present as that which it is if there is a *real* "subjective awareness" of it in the sense of a mind having been initiated into it, that is to say, having itself, by going under, attained the logical form.[50]

Giegerich indicates that what separated Jung from this understanding was his interpreting "his own century in terms of evil (on account of its many horrors), rather than as part of an *objective* historical initiation into Love."[51] This Giegerich found astounding for a soul-scholar of Jung's caliber.

Holocaust

It was estimated that by the end of the 20th century, the materials produced on the Holocaust would have equalled or exceeded the amount of material produced on any other subject in human history.[52] What more is there to say? Hence, I have not said much regarding the Holocaust because frankly I am allergic to the narratives, depictions, and dramatizations. In-short, I steer clear of them essentially because no matter what has been written, or represented in pictures, museums, and sites, as Elie Wiesel aptly states, "All this will not have brought you closer to the experience."[53] That said, I admit that my statements betray the contrary—that is, the inexpressible pain, and the conviction that neither *remembrance* nor *empathy* can call forth the real experience of the Holocaust, nor alter the barbarous defilement of human dignity endured by its victims.

---

[49] Jung, *MDR*, p. 353.

[50] Giegerich, *CEP* VI, p. 43.

[51] *Ibid.*.

[52] John C. Knapp, "The Nuclear Bomb Re-visited through the Eyes of the Shoah," in: Jennifer M. Sandoval and John C. Knapp, eds., *Psychology as the Discipline of Interiority: "The Psychological Difference" in the Work of Wolfgang Giegerich* (London and New York: Routledge, 2017), p. 155.

[53] Abrahamson, *Against Silence*, p. 30

Drawing on Freud's theory of the "psychic hole," which in contemporary psychoanalysis connotes a deficit or absence, the psychoanalyst Ilany Kogan applies the term to the offspring of Holocaust survivors who "had undergone massive trauma and often conveyed their feelings of depression and aggression to their children in a manner beyond words." [54] Her definition of the psychic hole is not connected to what Andre Green calls the "problem of emptiness" or the "work of the negative," which hypothesizes a dialectic interplay of absence and presence in the human psyche. She believes that in the case of the offspring of Holocaust survivors, the psychic hole does not remain empty but is filled with the unconscious fantasies pertaining to the parents' traumatization, too painful to be integrated into the victims' cognitive and affective framework. These traumatic fantasies residing in the offspring's "psychic holes" are "primitive identifications" connected to themes of "death and survival," that often get enacted. [55] I give this simplified version of an otherwise exhaustive psychoanalytic oeuvre to allude obliquely to my story, which I have never spoken of in public, but which dominated my entire life. The truth of the burden of such a legacy was, for me, always reserved for the confidential psychoanalytic hour. That said, I was born with a spirit that could never be deterred from a deep reverence for Love. In the absence of it, in the longing for it, in the sanity sought, was its presence, and I believe it was that that was captured by Giegerich's comments on the soul's perspective on the Holocaust.

As regards the state of consciousness and historical locus one finds oneself in, Giegerich declares that "there is no choice. We have to go all the way through with our real psychological situation, even if it appears as an impasse or as a dragon obstructing the way to the water of life." [56] Reading this passage brings to mind a dream I had at the beginning of this year:

---

[54] Ilany Kogan, "From Psychic Holes to Psychic Representations," in: Mary Kay O'Neil and Salman Akhtar, eds., *On Freud's "Negation"* (London: Karnac Books, 2011), p. 202.

[55] *Ibid.*, p. 204.

[56] Giegerich, *CEP* VI, p. 43.

I am in an endless ocean all alone. No land in sight, only the horizon in the distance appearing to connect heaven and ocean. As far as the eye can see, I am surrounded by water, reclining calmly, floating on a small white pillow with a thin white cable running underneath the water stretching into the distance— possibly to where I came from. Suddenly, gigantic, tall waves catapult me up from the horizontal position to a vertical one. Holding on to the small pillow, I am raised up against the immense waves towering over me. Looking down into the ocean's depths, I am terrified of falling into it. Yet, to my amazement, I am held in place and do not fall off.

When the soul speaks about itself in such a dramatic way, the attention it commands offers the possibility for us "to align our factual thinking with the inner logic of our real situation."[57] To sit calmly, alone in a vast ocean, and suddenly come under the sway of a formidable *force majeure*, only to discover an immanence of mercy and love—is a realization attributable to the timeless supervention of the soul. Apprehending the Holocaust as the soul's initiation into the spirit of Love has to be left *alone* to undergo the phases that precede its gradual historical realization; for as the lyrics of the classic Motown song say, "*You can't hurry Love. No, you just have to wait.*" We have to calmly wait, says Giegerich, "even if we as individuals might not live to see it—for to live, to truly live, means to be devoted to the present, to the next step, and to leave the future development to its own fate, in other words, to let it develop itself."[58]

---

[57] Giegerich, *CEP* III, p. 167.
[58] *Ibid.*, pp. 165-166.

7

The Creation of Outer Space and the Birth of Man in Japan

KENJI KANESHIRO

Introduction

We live in the age of space exploration. We know that the stars have a lifespan, and that the earth and the sun will one day cease to exist. Whether the universe itself has a lifespan is still under debate, but it has been observed that space is still expanding. And nowhere else in that expanding space is there a living being. Even if we cast the light of our consciousness to the edges of space, we can find only lifeless materials. Hence, man dwells with himself alone, "where, in the cold light of consciousness, the blank barrenness of the world reaches to the very stars."[1]

Outer Space is an archetypal image that is important to modern humans.[2] Humans developed rockets to explore space. This was an important event not only for science, but also for psychology, because it was related to the birth of Man. Giegerich analyzed the image of rockets as depicting the leap from the imaginal to reality. The speculative idea of the rocket created beneath itself the solid ground from which it was launched. And it was Christianity that gave man the idea of this solid ground. Through Christianity, the Western soul launched itself into Outer Space and came to see the earth from the outside. This represents a position where consciousness sees itself

---

[1] Jung, *CW* 9i § 29.
[2] Wolfgang Giegerich, "The Rocket and the Launching Base, or The Leap from the Imaginal into the Outer Space Named 'Reality'," *CEP* II, pp. 117- 135.

from the outside, even as it shows the stage where consciousness has become conscious of itself as Man.[3]

Even in the East, where the history of the soul is different from that of the West, the importation of Western science has had a significant impact. Japan, in particular, was one of the countries that actively adopted Western science and rapidly developed technology. This rapid development of science and technology in Japan has been a remarkable psychological phenomenon. The creation of the concept of Outer Space was a consequence of the same historical development that in the West produced Christianity. In the course of this long history, Western Man dug himself into this singular archetype, Outer Space, the zero. The Japanese soul, on the other hand, has taken in the natural sciences from the West and incorporated them into its own constitution without going through Christianity. This is probably due to the Japanese soul's tendency to compartmentalize and incorporate the foreign into its own composition.[4] However, Western science has brought about changes so great that the Japanese soul cannot compartmentalize without suffering its own distortions. This has caused conflicts with the traditional Japanese soul and has led to the emergence of neuroses.

One of the neuroses that is unique to Japan is anthropophobia. Anthropophobia is anxiety about the self being looked at by others. It is characterized by the fact that the value of the self does not depend on one's own evaluation, but on the external evaluation of others.[5] Just as the Judeo-Christian monotheistic God with his All-Seeing Eye was alchemically distilled and converted into the notion of the I,[6] I speculate that this being looked at from an external

---

[3] Wolfgang Giegerich, "The End of Meaning and the Birth of Man: An Essay about the State Reached in the History of Consciousness and an Analysis of C. G. Jung's Psychology Project," *CEP* IV, p. 218.

[4] Wolfgang Giegerich, *Pitfalls in Comparing Buddhist and Western Psychology: A Contribution to Psychology's Self-clarification* (London, ON: Dusk Owl Books, 2018), p. 24.

[5] Bin Kimura, *Hito to hito tono aida: Seishinbyorigakuteki nihonron* (Tokyo: Kobundo, 1972), pp. 185-201.

[6] Wolfgang Giegerich, *The Historical Emergence of the I: Essays about One Chapter in the History of the Soul* (London, ON: Dusk Owl Books, 2020), pp. 152-155.

viewpoint in anthropophobia could be a precursor of psychological consciousness in Japan.

Japanese neurotics fear the gaze of others. Then, who are the others? It is not someone in particular, but unnamed others. The Japanese critic Shichihei Yamamoto captured this ambiguous existence in the concept of "air."[7] He observed how, when making decisions, Japanese people would avoid taking responsibility and make excuses, saying that they had no choice but to go with "the air" of the moment. It is very vague and ambiguous, but it controls the Japanese psyche. Japanese neurotics are afraid of this "air." In Japanese, there is an expression *"kuuki wo yomu"* (reading the air), which means to be aware of the air and conform to it. In anthropophobia, the fear of being looked at by these nameless others, by this air, is prominent. Psychologically, it reveals the fear of being seen into, and along with this, the dread of the prospect of being ashamed if such an ocular incursion into one's own self were to happen.

It is interesting to note that the word "air" is associated with the neurosis peculiar to the Japanese culture. Air is something we are usually unaware of. It simply fills the space around us. We become aware of air when we feel suffocated; that is, when there is a lack of it. But so much for the literal air that we breath. The fact that the phrase "reading the air" has become widely used, and that people have become aware of air, is in itself an awareness of what enwraps the Japanese psyche. My hypothesis is that "reading the air" is a characteristic of the Japanese neurosis which has the potential to make an individual aware of his or her self being seen through, and thus, a challenging symptom that leads to the birth of Man in Japan.

Religion and "Air" in Japan

Psychology is the successor of religion.[8] The development which the Western soul went through during the course of its Christian history created the concept of Outer Space, turned Nature into physical facts, and led to that emergence of the modern subject from the form of myth that is called the birth of Man. In relation to

---

[7] Shichihei Yamamoto, *Kuuki no kenkyu* (Tokyo: Bungeishunjū, 1977).

[8] Wolfgang Giegerich, *Coniunctio: Reflexions on a Key Concept of C. G. Jung's Psychology* (London, ON: Dusk Owl Books, 2021), p. 88.

this, it is necessary to clarify Japanese religion if we are to understand how the Japanese soul has been dealing with Western technology.

Japanese religion is very ambiguous and has provoked much debate. Yamamoto pointed out that the air in Japan sometimes has a religious power that is irresistible.[9] On the other hand, when the air disappears, the substance disappears, and no one takes responsibility for it. It is elusive. Yamamoto thought that one of the reasons why the air has power is because of the animism of the Japanese, who see life in inanimate objects (hence, he said that "anima" or "pneuma" would be appropriate English translations of the word "kuuki"[10]).

Shintoism, characterized by animism and nature worship, has long existed in Japan, and it was followed by the introduction of Buddhism. Shintoism and Buddhism have coexisted since then.[11] However, there has been debate as to whether Shintoism should be considered as a religion or a set of rituals.[12] In fact, Shintoism builds shrines in places rich in nature and performs rituals to worship mountains, forests, huge rocks, and so on. Even after the introduction of Buddhism, Shintoism and Buddhism remained compatible through the explanation that the Buddha appears in the form of a variety of nature gods. And yet, the reason why Shintoism is said to be not a religion is because of the naturalistic emphasis on its rituals. Shintoism rituals are related to the activities of daily life, such as rice cultivation. Rituals serve as prayers to nature; they bring harvests and mitigate disasters. Shintoism does not have a metaphysical belief system. Therefore, it remains a stage of ritual rather than a religion. Shintoism rituals are directly related to people's lives, and its rituals were intended to maintain and bring prosperity to the community. It can be said that the soul of Japan has always had its place in the community that performed these rituals.

Folklorist Kunio Yanagita explained this Japanese spirituality with the concepts of "*ie* [home]" and ancestor worship.[13] The idea is that

---

[9] Yamamoto, *Kuuki no kenkyu*, p. 32.

[10] *Ibid.*, p. 59.

[11] Akio Yoshie, *Shinbutsushūgo* (Tokyo: Iwanami shinsho, 1996).

[12] Yuunosuke Kimura, Mushukyo dato bunmeika ni eikyo? In Nihonjin musyukyosetsu (Chikuma eBooks, 2023), p. 21.

[13] Kunio Yanagita, *Senzo no hanashi* (Tokyo: Kadokawa Sophia Bunko, 1946/2013). [Fanny Hagin Mayer, trans., *About Our Ancestors: The Japanese Family System* (Santa Barbara, CA: Greenwood, 1988)]

the Japanese soul worships ancestors who have maintained "home" for generations. In Japanese ancestor worship, the emphasis is on home. People become members of the home and work for its preservation and prosperity. In this context, being a member of the home is even more important than being genetically related. After death, people join the ancestral spirits. The spirits envisioned here by the Japanese soul are not spirits that reflect individual personalities. It is like a mass of spiritual energy. There is no distinction among individuals. For example, in the communities around Mt. Gassan, it was believed that after death people become the spirits of their ancestors and climb the mountain.[14] Here, the sacred mountain is equated with a mass of spirits.

The ancestral spirits return home from the mountains once a year. It is the ancestral spirits identified with nature that bring prosperity to the descendants, and nature worship and ancestor worship point in the same direction. In other words, the worship of ancestor/nature brings about a good harvest, averts disasters, and ensures the prosperity of the descendants, even as the prosperity of the descendants enriches the ancestor/nature spirits. Thus, in Japan's longstanding ancestor worship, this earthly world and the beyond are interpenetrated. In the cycle of the four seasons, the descendants continue their rituals, and the ancestral spirits return to this world to bring a harvest. The Japanese soul had lived this circulation of spiritual energy since ancient times.

Western Civilization and the End of "Home"

The Japanese soul had been living in a world where everything circulated and shifted, never remaining in the same state. At first glance, the Japanese religion seems to be compatible with the idea of energy and ecology in Western science, and the contours of the Japanese religions were blurred accordingly.

But in truth, the two are not the same at all. While Western natural science is based on the speculative concept of Outer Space, which means being outside of Nature, for the Japanese soul, Nature was not clearly separated as an object. Rather, Nature *was* subject, and the

---

[14] Masataka Suzuki, *Sangakushinko* (Tokyo: Chuokoron-shinsha, 2015), p. 41.

Japanese soul dreamt in the state of being enwrapped by Nature. However, coming upon it from outside, Western science and technology cruelly violated nature and distorted it. The innocence of the Japanese soul was destroyed by this imposition. On an empirical level, this is related to the rapid development of industrial technology, during which a great deal of pollution occurred in various parts of the Japanese land, resulting in such afflictions as Minamata disease. Air and water were polluted. At that time it was realized by the Japanese soul that nature could be altered by man, and this caused serious conflict.

The Japanese soul innocently adopted Western technology, thereby destroying nature, which had been its home. Thus, the Japanese soul lost what had enveloped it and found nature to be nothing more than mere physical facts. Having lost the Nature that it had been enwrapped in, the Japanese soul then went through two stages to reach modern consciousness. In the first stage, the importance of the home, which had been equated with Nature, was redoubled and a desperate resistance to maintain the family arose. Now the home had become the battleground of the Japanese soul.

Earlier it was noted that Nature worship and ancestor worship were originally interwoven in Japan. In consequence of this, when the soulful, spirit-filled nature was destroyed by the introduction of natural science, the home still remained something that enveloped the individual. This was studied by Hayao Kawai as the "pathology of the maternal principle" in Japan, which refers to the tendency for a family or community to become so powerful that it erases the individual will.[15]

In the second stage, the soul tries to push off from the home of the first stage. This is a transitional stage: the soul leaves the home behind but creates "the air" as its substitute, enveloping itself. At this point, the Japanese "read the air" to maintain harmony with the group. However, when anthropophobia emerges, it makes the person conscious of "the air" and makes it impossible for him or her to identify with the group. As a result, he or she fears "being read by the air" and feels suffocated; that is, the person experiences the air as seeing into his or her own inner self, and is tormented by the anxiety of being ashamed. This is the modern situation of the Japanese soul.

---

[15] Hayao Kawai, *Boseishakai Nihon no byori* (Tokyo: Kodansha, 1976/1997).

Man in Japan is now a part of bare nature, as a human being separated from Nature. The "I" in the Western sense has not yet been established. In order to regain the home it had lost, the Japanese soul created "the air" in which it phobically enveloped itself and for which it pays in the currency of suffering such a heavy price.

Images of Outer Space and the Birth of Man

We have come to an understanding of the difficult situation in which the soul of Japan finds itself. From here, I would like to go a little further and discuss a possible way for the Japanese soul to face this conflict and move to a new logical constitution.

I speculate that the soul will push off from itself through the image/concept of "space without air," that is, Outer Space. This was predicted in a monumental poem by a young poet, published shortly after the war, in 1952. It was a poem by Shuntaro Tanikawa, one of Japan's greatest poets, who published his first collection of poems at the age of 20. The poem was titled "*Nijuoku kounen no kodoku*" ("Two Billion Light Years of Solitude").[16]

Mankind on a little ball,
sleeping, waking and working,
and sometimes they want a companion on Mars.

Martians on a little ball,
I don't know what they're doing.
(Or, I guess they are nellying, kirlooing or hurrahing.)
But sometimes they want a companion on Earth.
It is absolutely true.

Universal Gravity
is the power of solitude that attracts.

The universe is distorted.
That's why everyone seeks each other.

The universe is expanding more and more.
That's why everyone is anxious.

---

[16] Shuntaro Tanikawa, *Nijuoku kounen no kodoku* (Tokyo: Shueisha Bunko, 1952/2008) (my translation).

In the solitude of two billion light years,
I sneezed in spite of myself.

In this poem, Man finds himself on a little ball, the earth. Here, the poet's consciousness is already in Outer Space, looking at itself from the outside. All human activity is contained within this sphere. Man seeks Martians, but the emphasis, as the title suggests, is on the sense of loneliness. As the line "I don't know what they're doing" clearly expresses, the "Martians" in this poem represents the Other (hence the Martians' speaking a language that makes no sense).

The poet's consciousness has already reached a place without air. I want to point out that this place is imagined via the archetypal image of Outer Space. When the soul goes deep into this archetypal image, it will be, let us surmise, to open up the possibility of Man being born as consciousness. The space imagined here is in sharp contrast to "the air" that enwraps the Japanese psyche. The space in the poem is distorted and expanding, causing loneliness and anxiety. In contrast, "the air" in Japanese neurosis envelops people, erasing the space between individuals in the name of "harmony" and suffocating them.

This poem also refers to love, in that people seek each other out of loneliness. Needless to say, Love is the theme of the modern soul. The more we seek, the more the space expands, and the more we come to realize that conjunction is impossible. It is in this uncertainty that modern man becomes anxious. And the poem suddenly ends with a sneeze. This is the moment of the birth of Man. It is the moment when the universe, which was born from the Big Bang, is interiorized into itself, which is hinted at by the little Big Bang, that is, the sneeze.

This poem describes one of the possible ways in which the Japanese soul deals with the conflict with natural science and comes to its version of what in the West has been the birth of Man. The Japanese neurosis pushes off from itself as "the air," and in so doing finds airless space. There is no nameless ambiguous other, but the solitude and the possibility of Love. More than half a century ago, a poet predicted the possibility of the birth of Man in Japan. This is a process that is still ongoing and is therefore observed in clinical cases. Finally, I will illustrate, with the case of a young Japanese man who suffered from anthropophobia, the birth of Man at the level of the individual.

Case Material

When I first met him, he was a young man of fifteen. He was brought to my counseling office by his parents. His parents requested to be present for the first session. When they were present, it was they, not he, who explained his condition. At that point, his self was buried in what earlier in this essay was discussed under the heading "the Home." The first task of psychotherapy was to challenge this situation. The initial outcome was that he was emboldened to resist his parents. After that, his anthropophobia came to the fore.

Three years later, when he was eighteen years old, he was preparing to enter an art college. At that time, he rarely talked to his friends or family and kept to himself, either surfing the Internet, studying, or reading books. His task, at that juncture, was to create and submit a piece of artwork as part of an entrance exam. But he could not show his work to anyone, including his therapist. He was afraid of being criticized or ridiculed by others. Even in everyday life, he complained that people he passed by on the street were saying bad things about him. His fear of other people sometimes took on a paranoid character. However, I must add that he had the intelligence to reflect and talk about himself when such was the case, saying that this fear might be his own assumption. During this time he reported a dream.

Dream 1:

> *I go to the infirmary and see a girl with hairy lips. At first I am horrified, but I think it could be her personality.*

The girl in the first dream seemed to represent, in the manner typical of such anima figures, the dreamer's self-relation. Her lips are apart, suggestive of kissing, and show in this way the possibility of his relating to himself. However, his psyche at that time was too sensitive and needed hair to cover the lips. He feels a strong sense of anxiety, but tries to calm himself down by thinking that this is just her personality.

Dream 3:

> *I am going to eat a cat in a pot. My cat is cut into pieces. The cat is meowing and I feel sorry for it. I yell that we shouldn't do such a terrible thing, but my parents say that it happens all the time, that it's no big deal, and that it can't be helped, and they cut it up.*

This dream has an initiation character. He is to take into his body, an animal covered with hair (which he associated with an animal of freedom). His parents appear as beings who have already accepted this transition. Through the initiation, he dissolves the state of being covered and protected by hair. It suggests the need for him to accept the freedom and responsibility of self-determination.

Dream 5:

> *I am skiing for the school club. I am about to be eaten by a big bear. I escape into the back of a truck. There is a bear who protects me and saves me from being eaten.*

In this dream, there are two kinds of bears. One is a terrifying bear that tries to eat him, and the other is a bear that protects him. Now he should be eaten and dismembered, but he is not ready for it. It is unusual for a bear to protect a man from another bear, which seems to indicate his wishful thinking to be protected by hair.

By this time, his fear of others was diminishing, but he still could not let others see his artwork. He said he would make a distinction between "the artwork I make for people" and "the artwork I make for myself," and he would keep the latter a secret. But it did not go well. At that time I asked him to draw a picture of a tree (Tree 1).

When I asked him what would happen to the tree, he replied that it would grow thick and big, like a thousand-year-old tree in the desert. In the next session, he wanted to draw another tree.

He then drew a second tree with intricate lines (Tree 2). He said, "Some people may say this is not a tree, but if I say it is, it is a tree." This was indeed a tree that is not a tree, a *negated* tree. Next, I asked him to draw a fantasy tree (Tree 3).

Tree 1

Tree 2

He said about this tree, "I want it to grow infinitely. I want it to reach the edge of the universe. It is a tree that is unstable, but it stands firm."

Unstable stability! Drawing became a catalyst for him. Later, he made a work based on the image of that unstable tree and showed it to me for the first time. He described his art as a tree whose branches grow and extend into Outer Space, and when they are fully extended, they shrink back to the earth. He submitted this work and was accepted into the college. Although still angry with his parents and society, he said that this anger was lessening and disappearing. He also said that he should not just blame someone else, but also be a driving force to change society. The last dream he reported was the following.

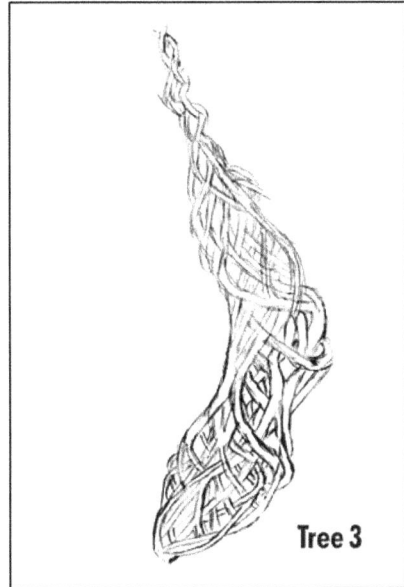

Tree 3

Dream 7:

> *I live with someone. I am in a house with about four beds. There are people I know and people I don't know. The person I know is a classmate who is the complete opposite of me. I don't know any girls. They all wear light blue clothes, like hospital gowns.*

Here we are presented with opposites: four beds, a person whom he knows, and persons whom he does not know. It is as if the girl with hairy lips in the first dream doesn't need hair to protect herself any more. That they are all in blue clothes suggests that they are in the middle of the healing process (the hospital gowns comparison). This concludes our discussion of his dreams. After he entered the college, he made friends there and became a member of the art group. That was the end of his psychotherapy.

He had had anthropophobia and could not show his artwork to anyone because he was afraid of being looked at by "the air," the nameless others. During psychotherapy, he became aware of his own anger towards his parents and Japanese society. However, he was unable to break out of this state. The turning point came when he drew "a tree that is not a tree." In the course of doing this he stretched the branches of the tree to fill the space of the paper. It was, so to speak, the explosion of the tree and of the imaginal that had enwrapped him. This imaginal world was his neurosis, the air. He destroyed the imaginal by drawing the imaginal.

That the Japanese soul is still enveloped in the imaginal is reflected in the interest of Japanese artists in constructing imaginary worlds. This is evident, for example, in the fact that Japanese animation works are widely appreciated throughout the world. What is interesting here is that the patient from our case example needed an image to blow up the imaginal. In order to push off from "the air," which is very vague and ambiguous, he had to fill the space with a substance. That is probably why the second tree was drawn, the image of exploding and spreading its branches.

If he had just deleted the image here and created an empty space, he would have remained at the stage of the aesthetic resolution of conflict,[17] which is often seen in traditional Japanese culture. The Japanese soul creates a void and undoes the negation by hypostatizing nothingness. It is a negation of negation that does not bring about any change in the logical constitution of soul. It is like putting white paint on a canvas to erase a painting. The imaginal basis, the canvas itself, is not negated.

On the other hand, in his drawings, the patient filled the space with images and thus negated it. It was necessary to be very aware of the presence of the canvas to negate it. It was to become engulfed within, like the tree in the third drawing, and to disappear into itself. After the explosion, it shrinks. This is the same kind of movement that Tanigawa's poem abruptly turns into the sneeze. Giegerich says: "The move into the outer space beyond consciousness in order to see it from the outside is dialectically the interiorization (*Er-innerrung*) of the whole of the former consciousness into itself. It is similar to an involution."[18] The drawing of the third tree is exactly a representation of this involution.

Of course, this is a soulful development occurring at the level of individual neurosis. Whether a similar development will occur at the collective level of the Japanese soul remains to be seen. But I see here the birth of Man in Japan, as the poet Shuntaro Tanikawa described it about 70 years ago. Man discovers himself, not only in solitude, but also in the possibility of Love with the Other. And just as a sneeze is a reaction to a foreign object touching one's body, so can the encounter between the I and its Other bring about a little Big Bang. It is the moment when "the air" is blown away and Outer Space and its starting point, the zero, are born, if only for now on the level of the *opus parvum*.

---

[17] Hayao Kawai, *Yume, Shinwa, Monogatari to Nihonjin* (Tokyo: Iwanami Shoten, 2022). [Hayao Kawai, *Dreams, Myths and Fairy Tales in Japan* (Einsiedeln: Daimon Verlag, 1995)]

[18] Giegerich, "The End of Meaning," p. 220.

8

The State of Psychology in Japan: The Historical Transition of the Soul as Seen in *Shinju* (Love Suicide)

TSUYOSHI INOMATA

Shinju (Love Suicide) and Interiority

When we think about where the soul resides, we can probably respond that it is within human activities, and in particular, in culture. In this paper, I would like to begin by considering it in the context of a specific culture, namely Japan. Of course, I would like to discuss it not only as a single isolated case, but also with the assumption that it is connected to the universality of the human psyche, transcending the boundaries of Asia.

I would like to discuss the state of the psyche in Japan. Especially in this context, I deepen this theme by paying particular attention to the historical evolution of the image of love suicide in Japan. However, you may wonder why I dwell on this topic today, since it is probably far away in some Asian country, and the theme of love suicide does not seem very contemporary to you. I start by explaining this point.

In English, the term "love suicide" is usually expressed as "double suicide," which is used especially to describe the suicide of a man and woman who are in love. In such a case, it is called a "love suicide." In the case of a family, it is also called "family suicide," and a suicide forced by one of the suicide partners is called "forced double suicide." All of these are referred to as "*shinju*" in Japan. No matter which expression you look at, the word "suicide" is always at the center. However, the Japanese word "*shinju*," translated directly into English, signifies "inside the psyche," i.e., etymologically speaking, the word has the meaning of "getting into the psyche." In other words, the emphasis in Japanese love suicide is not on dying. Rather, it is in particular the act of two people, a man and a woman, who love each other, giving up on the idea of being united in this world, and committing suicide together at the same time, which in essence means "entering into the psyche and being united in the psyche."

Now, turning with this in mind to the concept of "interiority," which is so central to our sense of psychology as "the discipline of interiority," we find it expressed in a German book by Giegerich with the word, "*Erinnerung*." Of this he writes as follows:

> In psychoanalysis, we distinguish between "remembering/*Erinnern*" and "acting out," whereby the acting out is seen as a form of defense through which psychology is prevented. This pair of concepts could be used to describe the difference between psychology and politics. What would be a necessity in psychology, "acting" and with it the vigorous will to act for change, is precisely the legitimate task and virtue of politics. The domain of psychology is the remembering, the interiority/*Er-Innerung*: the path into the depths of real phenomena as they are in themselves.[1]

The main task of psychology is not to act outwardly, but rather to sublate the phenomenon of interest to the state of interiority by inwardizing it into itself. This opens the way to engage the deeper realm called the soul. The psyche can never go outside of itself, but rather, moves in a circular movement around itself, internalizing itself into itself.

In this way, this concept of interiority seems to contain something similar to the Japanese concept of *shinju*. However, there are, of course, significant differences. The reason why I discuss *shinju* as a state of psyche in Japan is that I would like to clarify the similarities and differences between *shinju* and Interiority, and through this analysis, work on clarifying psychology itself. For surely, an examination of *shinju* and the interiority concept in the light of each other will provide an answer to the question that serves as the title for this book, "Where is soul?"—and an answer, also, to the one implied in its subtitle, "Where is the soul in modernity?"

---

[1] Wolfgang Giegerich, *Die Atombombe als seelische Wirklichkeit* (Freiburg: Raben-Reihe, 1986), p.12 (my translation of the original German).

A *Shinju* Story and Psychology in Japan

The story of *shinju* (love suicide) was first widely covered in Japan in 1703, when the playwright Chikamatsu Monzaemon published his play, "*Sonezaki shinju*," based on a real-life incident that had taken place in the forest of Sonezaki in Osaka just two weeks earlier. Here is a synopsis of the story:

It is the story of a love affair between Ohatsu, a prostitute, and Tokubei, a young man who works in his uncle's soy sauce shop. Because of his faithful work, he has gained the trust of his uncle, and his uncle has come up with the idea of marrying his daughter to Tokubei so that Tokubei can inherit the store. Tokubei refuses the marriage proposal because he is in love with Ohatsu, but his uncle proceeds with the marriage arrangements without telling him, and even goes so far as to pay the betrothal money to Tokubei's stepmother. Nevertheless, Tokubei persists in his refusal to go ahead with the marriage, so his uncle finally becomes angry and disowns him. Tokubei is ordered to return the betrothal money and is banished from Osaka. He manages to get the money back from his stepmother, but before he can hand it over to his uncle, his friend Kuheiji, who is in desperate need of money, asks him to lend him the amount he needs, promising to return it in three days.

Three days later, when Tokubei goes to Kuheiji to ask him to pay hm back, Kuheiji denies ever having borrowed any money from him and, on the contrary, publicly accuses Tokubei of being a swindler, beating him up severely. As a result, Tokubei loses the trust of the people. Tokubei sees Kuheiji's act as a terrible betrayal by the man he had trusted so implicitly that he could call him a brother. Tokubei decides that the only way to prove that he did not embezzle the betrothal money is to demonstrate his innocence by giving up his life, so he visits Ohatsu at the teahouse (brothel) secretly after dark to discuss his plan with her. For her part, Ohatsu is being strongly encouraged by her landlady to marry a wealthy man, and she, too, believes that the only way to be with Tokubei is to commit *shinju*.

At the teahouse, Ohatsu hides Tokubei under the porch so that the others will not see him, and they discuss the matter. In the meantime, Kuheiji shows up at the teahouse, but Ohatsu treats him with indifference, and he leaves, speaking ill of Tokubei. Listening under the porch, Tokubei learns of Kuheiji's infatuation with Ohatsu and listens angrily as Kuheiji boasts about how he cheated Tokubei out of the money he had borrowed.

When Tokubei comes out from under the porch, he tells Ohatsu that he is ready to die. Soon after midnight, Ohatsu and Tokubei take each other's hand and make their way unnoticed to the open-air god's shrine in the Sonezaki forest, the beginning of their journey to the underworld. They bind each other to a pine tree to confirm their resolve, but Tokubei hesitates to take the life of his beloved Ohatsu with his own hand. Ohatsu urges him to "hurry, hurry," and finally Tokubei takes Ohatsu's life using a dagger, only to end his own life by slashing his throat with a razor. The story climaxes with the death of the two, who meet their tragic end in this life with a firm promise to be united with each other in the next life: "They will become a model for future love fulfilled in Buddhahood." [2]

As the story goes, the two lovers are driven into difficulties one after another by family relationships, friendships, and financial obligations, and when they realize that each of these relationships is intertwined and unsolvable, they decide to commit love suicide into their psyche. In other words, they come to the conclusion that the only way to be free from family, friends, and finances is to enter the psyche via death.

When this play was written in the early 1700s, Japan was at the height of what is known as the Genroku culture. It is said that this was a period of great cultural upsurge in Japan, comparable to the Renaissance in the West. At that time, there were few wars in Japan, and with the consequent development of commerce and the monetary system, people who were no longer involved in agriculture flowed into the cities, giving rise to a new class of urban dwellers. In contrast to farming, which involved a daily struggle with nature, life in the cities gave people more free time. Moreover, the absence of war and the development of a monetary economy made life comfortable and stable. Supported by such freedom and affluence in the cities,

---

[2] Chikamatsu Monzaemon, *Sonezaki shinjū* [*The Love Suicides at Sonezaki*] (Tokyo: Kadokawa, 2007), pp. 5-290 (my summarized translation).

various cultures emerged. In addition to *ningyo joruri* (puppet theatre), which was the main way in which this story of *shinju* was presented, haiku, painting, sculpture, and other cultural works were produced, and these works showed exceptional results.

But in the midst of such freedom and affluence, how did such a tale of love suicide come to be? It is understandable, of course, by looking at the content of this story. That is, it becomes clear that although people gained freedom from nature, they were not freed from human relationships, such as those involved in family and friendship. And furthermore, with the development of a monetary economy, they were also bound together in relationships through money. When we were enclosed by nature and engaged in agricultural daily work, we had to work together and cope with the fury of nature, and in this sense, we naturally had to provide mutual assistance to one another. However, as monetary transactions became a part of daily life, mutual support disappeared, and the very nature of human existence changed, with relationships now being mediated by money. At the same time, the communal relationships between people became less about mutual support and more about contractual relationships, in which people bound and controlled each other financially.

The female protagonist of this story, Ohatsu, was sold as a child to a brothel as a prostitute, while the marriage of the male protagonist, Tokubei, was determined by a betrothal gift. Moreover, the mistress of Ohatsu's brothel is kind, as is Tokubei's uncle, who is the president of the company Tokubei works for, and the protagonists' loyalty to these two people cannot be betrayed. In addition, Tokubei's friend Kuheiji, who easily betrays his friend's trust, seems to think that he can cheat his girlfriend by swindling her out of money, and looking at Kuheiji, the only way to live without loyalty is to be ruled by money. Furthermore, it could be said that Tokubei realized that he could not be a part of either of the two options. He could neither accommodate the wishes of his uncle, who tried to protect the family and live steadily, nor yield to Kuheiji, who tried to live individualistically as a profligate merchant. He therefore had no choice but to take the third path, which was to commit love suicide.

This third way of "double suicide" is not just a simple double suicide of lovers, as I explained at the beginning of this essay, but a way of "entering psyche." By dying together, the lovers open up the "world of soul," and a realm free from morality, humanity, and money can now be entered. Tokubei had no choice but to take the third way, which was to commit suicide. And the way to be released from this situation, adulterated as it was by demands for filial loyalty and modern economic concerns, was more difficult than it was for someone in earlier times to break free from the state of existence in which he was enveloped by nature. Here there was no other way than to die and put his hope in the next life. Or more acutely still, the only way was through love suicide to enter the psyche, where the two of them would be together.

At the beginning of this play, Ohatsu goes to 33 temples to pray and reads the following lyrical poem.

> Change Yourself in thirty-three,
> Leading the way with erotic beauty, teaching with mercy,
> Love is the bridge to bodhi,
> Kannon, the Goddess of Mercy, who saves us by crossing over,
> and whose vows are strangely gratifying.[3]

There is one more thing to note about "*Sonezaki shinju.*" This play is performed in Bunraku puppet theatre. The story of this *shinju* would be too emotional and intense if performed by flesh-and-blood actors, but the puppets, which are devoid of emotional expressions and perform only with gestures and movements, are very suitable as a method of expression for the theatre. The puppet stage opens up the possibility of reflecting essences from the world of human emotion in a less visceral manner.

As mentioned earlier, the difference between acting out and interiority was confirmed by quotes from Giegerich. In keeping with this distinction, we can say that if the play were performed by flesh-and-blood actors, it would have the merely literal character of being acted out, whereas when performed with puppets, "*shinju*" in its essential sense is expressed more clearly. The puppet reflects the human figure in a very stylized way. But as such, the puppet is stripped of the human-all-too-human things that accompany a person's daily life. This opens up the realm of the "soul," which is not visible to our eyes. The audience understands the play as if the puppet, not the

---

[3] *Ibid.* (my translation).

human being, has the psychic agency. In other words, the psyche is not in the actions of the human being, but in the puppet. Along with this, the audience additionally realizes that the psyche does not reside in the human being, but somewhere else. Even though a non-human, non-living being is playing the role of a human being, the audience perceives the deepest essence of human existence *in the performance* of the puppet. This is the true essence of *ningyo joruri* (puppet drama. In this way, the highly emotional drama of double suicide dramatically opens up the realm of the psyche, both in terms of content and in terms of the medium of puppet theatre, bringing the psyche into real existence and making interiority explicit.

Chikamatsu Monzaemon wrote an essay, "Kyojitsu Himaku Ron" [The Skin Membrane Theory of Fiction and Reality], in which he said:

> Art resides in the interspace of the skin membrane between reality and fiction. It is true that people today prefer to reflect facts in a realistic manner. However, kabuki actors and puppets, for example, reflect the gestures and speech of the true patriarch, but their appearance is different from that of the true patriarch. ... Falsehood is not falsehood, and reality is not reality, and there is comfort between the two.[4]

What is referred to here as "comfort" is not saying merely that the human mind is comforted by such art, but that it is moved from its deepest level. We may recall here the following words from Giegerich:

> The living soul is in the last analysis what is sparked off when a dead work and the right human subject touch. The soul is the spark that is ignited. The spark itself is bodiless. It is a happening. Momentary, lasting only for as long as it lasts. It is neither in the work or letter *per se*, nor in the human person, be it in his brain or in the interiority of his mind. No, it *is* only as the between, as and in their contact, which corresponds to what on the interpersonal level is the sharedness of meanings. It is the encounter between something dead and the human mind.[5]

---

[4] Chikamatsu Monzaemon, "Kyojitsu Himaku Ron" [The Skin Membrane Theory of Fiction and Reality], in: *Chikamatsu Joururi-syu*, (Tokyo: Iwanami, 1956), pp. 358-359, (my summary from the Japanese).

[5] Wolfgang Giegerich, *What Is Soul?* (New Orleans, LA: Spring Journal Books, 2012), p. 57.

At this point, the following becomes clear: This tale of a man and a woman's double suicide is not simply a love story between two human beings. Nor is it merely an attempt to realize a romantic relationship that cannot be established and continued in this world in the afterlife or the next world after their death. This play depicts an encounter with death that definitively leaves behind worldly reality, and as the audience watching it, we are touched by that real death and our hearts burst into sparks. As a result, it can be said that this work has the potential to open up the realm of soul. By depicting and expressing the moment of encounter with death as a work of art, this work of fiction, as Giegerich says, opens up the realm of soul in the psychological sense as a spark.

In this sense, it would not be an exaggeration to say that Japanese cultural works dealing with *shinju*, whether successful or not in their intentions, are works that aim to disclose the realm of the soul. After Chikamatsu's play in 1703, many *shinju* stories were spawned in Japan, such as *"Chushingura"* and *"Yotsuya Kaidan"* in the 1800s, and in the 1900s, *"Nigorie," "Shimabara Shinju," "Clown Flowers,"* and countless others. There are many masterpieces of the *shinju* works in Japan. In other words, through modern psychological stories, Japanese culture became explicitly aware, for the first time, of the interiority of the soul as a space to inhabit.

The Acting out of *Shinju* and Japanese Psychology or Religion

However, the artworks of *shinju* did not make their way only into the psychology of the Japanese. In the 1930s, just before the war, there was a period known as the "suicide season," when as many as 14,000 people a year committed suicide in the dark days leading up to the war. It is said that among them were many suicides between lovers, as well as suicides involving whole families. This trend continues to this day, and according to a 2023 survey,[6] suicide is the leading cause of death in Japan for those between the ages of 10 and 39, and it remains the second leading cause of death even among those in their 40s. In addition, suicide consistently accounts for 20 percent of all deaths in

---

[6] *Suicide statistics*, Japanese Ministry of Health, Labour, and Welfare, 2023.

Japan for those between the ages of 20 and 69. This means that people from adolescence to adulthood are regularly contemplating and committing suicide. However, nowadays, suicide by lovers is rare, and family suicide is also rare, and people are often choosing to die alone. In other words, the expectation of happiness after death and the desire to be together in the next life have disappeared, and people seem to be simply choosing death out of despair. However, even in such cases, it is difficult to say whether they are simply choosing death as individuals. It is remarkable that of the more than 20,000 suicides a year in Japan, nearly 4,000 people jump to their death in front of an oncoming train. While jumping into the path of an oncoming train is not love suicide, it does seem to send a message to the many people who use the trains that the person is dead, forcing them to share the experience of death with him or her. In any case, there is so much acting out of suicide in Japan that there is no longer any interiority or psychologizing of it.

While I mentioned the psychological importance of puppet theatre, we must not forget that puppets have traditionally been used ritually as a substitute. That is, we Japanese have been trying to free ourselves from human suffering, illness, and contamination by making the puppets serve as our stand-ins and doubles, and we have lived our lives using them as objects of ritualistic sacrifice. The figurative role of puppets is still prevalent in modern Japan, especially at children's festivals, where puppets continue to play an important role, taking the place of children and thereby protecting them from the evils of the world. In this way, the use of puppets in the expressive arts not only serves to provide an intermediary between the fictive and the real, but also leads to the pragmatic use of puppets as tools in an animistic view of the world. The destination to which this has come in present times is Japanese *manga* and *anime* culture, which promotes the acceptance of game-like avatars as self-images and AI characters as one's companion.

Thus, when we look at the situation surrounding suicide in contemporary Japan and the use of puppets for the benefit of human beings, we can understand that the human expression of *shinju* is not always an expression that opens up the realm of the soul, but rather can also include a movement away from psychology. The psychological understanding of suicide discussed by James Hillman in *Suicide and*

Soul[7] is not accepted by many, and suicide is usually regarded as something to be prevented and avoided. This kind of medical worldview, which places such importance on life, may counteract the idea that suicide opens up the realm of the soul, and may lead to humans once again being constrained by human relationships based on emotion, morality, and loyalty. Consequently, suicidal ideas and impulses cease to be about the manifestation of the soul and are rather to be understood as a simple acting out. And in this can be discerned a moving away from the puppet theatre-like moment, in which the encounter with the corpse becomes the spark through which the soul can be glimpsed.

As Giegerich said in *Buddhist and Western Psychology*,[8] the Japanese mind, while seeming to accept the Western mind's valuing of negation, does so only by splitting the mind into two compartments, one that accepts negation and one that excludes it. This compartmentalization is well expressed in the fact that while Buddhism, on the one hand, is pregnant with negation (as its dismissal of the natural world as *maya* and illusion shows), Shintoism, on the other, holds that even today all things have a soul, and that the world is filled with natural universal deities. This is truly evident in the fact that Shintoism and Buddhism are both established in Japanese culture at the same time.

What is even more characteristic is that many Japanese, when asked, "What is your religion?," usually smile a little and answer, "I have no religion," or, when pressed to say more, answer, "I believe in both Buddhism and Shintoism, a little bit. For funerals, I am Buddhist, and for New Year's and other celebrations, I am Shinto. Sometimes I believe in Christianity, for weddings." The reason this is possible is that such beliefs are not a matter of the real mind, but only concern one compartmentalized side, the side of technological modern society. As for the other compartment, the animistic world, in it the individual is not established in the first place, given that people consider it of primary importance to be in tune with the group or the community. To put this more precisely, when Japanese people talk in a group context, although it is thought that the group is made up

---

[7] James Hillman, *Suicide and the Soul* (London: Hodder and Stoughton, 1964).

[8] Wolfgang Giegerich, *Pitfalls in Comparing Buddhist and Western Psychology* (London, ON: Dusk Owl Books, 2018).

of individuals, in reality the group itself is like air and has no substance. This group does not have a firm identity as a group, and even if it has a defining characteristic or purpose, it is nevertheless still something that changes, without substance, like a jewel beetle. Or, you could say it is like a kind of vortex. That is to say, we Japanese are immersed in something like air, something like a vortex, something that is constantly changing color and is not fixed.

For example, Hideki Tojo, the Japanese Prime Minister during World War II, when asked if he was running a dictatorship, gave the following strange response:

> Dictatorship is often referred to. Tojo is a mere humble retainer of a grass-root farmer. I am not different from you. However, I have been given the responsibility of Prime Minister. This is the difference. This shines only when it receives the light of the Majesty of Japan. Without his Majesty's light, I would be nothing more than a pebble. I am in this position because I have His Majesty's trust, and I shine. This is what makes me different from the European lords who are called dictators.[9]

Japanese ultranationalism thus has no substance. But this lack of substance does not open the way to psychology, but only to a vortex with no clear center. The logic of the group is nowhere clearly manifested, and we might say that we are submerged in a kind of vortex, but without awareness of it.

Critical reflection, born of the negating action that consciousness visits upon itself, is an important factor, which gave rise to psychology in the West. This work of negation proceeds via collisions on the semantic level of what is visible to the eye in the outer world, which catapult the mind to the level of syntax, in which insights are to be had that are not visible to the eye. In Japan, however, one could say that by compartmentalizing and diverging from the inner world of the mind, this effect of negation has been destroyed. Thus, we see here the emergence of a form of psychology that stops in the middle of the path of psychological emergence, a phenomenon that perhaps also provides

---

[9] Masao Maruyama, "The Logic and Psychology of Ultra-Nationalism," in: *Selected Papers of Masao Maruyama* (Tokyo: Heibon-sya, 2010), p. 75 (my translation.)

a hint for considering how the emergence of psychology is interrupted in various cultures other than Japan.

There is one more thing that should be discussed here: the Japanese way of thinking about religion. In this connection, I have to wonder about my readers' familiarity with Confucianism. As mentioned earlier, Shintoism and Buddhism are the most popular religions in Japan. However, there is another hidden religion in Japan called Confucianism. I use the adjective "hidden" because I believe that Confucianism is indeed a religion that we Japanese are mostly unaware of. I was living in Europe from 1996 to 2003, and I still remember how surprised I was when a colleague I met in Europe said to me, "Japan is a Confucian country, isn't it?" At the time, I was not aware that I was a Confucianist, nor did I imagine that Confucianism was involved in my spiritual life in any way. Later, however, when I learned more about Confucianism and psychology, I came to realize that not only I, but the Japanese people as a whole, have accepted and practiced Confucian spirituality without being aware of it.

The following summary of Confucianism relies on the expertise of the Japanese Confucian scholar Nobuyuki Kaji.

The basic idea of Confucianism is ancestor worship, which is common to many shamanistic cultures throughout the world. The uniqueness of Confucianism lies in the fact that it has been developed into a theoretical system. Kaji defines religion as "an explanation of death and the afterlife," and the Confucian explanation differs from the Buddhist explanation of liberation from the suffering of life. At the heart of the Confucian view of life and death are invocation and rebirth rituals and shamanism, which recognize the existence of spirits and invite them to come and reanimate themselves in this life. How does one do such a thing? First, a person dies and becomes an ancestral spirit. Then, the living perform the ritual of inviting this ancestral spirit to return to this world, and every year, on a set day in the spring (analogous to All Souls' Day in the Christian tradition), the ancestral spirit spends some time in this world with the living. In this way, it is explained that although a person has died once, his or her spirit is repeatedly "resurrected." Through this invocative reanimation rite, the dead are realistically returned to their families, and the dead continue to live on in ancestor worship through the repetition of the rite.

The Confucian concept of "filial piety" is based on three elemental concepts: (1) respect for one's parents; (2) ancestral rites; and (3) procreation. In everyday life, the first of these three, respect for parents, encompasses both respect for the past (in the form of ancestral rites) and hope for the future (in the form of procreation), and these are incorporated into the worship of the family spirit. This creates the belief that one's present self has been alive for hundreds of years and will be alive in the family lineage for eternity, and will never be lost. If, as Kaji says, Confucianism concerns itself with teachings and practices relating to death and the afterlife, then it is characterized by its view of death and return, with ancestor worship at its core, and faith centered on the family. This life, the next life, and past lives are linked by this family and ancestor worship, and mortality is overcome through the idea of family.[10]

The reason for the coexistence of what is considered Buddhism and what is considered Shintoism in Japan, while compartmentalizing both, is that Confucianism secretly links these two religions in a profound way. Buddhism, a highly ideological religion, and Shintoism, a primitive animistic religion, are mediated by Confucianism, which theoretically makes family and ancestor worship religious, and this unconsciously shapes our Japanese religiosity. This is why we can profess explicitly to be non-religious, yet implicitly believe in all the various religions. This is also why Hideki Tojo could worship the emperor, but be unaware of what he was, and just call him "light." All are part of one's own family, and all are ultimately one in the end, the only difference being how distantly or closely related they are by blood. Moreover, this family belief is so far removed from our consciousness that even today we Japanese are hardly aware of our own Confucianism.

By elevating the idea of family to an ideology, Confucianism teaches that one can be free from the fear of death if one is with one's family, thus substituting ancestral beliefs for beliefs that benefit this world. It teaches that family and ancestors are the way to accept death and be with it, for no one in the family ever dies out completely, but is always revived in the family. However, in doing so, people actually

---

[10] Nobuyuki Kaji, *Jukyō to wa nanika* [What is Confucianism?] (Tokyo: Chuoukouron-sya, 1990).

associate and give meaning to the psychological moment of the spark of the soul being ignited by the encounter with the corpse, relating it to their family and ancestors, and then they extinguish that fire. In this way, the soul is sidelined by the family and ancestors, and soul-making is thwarted.

Furthermore, the elevation of family leads to Japan's optimistic view of history. In Japan, no matter how painful the past may have been, it is always dismissed as a temporary occurrence in the context of the long family history, and no matter how intense the anxiety about the future, it is always masked by a utopian sense of family togetherness, which leads to a pervasive present-life orientation that always focuses only on this present moment. As in typical positive psychotherapy, only the "here and now" is considered absolute.

Psychology and Love

In this way, we can see that the psychological image of the mind is re-read by behaviorization and Confucianism as being life-oriented and devoid of inner value. But then, when we hear the following words of Giegerich, it is remarkable to note that Confucianism does not merely split the Japanese mind into compartments, but rather plays a role in connecting these compartments in a roundabout way:

> We should also not misconstrue the separation and the union as two separate, consecutive steps, first the separation, thereafter the union. Both are equiprimordial, simultaneous: a dialectical unity that has the separation within itself, not outside of itself, the unity of I and me (me as the "stranger" to I), pure concept and real existence. It is one movement that at one and the same time goes in opposite directions.[11]

In this sense, perhaps paradoxically, it is important to take this ancestral belief in Confucian thought seriously from a psychological perspective and continue to think about it, even though it is an inevitable and painful path to take as a psychologist living in Japan. The psychological "I" holds separation. But on the other hand, those of us who live in the Confucian world live our daily lives with a unity that allows us to naively say, "I am." I am both the I that holds the

---

[11] Giegerich, *Pitfalls*, p.81.

division and the unified I. I am the kinetic movement that is in motion, holding the two Is at the same time.

Seen in this light, it is reasonable to say that despite its separateness, the compartmentalized state of contemporary Japan tends towards a psychological state of mind. Although there seems to be no hope at all for the actual achievement of such a state of mind in Japan, if we consider that this lack of hope is the foundation of the psychological "I", then perhaps it is important to be with this hopelessness. To put it simply, there is no hope at the moment for me as a psychologist to continue working on psychology in Japan. However, it may be said that this is only because it has not yet been revealed, and its meaning will become clear only at the end of the work. That is to say, it may be an activity that dives deeply into the image of *shinju*. I would like to conclude my essay by quoting a passage from Giegerich's *Animus-Psychologie* on love.

> Love as a response to Job, to Auschwitz, to the atomic bomb, however, does not mean a positive struggle for the realization of utopia according to the principle of hope, for the solution of all the terrible problems, not even, more modestly, an effort for an improvement of social conditions and for a little more humanity in the world. Love means, in purely negative terms, our understanding of love, which always includes our being understood by love. It means growing in the awareness of love ourselves, and thus gaining a more loving awareness (an awareness that looks more lovingly into the needy world). Love does not eliminate the need in the world, love does not solve problems outside of us; at best love "solves" us, our heart, our sense. Love means understanding: even Auschwitz and the atomic bomb have a place in love. Auschwitz (or our defensive reaction to Auschwitz) shows us how little we have understood of love and are understood by love, how small-hearted and narrow our consciousness is, so that it must think of Auschwitz as being outside of love or even opposed to love. But even this being distant from love is still encompassed by love[12].

In Japan, the story of *shinju*, love suicide, is outside of love, placed in opposition to love, and far removed from love. That is

---

[12] Wolfgang Giegerich, *Animus-Psychologie* (London, ON: Dusk Owl Books, 2021), p. 250 (my translation from the original German).

why, although the possibility of interiority has been opened up, it has been absorbed into the season of suicide, and it remains in a love that has never been realized in the compartmentalized culture that is the manifestation of the soul of Japan. However, even so, it would be a psychological task to continue working within this culture, knowing that "even this being distant from love is still encompassed by love."

9

Where Is Soul? A "Spiritual Problem" for Jung's Time and our Own?

PAUL BISHOP

Jung's essay entitled *Das Seelenproblem des modernen Menschen*, usually translated as "The Spiritual Problem of Modern Man,"[1] was first published in the *Europäische Revue* in 1928,[2] and then revised and expanded in *Seelenprobleme der Gegenwart*, a collection of papers published by Rascher in 1931. The text in the *Gesammelte Werke* is this revised and expanded version (which has significant differences from the first version).[3] Now in this essay Jung reveals himself to be a critic of modernity, fully the equal of the likes of Max Weber (the proponent of the notion of the "iron cage," or the bureaucratic domination that will resist any and all revolutionary upheavals) or Georg Simmel.

Jung begins by invoking the topos of modesty: precisely because of their modernity, he argues, the *Seelenproblem* of modern individuals is a question that is "incalculable," or "immeasurable," or "unforeseeable" (*unabsehbar*).[4] The problem of the modern—or the "modern problem"—

---

[1] Jung, *CW* 10 §§ 148-196.

[2] On the political orientation of this journal, see: Tillmann Heise, "'Konservative Revolution' transnational? Der *Kulturbund* und die *Europäische Revue* als Intellektuellennetzwerke der Zwischenkriegszeit," *Brücken: Zeitschrift für Sprach-, Literatur- und Kulturwissenschaft*, 1 (2022): 59-76.

[3] See: C. G. Jung, "Das Seelenproblem des modernen Menschen," *Europäische Revue*, 4, no. 9 (1928): 700-715; and C. G. Jung, "Das Seelenproblem des modernen Menschen," in *Seelenprobleme der Gegenwart* (Zurich: Rascher, 1931), pp. 401-435.

[4] Jung, *CW* 10 § 148.

is "a question which has just arisen and yet whose answer still lies in the future."[5] His next move is to make a shrewd distinction between those who are modern, in the sense that they simply happen to be alive at this particular historical moment, and those who are truly modern, in the sense that they "stand upon a peak or at the very edge of the world, above them the heavens, below them the whole of humankind with their history that disappears in primeval mists, in front of them the abyss of the future."[6] Those who belong to this second category, or "individuals of the immediate present," are said by Jung to be few, because "their existence demands the highest possible degree of consciousness, the most intensive and the broadest consciousness, [...] for only those are truly in the present who are fully conscious of their existence as human beings."[7]

To be a truly modern individual, in the sense of being "as conscious as possible of the present," is, however, to be a lonely individual. (Here a note is sounded that can also be heard in an entry in the *Black Books* for 18 March 1914, when Jung records that "a number of times I read in Nietzsche the expression 'ultimate solitude' [*letzte Einsamkeit*],"[8] and which recurs numerous times in *Memories, Dreams, Reflections*, where Jung frequently complains of being misunderstood.) Here, Jung explains this sense of isolation as arising from the decoupling from our "original, purely animal *participation mystique* with the herd, from submersion in a common consciousness [...] the all-embracing maternal womb of unconsciousness."[9] Jung sounds almost Nietzschean when he declares that modern individuals have become "unhistorical," in the sense that "the world of past levels of consciousness, their values and strivings" are of interest to us only

---

[5] *Ibid.*

[6] *Ibid.*, § 149, trans. modified. For further discussion of this moment, see Wolfgang Giegerich, "The End of Meaning and the Birth of Man: An Essay about the State Reached in the History of Consciousness and an Analysis of C. G. Jung's Psychological Project," *Journal of Jungian Theory and Practice*, 6, no. 1 (2004): 1-65.

[7] Jung, *CW* 10 § 149.

[8] C. G. Jung, *The Black Books, 1913-1932: Notebooks of Transformation*, ed. Sonu Shamdasani, trans. Martin Liebscher, John Peck, and Sonu Shamdasani, 7 vols. (New York and London: Norton, 2020) vol. 5, p. 203.

[9] Jung, *CW* 10 § 150.

"from a historical standpoint."[10] After all, in his untimely meditation on "The Uses and Disadvantages of History for Life" (1874), Nietzsche had invited the reader to meditate on the following proposition: namely, "*the unhistorical and the historical are necessary in equal measure for the health of an individual, of a people and of a culture*" (§11).[11]

For Jung, the modern individual has become "unhistorical," indeed: "'unhistorical' in the deepest sense" (*im tiefsten Sinne "unhistorisch"*), inasmuch as this individual is "estranged [*entfremdet*] from the mass of individuals who live only in traditional ideas,"[12] and becomes "completely modern" when "come to the very edge of the world, leaving behind all that has been discarded and overcome, standing before the acknowledged Nothing from which All may come [*das zugestandene Nichts, aus dem noch Alles werden kann*]."[13] In this final sentence, the editors of the *Collected Works* suggest, we have an allusion to another of Jung's favourite authors, namely, Goethe, and to the Mothers Scene in *Faust*, Part Two, when Faust tells Mephisto, "For in thy Naught I trust to find the All" (*In deinem Nichts hoff ich das All zu finden*) (l. 6256).

At this point, Jung pauses. Does this not all sound so grand that it risks becoming a banality? he wonders. And he concedes: the notion of the modern individual is "questionable and suspect," *and it always has been*—"beginning with Socrates and Jesus."[14] This identification of modernity with Socrates and Jesus is perhaps surprising, yet Jung is making the same point that the French philosopher Bertrand Vergely makes, when he argues that there are two false pictures one can have about modernity: the first is to diabolize modernity, the second is to declare it sacred.[15] On this account, those who diabolize modernity respond to the tensions of the present moment by creating a nostalgia for a past which they idealize, and in so doing forget that there has never been innovation

---

[10] *Ibid.*

[11] Friedrich Nietzsche, *Untimely Meditations*, trans. R. J. Hollingdale (Cambridge, UK: Cambridge University Press, 1983), p. 63.

[12] For further discussion of this crucial notion, see: Vicky Rippere, *Schiller and "Alienation"* (Bern, Frankfurt am Main, Las Vegas: Peter Lang, 1981).

[13] Jung, *CW* 10 § 151.

[14] *Ibid.*

[15] Bertrand Vergely, *Boulevard des philosophes: De la Renaissance à aujourd'hui* (Paris: Milan, 2005), pp. 119-122.

without tension, and that in the past there were the same tensions as there are for us today. By contrast, those who declare modernity sacred respond to the successes and triumphs of the present by idealizing the present, and in so doing forget that great things were achieved in the past, without which the innovations of today would never have seen the light of day. In other words, modernity is a much more complex phenomenon than it is usually understood to be— especially by postmodernists …

For what we have to grasp, as Vergely insists, is that modernity began a long time *before* modernity. In this sense, the first moderns were really the ancients, and this is an argument we find in Pascal and his *Préface sur le traité du Vide*: "Those whom we call ancient were really new in all things, and properly constituted the infancy of humankind; and as we have joined to their knowledge the experience of the centuries which have followed them, it is in ourselves that we should find this antiquity that we revere in others."[16] Pascal's point here is that the past is not something that is finished and over with the arrival of the modern world, but rather that it persists among us in thousands of different ways. (Elsewhere, Jung also makes this point, i.e., the ancients are not outside of us, in the past, but are still among us, today; this is the dimension that Jung refers to as *the archaic*.[17] As he once memorably put it, "we should never think we are living in modern times—we are living three or four hundred years behind our times, our feeling life is not up to date. […] You step into a streetcar in Zurich and there is a Neanderthal man sitting right opposite you, his psychological level of humanity."[18] In a sense, Jung's position is an eminently logical one; after all, as Dilthey

---

[16] Blaise Pascal, *Œuvres complètes*, ed. Louis Lafuma (Paris: Seuil, 1963), pp. 231-232.

[17] See Jung's essay "Archaic Man" (1931) (Jung, *CW* 10 §§ 104-147). For an exploration and a defence of the notion of the archaic, see Paul Bishop (ed.), *The Archaic: The Past in the Present* (London and New York: Routledge, 2012).

[18] C. G. Jung, *Visions: Notes of the Seminar given in 1930-1934*, ed. Claire Douglas, 2 vols (London: Routledge, 1998), vol. 1, pp. 59-60.

argued, "the present never *is*; what we experience as present always contains the memory of what has just been present.")[19]

Thus even to identify oneself as modern is, in Jung's words, to make a "voluntary declaration of bankruptcy," to take a "vow of poverty and chastity," to renounce "the halo of sanctity which [...] history bestows"—and to commit the "Promethean sin of being unhistorical," for "*higher consciousness is therefore guilt*."[20] To attain the ultimate consciousness of the present, one must have overcome the stages of consciousness of the past and have fulfilled the tasks enjoined upon one in that world; in other words, one must be a virtuous (*tugendhaft*) and capable (*tüchtig*) individual, even if the concept of being capable (*Tüchtigkeit*) is abhorrent to the pseudo-moderns (*Auch-Modernen*) of our time.[21] (As Jung goes on to observe, "many people call themselves 'modern'"—and "especially the pseudo-moderns.")[22]

Yet the criterion of *Tüchtigkeit* is indispensable for the modern individual, since without it the modern individual is nothing other than an "unscrupulous speculator." For unless it is replaced by "creative ability," the unhistorical is, Jung insists, "a mere infidelity to the past."[23] "Today only has a meaning if it stands between yesterday and tomorrow," he explains, because "today is a process, a transition, taking leave from yesterday and going toward tomorrow," and "only those who are conscious of the present in this sense can call themselves *modern*."[24] As a result, the following paradox emerges: the "really modern" moderns (*die wirklich Modernen*) are often to be found among those who call themselves "old-fashioned" (*altmodisch*), and who do so for two reasons. First, in order somehow to "redeem [*wett machen*] their guilt-laden overcoming of the historical [*jene schuldhafte Überwindung des Historischen*] by a heightened emphasis on the past [*eine verstärkte Betonung der Vergangenheit*]"; and second, in order to avoid

---

[19] Wilhelm Dilthey, *The Formation of the Historical World in the Human Sciences* [*Selected Works*, vol. 3], ed. Rudolf A. Makkreel and Frithjof Rodi (Princeton, NJ, and Oxford: Princeton University Press, 2002), p. 216.

[20] Jung, *CW* 10 § 152.

[21] *Ibid.*, §§ 152-153.

[22] *Ibid.*, § 154.

[23] *Ibid.*, § 153.

[24] *Ibid.*

being mistaken for pseudo-moderns. Jung goes on to say that a "feeling of elation" (*Hochgefühl*)—the feeling of being the apogee of all past human history, the fulfillment and the end-product of countless millennia—that often accompanies the "consciousness of the present" (*das Gegenwartsbewußtsein*) can be "rendered illusory" by the "painful fact" that "nothing good can come into world without immediately producing its corresponding evil."[25]

In "The Work of Art in the Age of its Technological Reproducibility" (third version) (1939), Walter Benjamin made the same point very powerfully:

> Imperialist war is an uprising on the part of technology, which demands payment in *human material* for the natural material society has denied it. Instead of draining rivers, society directs a human stream into a bed of trenches; instead of dropping seeds from airplanes, it drops incendiary bombs over cities; and in gas warfare it has found a new means of abolishing the aura.[26]

In the case of Jung, this point is made more succinctly, yet just as powerfully: "Think of two thousand years of Christian history and, instead of the parousia and the millennial kingdom, the World War of Christian nations with barbed wire and poison gas … What a *débacle* in heaven and on earth!"[27]

Jung brings the principle that "every good has its corresponding evil" (*neben jedem Guten steht sein entsprechendes Böses*) to bear as an optic on human history. Science, technology, and organisation can be beneficent, but also catastrophic; the principle of "in times of peace, prepare for war"—derived from Vegetius's tract *De re militari*, but also found in Plato (*Laws*, 628c-e)—has led Europe to rack and ruin; in short, humankind is at once "the final end-product of an age-old development," *and* "the greatest conceivable disappointment of all humankind's hopes."[28] Writing in 1928—that is, just ten years after the end of the Great War—Jung wonders whether humankind has

---

[25] Jung, *CW* 10 § 154.
[26] Walter Benjamin, *Selected Writings*, vol. 4, *1938-1940*, ed. Howard Eiland and Michael W. Jennings (Cambridge, MA: Belknap Press, 2003), p. 270 (Benjamin's italics).
[27] Jung, *CW* 10 § 154.
[28] *Ibid.*, § 155.

really learned anything from this devastating experience: for we see, he says, "the same optimism, the same organisations, the same political aspirations, the same phrases and catchwords at work."[29] The sheer inadequacy of this response, Jung argues, not only means that these phrases and catchwords will inevitably prepare the way for "further catastrophes," but more generally that "modern consciousness can be compared with the soul [*Seele*] of someone who has suffered a fatal shock, and as a consequence has become fundamentally uncertain [*wesentlich unsicher*]."[30]

At this point, Jung pivots to a more self-referential mode: he is speaking, he avers, as a medical doctor [*Arzt*], and from his medical experience.[31] As a result, he continues, he can only paint a "onesided picture" (*ein bloß einseitiges Bild*), for "everything lies *in the soul*, it is so to speak all *inside*" (*es liegt alles in der Seele, alles sozusagen auf der inneren Seite*).[32] This is, Jung adds, "remarkable" (*eigentümlich*), because it is not *always* the case that the psyche is to be found on the inside. (In the case of ancient civilizations in general and Egypt—"with its magnificent objectivity and its just as magnificently naïve, negative confession of sins"—in particular, the reverse is the case. There is no "psychic problematic" to be detected lurking behind the spirit of the Apis tombs of Saqqara and the Pyramids, any more than there is behind the music of Bach, he adds.)

Jung goes on to explain what he means when he says that the psyche is "outside" and there is no "problem of the soul" (*Seelenproblem*). In such cases, we find a "living religion" (*eine lebendige Religionsform*), or "an ideal and ritual form, in which all yearnings and hopes of the soul are taken up and given expression."[33] Although the discovery of psychology is an event of the early decades of the twentieth century, its "psychological facts" had been known for centuries before that. But the "spiritual need" (*spirituelle Not*) of our time that produced the discovery of psychology, just as—in the technical realm—the mechanical principles and the physical facts required to construct a steam engine had been known to the Romans,

---

[29] *Ibid.*
[30] *Ibid.*, § 156.
[31] *Ibid.*, § 156 and §158.
[32] *Ibid.*, § 158.
[33] *Ibid.*, § 159.

but it was the division of labour and the growing specialization of the
nineteenth century that had improved on the device made by Heron
of Alexandria, sometimes hailed as the "greatest experimentalist of
antiquity." Thus the very existence of psychology as a discipline is itself
a "symptom"—a sign of "profound convulsions in the collective soul"
(*tiefgreifende Erschütterungen der allgemeinen Seele*).[34]

The catastrophic consequences of the First World War have been,
Jung insists, psychological consequences: a "shock" to modern
consciousness, on the one hand, and, on the other, the "moral shock
to our belief in ourselves and in our goodness [*an uns selbst und an unsere
Güte*]."[35] On Jung's own part, his belief in the "rational organizability
of the world," otherwise known as the "old dream of the millennial
kingdom where peace and harmony reign," had begun to falter.[36] Jung
sketches two mutually contradictory portraits. First, the worldview of
the medieval individual: "Here the earth lay in the center of the
universe, eternally fixed and at rest, encircled by a solicitous, warmth-
bestowing sun, the Caucasian race represented the children of God,
lovingly overseen by the Most High and brought up for eternal
blessedness, and all know exactly *what* one should do and how one
should conduct oneself in order to leave earthly evanescence and to
attain an eternal, blissful existence."[37] And second, and by contrast,
the realization that "of such a reality," as he wistfully remarked, we—
the moderns—"cannot even dream," for "science has long ago torn
this lovely veil to shreds": "All the metaphysical certainties of the
medieval individual have disappeared, and in exchange we have the
ideal of material security, general welfare, and humanitarianism."[38] (In
Nietzschean terms, the modern individual is *der letzte Mensch* ....)

Yet precisely security, says Jung (in words that, nearly a century
later, have an uncanny echo about them), "has gone," as "external
progress" (*Fortschritt im Äußeren*) goes hand in hand with a "steadily
increasing possibility of even greater catastrophes."[39] "What does it,
for example, say," Jung asks, "if great cities are today planning, or

---

[34] *Ibid.*, § 160.
[35] *Ibid.*, § 162.
[36] *Ibid.*
[37] *Ibid.*
[38] *Ibid.*, §§ 162-163.
[39] *Ibid.*, § 163.

even practising, defences against poison gas attacks?"[40] (In the 1960s and 1970s, the UK government produced booklets to advise the general public on what to do in the event of nuclear attack ... And in the United States of our own time, schools practice emergency measures to be carried out when a gunman runs amok ....) Even in the pre-nuclear age, Jung is aware of the dangers faced then—and *a fortiori* now—by humankind:

> The dawning intuition of that terrible law which governs all that blindly happens, for which Heraclitus coined the concept of *enantiodromia*, of running toward the opposite, fills the subterranean levels of modern consciousness with chilling horror and paralyses all belief in the possibility of facing these monstrosities with social and political measures.[41]

Or as Jung put it many years later on October 22, 1959, in his famous interview for the BBC's *Face to Face* programme, "the only danger that exists is man himself—he is the great danger, and we are pitifully unaware of it."

In such times, the very role of psychoanalysis itself has become compromised: thanks to Freud, we have discovered "bleak darknesses" in ourselves, with the result that science has destroyed a "last refuge," turning what should have been a "sheltering cave" into a "cesspit." In so writing, Jung does not mince his words, nor should he—in a world where newspapers see themselves as empowered to point to the "unconscious evil" motives of politicians, and to urge them, "Please have yourself analysed. You are suffering from a repressed father-complex."[42]

However grotesque such examples might be of the absurdities to which the illusion gives rise that, because something is psychic, it is therefore under our control, Jung nevertheless believes that a turning on the part of modern consciousness away from material externalities (*materielle Äußerlichkeit*) and toward subjective interiority (*subjektive Innerlichkeit*)—that key concept for the organisers of this conference—can be found in the growth of a global interest in

---

[40] *Ibid.*
[41] *Ibid.*, §164.
[42] *Ibid.*, § 165.

psychology.[43] As further evidence of this shift, Jung points in a brief
aside to the case of Expressionism: in a rare excursus into art theory
or art appreciation, he applauds its "prophetic anticipation" of this
development, acknowledging that "art always intuitively anticipates
such imminent changes in general consciousness."[44]

Yet the "psychological interest of our time" does not necessarily
take a strictly religious form, and Jung cites, not just the example of
Freudian psychoanalysis, but the widespread growth of interest in such
examples of psychic phenomena (*seelische Erscheinungen*) as spiritualism,
astrology, Theosophy, parapsychology, etc. "Since the end of the
sixteenth century and the seventeenth century," an astonished Jung
observes, "the world has seen nothing like it"![45] If a parallel can be
found, then it is in the flowering of Gnosticism in the first and second
centuries C.E., and Jung detects a "deep affinity" between early
Christian Gnosticism and contemporary spiritual currents. Yet Jung is
suspicious: citing the example of an Eglise gnostique de la France, and
two Gnostic schools in Germany, Jung—who will later express outrage
when Martin Buber accuses him, Jung, of Gnosticism[46]—is as
dismissive of them as he is of the growth in Theosophy and its
"continental sister," Anthroposophy—both Gnosticism in an Indian
guise (*eine indisch zurechtgemachte Gnosis reinsten Wassers*), he sniffs.

---

[43] Note that "psychology as the discipline of interiority" in the sense used
by the ISPDI does not refer to the psychic inner in individual persons;
rather, such subjective inner images, emotions, etc., are positivities. True
interiority requires that such positivities be "interiorized into themselves" or
apperceived as "negated from the outset," that is, "thought" (in the Hegelian
sense). This conceptual meaning of "interiority" can be found in such
statements by Jung as those in his letter to Josef Goldbrunner of 14 May
1950 that "the individual in my view is enclosed in *the* psyche (not in *their*
psyche)" [i.e., *in der Psyche (nicht in seiner Psyche)*] (Jung, *Letters 1*, p. 556) and
in his "Commentary on 'The Secret of the Golden Flower'" that "the psyche
is a world in which the ego is contained" (i.e., *die Seele [ist] eine Welt, in der das
Ich enthalten ist*) (Jung, *CW* 13 § 75). I am grateful to Greg Mogenson for
highlighting this crucial definition.
[44] Jung, *CW* 10 § 167.
[45] *Ibid.*, § 169.
[46] See: Martin Buber, *Eclipse of God: Studies in the Relation between Religion
and Philosophy* [1952] (Princeton and Oxford: Princeton University Press,
2016), pp. 65-78, cf. pp. 113-117.

The problem with Theosophy and Anthroposophy, it turns out, is that they are false forms of gnosis; true gnosis—as, if anyone, then Jung would know!—bases itself exclusively on "subterranean phenomena" (*Hintergrundsphänomene*) and extends in its morals into "dark depths" (*dunkle Tiefen*), as, for example, Kundalini Yoga does in its European guise.[47] Jung is particularly scathing about the way Rudolf Steiner (1861-1925) describes Anthroposophy as a *Geisteswissenschaft* (or, as the translators add for good measure, Mary Baker Eddy proposes a "Christian Science").[48] These claims to scientificity only serve to reveal how disreputable (*anrüchtig*) religion has grown; almost as disreputable, Jung adds for good measure, as politics and world reform ….

And now Jung unveils his critique of these contemporary movements (which are also, in a sense his competitors): unlike the consciousness of the nineteenth century (with its most intimate and weightiest expectations), the modern consciousness turns to the soul, not in the sense of any sort of traditional confession, but in a Gnostic sense. What does Jung mean by this? For Jung, the claim of these movements to the status of a science demonstrates the priority they place on knowledge (*Erkenntnis*), in strong contrast to Western forms of religion, which place an emphasis on *belief* or *faith* (*Glauben*). In fact, Jung goes so far as to declare that "modern consciousness abhors faith" (*das moderne Bewußtsein perhorresziert den Glauben*), and consequently it abhors those religions based on it. Instead, modern consciousness is after something else: "it wants to *know*, that is, have a primordial experience" (*es will wissen, d.h. Urerfahrung haben*).[49] (In a conversation with Aniela Jaffé, Jung

---

[47] For further discussion, see: C. G. Jung, *The Psychology of Kundalini Yoga: Notes of the Seminar given in 1932*, ed. Sonu Shamdasani (London: Routledge, 1996).

[48] This reference to Steiner might prompt one to recall the important discourse of the soul in Steiner's thought, symbolized for Steiner (in a lecture given in Berlin on 29 April 1909) by the figure of the Virgin in Raphael's *Sistine Madonna* ("Isis and Madonna," in *Isis Mary Sophia: Her Mission and Ours*, ed. Christopher Bamford [Great Barrington, MA: Steiner Books, 2003], p. 94).

[49] Jung, *CW* 10 § 171. For further discussion of (the need for) *Urerfahrung des Geistes*, see: Jung, "Psychotherapists or the Clergy," *CW* 11 §535, and "Freud and Jung," *CW* 4 § 780.

identifies his own *Urerfahrung* of 1913 to 1917 as a kind of mystical experience or even Gnosis. [50])

At this point, Jung pivots again, this time to a consideration of the historicity of the notion of the unconscious. Since the beginning of the nineteenth century, he argues, and more precisely since the time of the French Revolution (1789), [51] the psyche—or what Jung calls *das Seelische*—has moved "with steadily increasing power of attraction into the foreground of general consciousness." [52] As an emblem of this shift, Jung cites the enthronement of *La Déesse de la Raison* in the cathedral of Notre Dame in Paris; a "symbolic gesture" which, he claims, has a similar significance for the Western world as the hewing down of Wotan's oaks by Christian missionaries. On neither occasion did an "avenging bolt strike down the blasphemer," Jung notes with palpable irony.

In this essay Jung voices a profound concern: the "soul of the West" (*die Seele des Abendlandes*) is in a worrying predicament, and all the more worrying, because we "still prefer illusions about our inner beauty [*unsere innere Schönheit*] to the merciless truth." [53] As a result, Westerners live in a "positive cloud of smog of self-incensing [*Selbstberäucherung*]" that obscures their "real face," but what do people in China and India think about us? What do Africans think about us? And—here Jung begins to reveal a decolonializing dimension to his thought—what do all those think of us whom we exterminate with schnaps, venereal disease, and with expropriation of their lands? [54] As an aside, Jung relates an anecdote from his visit to Mexico in 1925, when he met the Pueblo Indians (that, is the Puebloans or Pueblo

---

[50] In Aniela Jaffé's words, this *Urerfahrung* can be described as "*eine mystische Erfahrung oder eine Gnosis*" (Aniela Jaffé, "Die schöpferischen Phasen im Leben von C. G. Jung," in *Parapsychologie—Individuation—Nationalsozialismus* (Zurich: Daimon, 1985), pp. 9-45 (p. 30).

[51] For further discussion of the impact of the French Revolution on psychology, see: C. G. Jung, *History of Modern Psychology* [*Lectures delivered at ETH Zurich*, vol. 1], ed. Ernst Falzeder, trans. Mark Kyburz, John Peck, and Ernst Falzeder (Princeton and Oxford: Princeton University Press, 2019), pp. 27 and 29.

[52] Jung, *CW* 10 § 174.

[53] *Ibid.*, § 182.

[54] *Ibid.*, § 184.

peoples, as we would say today). He records one of them saying that the "Whites" are always restless, always searching for something, and have such cruel expressions; for the Puebloans, Westerners are mad!

In so speaking, Jung remarks, his Puebloan acquaintance has correctly identified the "Aryan bird of prey and its insatiable lust for loot [*unersättliche Beutegier*]," an intuition which many years later, in *Memories, Dreams, Reflections*, he describes almost in terms of a vision—a "long meditation," in which he saw Roman legions "smashing into the cities of Gaul" and "the Roman eagle on the North Sea and on the banks of the White Nile"; St. Augustine "transmitting the Christian creed […] on the tips of Roman lances," Charlemagne's "forced conversions of the heathen," and the "pillaging and murdering bands of the Crusading armies"; followed by Columbus, Cortes, and the other conquistadors with "fire, sword, torture, and Christianity"; and the peoples of the Pacific islands "decimated by firewater, syphilis, and scarlet fever carried in the clothes the missionaries forced on them."[55] And Jung rehearses exactly the same point that he makes in 1928 when, in *Memories, Dreams, Reflections*, he concludes: "All the eagles and other predatory creatures that adorn our coats of arms seem to me apt psychological representatives of our true nature."[56]

And this image—this almost Nietzschean image of the bird of prey—prompts on Jung's part an impassioned outburst against the evils of colonialism, citing as examples the Christian missions in China and in Africa (describing the latter as a "pitiful comedy"), the abolition of polygamy and the consequent rise in prostitution, and the "blessings" of the opium trade in Polynesia.[57] And this sight of the Europeans, when the cloud of moral fog is lifted, is not a pretty one: which explains, Jung continues, why the "excavation of our soul" resembles nothing more than a sort of "drainage operation"—an "unclean job" of a kind to which only a "great idealist" such as Freud would dedicate the whole of his life. True, Jung admits, it is not *entirely* Freud's fault: "it was not he who caused the bad smell," he concedes, "but all of us, who think of

---

[55] Jung, *MDR*, pp. 276-277.
[56] *Ibid.*, p. 277.
[57] Jung, *CW* 10 § 185.

ourselves as so clean and decent, yet do so out of pure ignorance and gross self-deception."[58]

In a twist on the topos of modesty, Jung now accuses himself of one-sidedness (*Einseitigkeit*), admitting that he has passed over in silence "the soul of our worldliness" (*die Seele unserer Weltlichkeit*)— what in his *Red Book* he called *der Geist dieser Zeit*—, a spirit about which most people love to talk because it is so clearly obvious to all.[59] But what does this "soul of worldliness" or the "spirit of the times" look like? In these concluding paragraphs, Jung reveals himself to be just as astute a *Kulturkritiker* as were the members of the Frankfurt School (and notably Theodor W. Adorno), declaring that "the soul of our worldliness" (*die Seele unserer Weltlichkeit*) reveals itself in the "international or supernatural ideal, embodied in the League of Nations and the like, as well as in sport and lastly and tellingly in cinema and in jazz."[60] Like Adorno, Jung connects these cultural phenomena with our "psychic condition"; unlike Adorno, however, who gets his psychoanalytic theory from Freud, Jung sees in this rediscovery of the body—a topic to which he will return in his seminar on Nietzsche's *Zarathustra*[61]—a chance for something positive. "The fascination of the soul" (*die Faszination der Seele*), Jung claims, is "nothing other than a new self-contemplation [*eine neue Selbstbesinnung*], a return to fundamental human nature [*eine Rückbesinnung auf fundamentale menschliche Natur*]."[62] On Jung's account, "it is no surprise that this leads to the body, which for so long was held in low esteem vis-à-vis the spirit [*gegenüber dem Geiste*], being rediscovered," and sometimes, he added, "one almost feels tempted to speak of a *revenge of the flesh on the spirit*."[63]

Finally, in the final lines of the revised version of his paper, Jung draws comfort—as did, each in his own way, Heidegger and Adorno— from the poem "Patmos" by Friedrich Hölderlin, whose famous lines, "*Wo aber Gefahr ist, wächst / Das Rettende auch*" ("Where danger

---

[58] *Ibid.*, § 186.

[59] *Ibid.*, § 195.

[60] *Ibid.*, trans. modified.

[61] See: *Jung's Seminar on Nietzsche's "Zarathustra": Abridged Edition*, ed. James L. Jarrett (Princeton, NJ: Princeton University Press, 1998), pp. 197-198.

[62] Jung, *CW* 10 § 195, trans. modified.

[63] *Ibid.*

is, / Arises salvation also"), Jung quotes.[64] Such comfort is, however, sorely needed, as the world begins to adjust to a new tempo that Jung associates, as did Adorno, with America: "And indeed we see how the Western world strikes up a more rapid tempo, the American tempo, the opposite of quietism and world-negating resignation," Jung concludes, adding: "An unprecedented tension arises between outer and inner or, more precisely—between the objective and the subjective, perhaps a final race between aging Europe and youthful America, perhaps a healthy or a desperate attempt to escape the might of dark natural laws and achieve a yet larger and more heroic victory of wakefulness over the sleep of nations."[65] Likewise, in *The Science of Character* (1926) Ludwig Klages (1872-1956) identified America as the battleground for the conflict, as he saw it, of the soul versus *Geist*: "America, where more rapid 'progress' allows us to foresee the future day to day, has established a considerable lead in the standardization of thought, amusement, and so on. […] These 'free citizens' are in fact puppets who imagine that they are free, and a single glance at American methods of work or American methods of amusement is enough to show that *l'homme machine* ['the man-machine'] is no longer imminent, but has already become reality there."[66] Klages's critique of "standardization" or *Schablonisierung* constitutes a counterpart to Jung's notion of "identification with the mask" or what the Existentialists called a lack of "authenticity," a term whose use as a piece of philosophical jargon Adorno was wont to decry.[67]

In 1928, Jung concluded his paper by emphasizing the individual subjectivity of his analysis of the spiritual problem of modernity: "My voice," he wrote, "is only *one* voice, my experience is just a drop in the ocean, and my knowledge is only as large as the circumference of a microscopic field of vision, my spiritual eye [*mein geistiges Auge*] a little mirror which depicts a tiny corner of the world, and finally

---

[64] *Ibid.*

[65] *Ibid.*, § 196.

[66] Ludwig Klages, *The Science of Character*, trans. W. H. Johnston (London: Allen & Unwin, 1929), pp. 160-161.

[67] See: Theodor W. Adorno, *Jargon der Eigentlichkeit: Zur deutschen Ideologie* (Frankfurt am Main: Suhrkamp, 1964); and *The Jargon of Authenticity*, trans. Knut Tarnowski and Frederic Will (Evanston: Northwestern University Press, 1973).

my idea—a subjective confession."[68] In 1931, however, Jung cut this paragraph and replaced it with a shorter, and terser, conclusion: with reference to the possibility of a race between Europe and America, or between the might of dark natural laws and the heroic victory of wakefulness, he commented ominously: "This is a question which history will answer" (*Eine Frage, welche die Geschichte beantworten wird*).[69] How history decided to answer the question can be gauged by some of the other titles in *Collected Works*, volume 10, namely:

- "Wotan" (1936)
- "After the Catastrophe" (1945)
- "The Fight with the Shadow" (1946)

while such other titles as "The Undiscovered Self (Present and Future)" (the English translation of *Gegenwart und Zukunft*, published in 1957) and "Flying Saucers: A Modern Myth of Things Seen in the Skies" (1958) hint at the wider themes that Jung's thinking would embrace over the coming decades. Yet the soul as a problem persists in Jung's thought as it does in our own day, as witnessed by a return of the concept of the soul in contemporary French discourse (this exemplified by two entirely ideologically opposed thinkers, Michel Onfray and Bertrand Vergely),[70] and by the title of this very conference.

---

[68] Jung, "Das Seelenproblem des modernen Menschen," *Europäische Revue*, p. 715.

[69] Jung, *CW* 10, § 196; cf. Jung, "Das Seelenproblem des modernen Menschen," in *Seelenprobleme der Gegenwart*, p. 435.

[70] See: Michel Onfray, *Anima: Vie et mort de l'âme* [*Brève histoire de l'encyclopédie du monde*, vol. 4] (Paris: Albin Michel, 2023); and Bertrand Vergely, *La Puissance de l'âme: Sortir vivant des émotions* (Paris: Trédaniel, 2023).

10

Aurum Vulgi: A Reflection on *Simulation* in Psychology and Its Philosophical and Historical Backdrop[1]

MICHAEL WHAN

In an insightful report prepared for the Heritage Foundation by the late English conservative philosopher, Sir Roger Scruton, entitled "The Future of European Civilization: Lessons For America," reference is made to Oswald Spengler's having argued in his book, *The Decline of the West*, that "the culture of the West [...] will dwindle to a purely mechanical simulacrum of its former greatness before disappearing entirely."[2] I mention this reference to simulacrum only to point out that the idea of simulation was, as it were, already foreshadowed as the fate of Western modernity. I know not whether Scruton's use of this idea is taken from Spengler's original text, or is Scruton's own.

Turning now to what I have to offer about the *simulation* topic, I want first to state that this falls within the historical shadow of the cultural portent laid out by these authors. But my focus is specifically *Jungian psychology*. In this context, simulation needs to be understood not only as the work of misguided and deceived Jungian analysts trying to oppose the prevailing mood of the "disenchantment of the

---

[1] This is a revised version of a talk with the same title given at the ISPDI Conference, "Where Is Soul? Psychology in Modernity," Berlin, August 2024.

[2] Roger Scruton, "The Future of European Civilization: Lessons for America," The Heritage Foundation, 8 December 2015, https://www. heritage.org/europe/report/the-future-european-civilization-lessons-america.

world."[3] Rather, it needs to be understood as the soul (*Geist*) having *surpassed* the mythic, religious, and metaphysical forms of its previous modes of expression. Simulacra, it follows, are the soul's showing of the obsoleteness of these former forms of itself to itself in a speciously literalized manner. Thus, it presents them as if they were facts of existence, facts of the psyche, still operative and determinative in the modern psyche. From this perspective, Jungian analysts under the sway of the soul unconsciously or innocently draw upon the simulacra of these obsolescent forms, conceived *naturalistically*, as if inherent empirical factors of the psyche. Why, though, does the soul still manifest in psychology in such a way? What is going on that the soul manufactures the pretence of "an event of truth, of soul,"[4] presenting itself to itself as "the fair memory of things that once were."[5] What George Steiner has termed a "nostalgia for the absolute."[6] In modernity, the soul has emancipated itself from its former truths, its "historical move [is] one of *kenôsis*, a relentless being emptied of whatever claim to mythic or divine stature"[7] it once had. Nevertheless, the soul cannot simply, innocently, suddenly leave all it has been behind. It needs to repeatedly

---

[3] Wolfgang Giegerich, "The Disenchantment Complex. C. G. Jung and the Modern World," *CEP* V, pp. 67-90; also see, Michael Whan, "Myth, Disenchantment, and the Loss of Sacred Place," *International Journal of Jungian Studies*, 4, no. 1 (2012): pp. 34-40.

[4] Wolfgang Giegerich, *What Is Soul?* (New Orleans, LA: Spring Journal Books, 2012; now also, London: Routledge, 2020), p.143.

[5] Jung, *CW* 9i § 50.

[6] George Steiner, *Nostalgia for the Absolute*. Massey Lecture Series (Toronto: House of Anans Press, 1999). Also, Giegerich, *What Is Soul?* p. 164: In the process of neurosis, the functioning of simulation is to install the neurotic "'The Absolute': it is [the soul's] former truths in the plural, that make themselves felt in their simulation [...]." However, "[...] it is only the naked abstract concept of 'The Absolute' in the singular, into which former metaphysics *as a whole* has been contracted or reduced, metaphysic's [*sic*] zero stage [...]." This is the key element. In psychology, the "absolute" principles that arise are basically fake absolutes, fundamentally different to the neurotic "The Absolute." Unlike in neurosis, in which "The Absolute" inflicts real suffering, the fake absolutes of psychology have in the long run a *consoling*, affirming, and reassuring *effect*.

[7] Giegerich, *What Is Soul?* p. 293.

work off, slowly shed its past forms, namely a *working through* of it all. Henceforth, for the soul

> [...] it is obviously not enough to simply (easily, 'just like that') *outgrow* metaphysics in a natural developmental process (metaphysics as the historical successor to myth). [...] It has to actively, systematically, in detail and in full awareness *work off* its own fascination and infatuation with the metaphysical, the mythic, the numinous, and the suggestive power of the imaginal. [...] The soul needs to concretely, as a hard core reality, *put before itself* once more that from which its natural development has already long removed it, and to give it a new artificial presence so that it (the soul) is forced to psychologically, explicitly depart from it.[8]

Thus, too, does *psychology itself* have to work off its "fascination and infatuation" with the mythic, the metaphysical, and numinous.

On Simulation

This process of the soul working off its obsolescent forms of logical life has, however, to be differentiated from the soul's workings in *neurosis*, as already noted above.[9] Though simulation's functioning in psychology's thinking and theorizing has a certain superficial resemblance to that of neurosis, there is a crucial difference. In psychology, simulacra have mainly a *syntonic* effect. They appear to harmonize with a certain wishful, *restorative* ideology, that is reactionary to modernity, which many Jungian analysts adhere to, as often did Jung. Even so, simulation still remains the work of the soul upon itself. Jungian analysts are unconsciously expressing the soul's work in (mis)taking simulacra as authentic soul phenomena. For instance, with the appearance in therapy or a dream of a simulated mythic-like image, the image needs to be understood purely *semantically*. The form or *syntax* of the consciousness in which it appears is *not* mythic. As a simulation it is utterly modern. And therefore semantically it contradicts the syntax of the consciousness in which it manifests. If it were truly a mythic image, it would be semantically *and* syntactically of the same logical constitution.

---

[8] *Ibid.*, p. 332.
[9] See footnote 6.

Awareness of this duplicitous contradiction, then, hardly factors in much of psychology's thinking.

Neurosis, however, "is not a simulation of the metaphysical within the modern world. [...] Neurosis does not play, not pretend, not make-believe. [...] It is the existing contradiction between 'soul' and modern empirical reality, between metaphysics and modernity."[10] The shared resemblance between neurosis and simulation is their restorative element: "neurosis has a character of a restoration." As an example, the French Revolution literally and symbolically killed off the *ancien regime*. No longer naïve, the soul well "experienced and understood"[11] this. But what it installed following this historical rupture was "not a restoration in the sense of a repair or maintenance of some old tradition."[12] Rather, it turned toward "the *modern* imagination, imitation, simulation, of the old." Henceforth, what actually "happened was the reactionary spiteful new installation of the abstract concept of a decidedly *former* tradition, a ghost that is, however, passed off as alive."[13] Thus, neurosis does have the character of simulation in that

> [...] in the logical status of positivity and the physicalness of neurotic symptomology [...] what thus appears as a quasi-natural fact has in truth nevertheless only the character of an absolute demand or claim about how real events or phenomena absolutely ought to be and how the subject *must* under all circumstances behave [...]. [N]eurosis is the *psychic* simulation of *physical* positivity and necessity. It is the attempt to *sink* the mind and the metaphysical into the mindless status of a positive fact.[14]

Therefore, the neurotic soul in this sense is "not a refusal to leave this status [of obsolescent forms] because the latter has already been left all along."[15] Rather, it is "the simulation of the soul's still being in

---

[10] Wolfgang Giegerich, *Neurosis. The Logic of a Metaphysical Illness* (New Orleans, LA: Spring Journal Books, 2013; now also, London, Routledge, 2020), pp. 43-44.

[11] Giegerich, *Neurosis*, pp. 297-298.

[12] *Ibid.*

[13] *Ibid.*

[14] *Ibid.*, p. 305.

[15] *Ibid.*, p. 430.

this status, the regressive restoration of that which is already known to have once and for all been overcome."[16] What happens in neurosis is essentially the installation of the absolute principle. The neurotic patient then feels the *absolute demand* through the pull of the neurotic symptoms. In that case, their experience is a deeply dystonic one. The patient really suffers. And it is the inescapable neurotic demand of the simulated metaphysical absolute principle, acted out in empirical reality, that inflicts such a plight. Nevertheless, as with the working off process of the soul's simulating operations within psychology, neurosis, too, as a *cultural* phenomenon, seeks to bring about a "redemption within itself. It is aiming all by itself at disapproving its own initial absolute principle and, thereby, making itself unnecessary."[17] Within psychology, analysts and psychotherapists may then be deceived by such simulacra, perceiving these as an instance of (*semantic*) healing, repair, as a way of restoring a sense of meaning and connection to the "numinous"[18] level of mythopoetic "primordial experience."

---

[16] *Ibid.*

[17] *Ibid.*, p. 351.

[18] On this matter, Giegerich quotes Jung: "[…] [I]nasmuch as you attain to the numinous experience you are released from the curse of pathology" (Jung, *Letters 1*, to P. W. Martin, 20 August 1945, p. 377). Responding to this therapeutic prescription, Giegerich, offers this critique: "Neurosis invites yet another comparison, the comparison of 'The Absolute' with the popular term and idea of numinosity. The numinous is, it seems to me, the *sublated* version of the neurotic 'The Absolute.' Just as with the term 'the unconscious' something neurotic (the decided mindlessness of The Absolute) was raised to the level of psychological theory, so the idea of 'the numinous' uplifted the neurotic surplus significance from the wretched sphere of actual personal illness to the universal level of theory and thus gave it higher honors. […] However, in truth 'the numinous' is a cheap, unworthy version of the neurotic 'absolute significance': just idle talk, empty simulation. The neurotic's 'The Absolute,' which has its real place in his symptoms, has a much higher, namely, a real dignity because *he* [the patient] dearly pays for the absolute significance achieved through his neurosis in hard psychic cash: in his suffering from his symptoms and the severe restrictions they impose on him. […] The modern cult of the numinous in psychology, of 'personal myth,' of 'gods/goddesses in every man and

That simulation plays out both in psychology itself *and* in neurosis raises the question as to neurotic factors in the very nature of Jungian psychology as presently constituted. Giegerich addresses this concern as follows: he points to the neurotic element in psychology, proposing that psychology fell for neurotic rationalizing in its initial constitution.

> [...] [D]uring the late 19th and the 20th century psychoanalytical psychology came up with the concept of 'the unconscious' by way of an explanation of neurosis. Psychology fell for the neurotic 'arrangement' and *mise en scène*, took it literally, at face value. [19]

In consequence, psychology raised this neurotic absolute concept to the higher level of theory, designating it as the causal hinterland of neurosis. Again, the idea of "the unconscious" as a "truth of nature," simulated the *facticity* of physicality, of empirical reality. Nonetheless, psychology in this sense is not neurotic in the same way as the neurotic patient, who suffers because of their symptoms and pathological behaviour. Despite this critical difference, psychology "is neurotic (neurosis-syntonic) in that it, of course unwittingly, harbours within itself and *celebrates* the neurotic structure." [20] When psychology claims *empirical* status, asserting that it deals in "psychic *facts*," it is simulating these supposed *facts* as if they were literally, empirically real. [21] Namely,

---

woman,' by contrast, functions via crass overspending, buying on credit." *Neurosis*, p. 63, fn. 28.

[19] *Ibid.*, p. 59, fn. 27.

[20] *Ibid.*

[21] R. D. Laing, *Self and Others* (Harmondsworth: Pelican Books, 1969), p. 45. Laing puts forward the idea of "elusion," which is "a relation in which one pretends oneself away from one's original self; then pretends oneself back from this pretence so as to appear to have arrived back at the starting point. A double pretence simulates no pretence." This strikes me as the way simulation conceals its own nature, a "double pretence" *simulating* "no pretence." For a different angle on this, see: Niel Micklem, *The Nature of Hysteria*, in the chapter "Help at All Costs' (London: Routledge, 1996), pp. 110-111. Micklem writes, that hysteria "now appears as prominently in the treatment as in earlier times it did in the course of disease [...]." Psychotherapy, in its many different modalities, "[...] is a model of hysteric infection. [...] The characteristics are in every respect similar to those found previously in the causes and presentations of disease. Strong emotionality,

the soul simulates a mythic image as if it still expressed itself today in mythic terms. That is to say, it is supposed that myths are still the living "truth" of the soul. This "regressive restoration" of the soul's long-ago superseded forms of self-display is a simulated "truth event." It pretends that these are still psychically "living, existing" modes of being-in-the-world, "the living symbol," whilst simultaneously pretending itself away from its knowing full well that it has long ago surpassed them, emptied itself of them.

Psychology, though, is itself but one locus of the phenomenon of simulation, which pervades and consumes today's world. This consuming character of the simulacrum is well described by Baudrillard,[22] who charts the "successive phases" of the image. Accordingly at first, the image "is the reflection of a profound reality."

---

deception, some dissociation and, above all, exaggeration are all there, making the realities of therapy not quite what they seem to be. […] Psychotherapy in one form or another has broken out and spreads like an infectious disease or—more appropriately—like hysteria. […] [A]n 'hysterical gold-rush' has transformed the whole field of therapeutics into a caricature of its former self." We need to remember that a dominant feature of hysteria is its subtle ability to *simulate*, mimic, what is *other* than itself. What Micklem here suggests is that contemporary modes of psychotherapy simulate their previous, historical forms. Thus, are Jungians actually in some way simulating Jung? For instance, see Jung's "Parable of the Mandala," at the end of this essay (p. 146 below). Are we caught in a culture of unconscious identification and transference to the fantasy figure of "Jung" that we bear within ourselves professionally and individually. See Wolfgang Giegerich, "Jungian Psychology: A Baseless Enterprise: Reflections on Our Identity as Jungians," *CEP* 1, pp. 153-170, for a masterful discussion on the dialectical nature of Jungian identity, our transference styles, and much more. For instance, "'*Our* identity' as Jungians requires that *as* Jungians we maintain our own and do not castrate ourselves by subordinating ourselves to the authority of our master; 'our identity *as Jungians*' on the other hand requires that Jungian thought come into its own in our thought and is not arbitrarily selected and fashioned after our personal tastes […] and the masterpiece will be able to find an identity style that brings both opposites into agreement, an identity that is the oneness of identity and non-identity. I must remain myself and yet at the same time be not myself." *Ibid.*, p. 163.

[22] Jean Baudrillard, *Simulacra and Simulation* (Ann Arbor, MI: The University of Michigan Press, 2010), p. 6.

Typically, this is the Jungian approach to the image as *symbol*. In its next phase, "it masks and denatures a profound reality." In the following historical stage, a further transformation occurs, "it masks the *absence* of a profound reality." In the latter, we can see, for instance, the commodification of images, as with advertising and other commercial uses, or indeed in the contemporary practice of "selfies," along with much online phenomena. And finally, the image comes to have "no relation to any reality whatsoever: it is its own pure simulacrum."[23] As Baudrillard conveys, this fateful character of simulation has overshadowed the logical constitution of the image in modern times. To what degree is it though? A question that can be answered as follows:

> Whereas representation attempts to absorb simulation by interpreting it as a false representation, simulation envelops the whole edifice of representation itself as a simulation. […] [I]t is no longer of the order of appearances, but of simulation.[24]

Or as Pascal Bruckner writes, our time is the "reign of the 'just like.' […] But isn't it, in reality, just like nothing."[25] Within modernity, the logical status of image has undergone profound changes reflected not only in psychology, but within the culture at large.[26] Obviously, for Jungians such changes are critical for an understanding of their own psychology, since for Jung "image *is* psyche."[27] Can the very way we as Jungians understand our own psychology account for and comprehend these historical, cultural changes woven into the very fabric of our psychology? Are we Jungians still treating images as if they had today the same logical constitution as they once had in past times, when already in modernity that very logic of the image has undergone a profound transformation and rupture with its past forms?

---

[23] *Ibid.*

[24] *Ibid.*

[25] Pascal Bruckner, *The Triumph of the Slippers: On the Withdrawal from the World*, trans. Cory Stockwell (Cambridge, UK: Polity Press, 2024), p. 23.

[26] Michael Whan, "The Logic of the Image," a paper given at the International Society for Psychology as the Discipline of Interiority Conference, "Interiority, Truth, and Psychology," in Malibu, April 2015.

[27] Jung, *CW* 13 §75.

This state of affairs results from the way psychology itself is today in the main logically constituted, namely as *positivity*. As such, simulation ideally fits into this positivistic mode and deceivingly mimics it. Take for instance the idea of "primordial experience" or "primordial image," so fundamental in Jungian thinking. In modernity, the soul has lost its primary unity with itself. The soul has projected itself outside of its itself, it now exists "in the logical status of externality."[28] Thus to talk in psychology of "primordial image" or "primordial experience" can only happen as a simulated form of talk. Even when we substitute terms like "archetype," there is no "direct encounter."[29] Rather, what has happened evinces the positivistic and simulated way of speaking that suits and satisfies the ego:

> It is not an event of truth, of soul. [...] [I]t is [...] the *simulation* of a soul truth, a truth translated from the language of the soul into the language of the positivistic ego [...]. As such, the ego manages to take possession of the abstract contents—the memory images— of the former truths for itself, while ipso facto giving up their *truth* character.[30]

Psychology has fallen for the soul's beguiling sleights of hand, satisfying thereby the ego's longing for "symbol," the "imaginal," "the numinous," a longing seemingly for direct experience of soul.

> Why? Because 'the unconscious' and 'the imaginal' have the logical form of 'ego,' although they of course pretend to be 'non-ego' (and, semantically viewed, are indeed non-ego). They speak immediately to the ego, presenting it with easily accessible contents and evoking emotions of mystery, bewilderment, thrill, fear, guilt, shame, exaltation, higher meaning, deeper significance. They appeal to the ego's desire for what can be sensibly imagined. This is even true in those cases where imaginal psychology penetrates precisely to the very opposite of visibility, to alchemy's 'Black Sun,' to the ideas of

---

[28] Giegerich, *What Is Soul?* p. 164: In modernity the soul "was ousted from within itself, alienated from its primordial unity with itself, exteriorized, and thus came under the sphere of jurisdiction of the ego. It is the soul on the level, or in the logical *status* of externality, the soul in the element of modernity and this means ego."

[29] *Ibid.*, p. 143.

[30] *Ibid.*

the Unassimilable and Unspeakable, the Void. Those are all merely the *semantic* and in itself *imaginal* negation of the visible and sensibly imaginable, not the syntactical negation, and as such they celebrate the semantic orientation while seemingly transcending or destroying it. They are well suited to satisfy the ego's mystical longings, as Mogenson insightfully pointed out.[31]

Jung, too, in one of his letters addresses this issue of imitation—though he doesn't speak of simulation. Therein, Jung remarks of an "enduring effort" by way of "a deliberative, imitative arrangement of the analogous circumstances" to restore an "original situation."[32] He continues, how "a genuine and original inner life" can succumb to the "sensualism and rationalism of consciousness, i.e., to literal-mindedness." Though Jung's words address the inner life of the individual, his words can also be related to the dominant "sensualism" and "literal-mindedness" of psychology itself, namely the way simulation smuggles itself into the very fabric of psychology. That is, the way simulacra as logically semantic forms expressly imitate the "symbolic forms and imagery." We have to hold onto the insight that simulation exercises a mercurial duplicity, a "double pretence" simulating no pretence. For, a "true simulation is simulation only to the extent it manages to conceal its simulation character and forcefully gives itself out as absolutely authentic."[33] Simulated soul phenomena are "of a much higher logical complexity than innocent ones."[34]

Simulation and the Feeling Function

The mercurial duplicity of simulation brings with it the challenge of how to differentiate authentic soul phenomena from simulated ones. What is needed for this is a highly differentiated *feeling*.[35] Jung also raised this issue in relation to the differentiation of a symptom from a symbol, drawing attention to "two distinct and mutually

---

[31] *Ibid.*, p. 150. See also: Greg Mogenson, "Marlan's Bardo Thödol," in *San Fransisco Jung Library Journal*, 24, no. 4 (2005), pp. 6-16.
[32] Jung, *Letters 2*, to Melvin J. Laskey, 19 October 1960, p. 607.
[33] Giegerich, *What Is Soul?* p. 205-206.
[34] *Ibid.*
[35] *Ibid.,* p. 206.

contradictory views." [36] He noted that perception of the "meaning and meaninglessness of things" is dependent upon which view is acted on. Thus, something can be seen either as a symptom or symbol, as a function of which view holds sway. What Jung points to here is the exercise of feeling and what was once called "clinical intuition."

When talking of feeling, psychology has to differentiate *subjective* from *objective* feeling. A ready example of this is our differentiating the objective feeling-tone of a dream from our egoic reactions to it. We may react to the dream, judging it negatively, which may more represent our subjective feeling response ("I had a horrible dream"), rather than the objective feeling-tone of the dream. For, dreams have their own feeling-tone, mood, nuances, and atmospherics. Psychology has the task of discerning the *objective* feeling of dreams. This necessitates a

> well differentiated feeling function, which is, as Jung stressed, a *rational* function, and has nothing to do with personal *feelings*. The feeling function, by contrast, is really a function, something that is exercised[,] [...] a value judgment or assessment about something real, in our context a dream image[,] [...] the objective 'feel' of it, and has nothing to do with what we may feel. [37]

We let the dream have *its say*, which is the methodological principle for working with soul and dreams. The predicament, however, is to discern *when* it is speaking authentically and not so. [38] This is the

---

[36] Jung, *CW* 6 § 822.

[37] Wolfgang Giegerich, *Working with Dreams: Initiation into the Soul's Speaking about Itself* (London: Routledge, 2021), p. 132.

[38] Giegerich, *What Is Soul?* pp. 206-207. Elaborating on the difficulty of a feeling discernment, Giegerich writes: "[...] [T]he difference is no longer 'semantic' but 'syntactical,' we cannot rely on the external material characteristics of the phenomena. There is nothing tangible, obviously discernible and demonstrable, not anything countable that would unambiguously relieve us of the burden of a decision. What belongs to the one side may *look just like* what is other, just as symbolic, mythic, archetypal. The change from the semantic to the syntactical means that also the locus of the decision is interiorized from 'out there' (one's dwelling on the phenomenon itself) to the interiority of the soul, from the 'external' sense to a finer inward sense: it is a move from seeing to feeling, a feeling sensitivity[,]

veritable "Gorgon's Knot" that psychology faces in relation to discerning the authenticity or otherwise of what the soul produces.

The Philosophical Backdrop to Simulation as a Psychological Phenomenon

The manifestation of simulation within psychology is the flipside, as it were, of the end or going under of metaphysics as the condition of modernity. Not only is this the so-called "end of metaphysics," the backdrop to simulation in its contemporary form, but it is the condition for the emergence of psychology itself. Since psychology is "*sublated* metaphysics, irrevocably *sublated* metaphysics. But also sublated *metaphysics*."[39] Jung recognized this condition of modernity when he wrote of how symbols had become empty, abstract signs— not symbolic but semiotic. He wrote:

> [...] [T]he growing impoverishment of symbols has meaning. It is a development that has an inner consistency. [...] It seems to me that it would be far better stoutly to avow our spiritual poverty, our symbol-lessness, instead of feigning a legacy to which we are not the legitimate heirs at all. [...] Anyone who has lost the historical symbols and cannot be satisfied with substitutes is certainly in a very difficult position today: before him yawns the void, and he turns away from it in horror.[40]

Jung continues, that it is better and more truthful "to renounce the false riches of the spirit [...] in order, finally, to dwell with itself alone, where, in the cold light of consciousness, the blank barrenness of the world reaches to the very stars."[41] Adding, elsewhere, that "I am not exaggerating when I say that modern man has suffered an almost fatal shock, psychologically speaking, and as a result has fallen into a profound uncertainty. [...] Modern man has lost all the metaphysical

---

[...] a highly developed, differentiated *feeling function*, an organ capable of discerning differences in degree of otherwise imperceptible qualities, as depth, dignity, status, rank, and value."

[39] *Ibid.*, p. 307.

[40] Jung, *CW* 9i §§ 28-29. See also: Michael Whan, "Archaic Mind and Modernist Consciousness," *Spring 56*, pp. 40-52.

[41] Jung, *CW* 9i §§ 28-29.

certainties of his medieval brother."[42] What Jung here describes is the other side of the coin for the manifestation of simulation, the "symbol-lessness," the "void," the loss of "all metaphysical certainties": its preparatory conditions. In a way, simulation is precisely that "feigning a legacy," but a "feigning" that is the soul's work on itself—and on psychology. The soul, *through* psychology, deceitfully employs psychologists on behalf of its work, unless, that is, a differentiated feeling and thinking have been achieved to determine the difference between simulation and authentic soul phenomena. Simulation feigns "the fair memory of things that once were."[43]

If there is a philosophical, literary occasion that announces this radical rupture and transformation, then surely it is Nietzsche's *Twilight of the Idols, Götterdämmerung*. There, declares Nietzsche, "We have abolished the real world: what world is left? The apparent world perhaps? [...] But no! *with the real world we have also abolished the apparent world*."[44] With the end of Platonic-Christian metaphysics, its *other*, namely "appearance" or the "apparent world," has also been abolished. As Baudrillard has written, simulation has *consumed* representation, abolished the "order of appearances."[45]

Concerning the above, I want now to turn to Heidegger's commentary on this passage of Nietzsche's, for the "overturning of metaphysics" leaves "for metaphysics nothing but a turning aside into its own inessentiality and disarray."[46] The closure of metaphysics leaves the soul free to *feign* an *empty, abstract, fake absolute*. The end of the suprasensory realm hence marks the end of the *essence* of the sensory (empirical and imaginal) realm. This results, so that the suprasensory is "transformed into an unstable product of the sensory. And with such a debasement of its antithesis, the sensory denies its

---

[42] Jung, *CW* 10 §§ 155-163.

[43] Jung, *CW* 9i § 50.

[44] Friedrich Nietzsche, *Twilight of the Idols, Götterdämmerung*, trans. R. J. Hollingdale (Harmondsworth: Penguin Books, 1968), pp. 40-41. Nietzsche announces the closure of Platonic-Christian metaphysics and the collapse of the division of Being as the suprasensory and sensory.

[45] Baudrillard, *Simulacra*, p. 66.

[46] Martin Heidegger, "The Word of Nietzsche; 'God is Dead'," in *The Question Concerning Technology and Other Essays* (New York: Harper and Row, 1977), pp. 53-54.

own essence." All of which leads to a condition of "meaninglessness," the loss of the suprasensory culminating in "blind attempts to extricate [...] from meaninglessness through the mere assigning of sense and meaning."[47] "Meaning" is no longer a *fact of existence*, but an act or product of the ego. That is, the "suprasensory" has become an "unstable product of the sensory," as with the rise of simulacra.

Jung's talk of "symbol-lessness" and the "void" compares with what Nietzsche defined as *nihilism*. The latter wrote, "Nihilism stands at the door: whence comes this uncanniest of guests."[48] In the German, *the uncanny* is "*Die Unheimlichkeit*," literally, the *unhomely*. For Heidegger, this was the fundamental ontological mood of modernity, our no longer being *at home* in the world. Psychologically, modern man has been projected by the soul *out* of the *a priori* condition of embeddedness in the world, in nature, no longer having a profound sense of *in-ness*. We can no longer find meaning as in times past *in* myth, religion, or metaphysics as a fact of existence, of nature, as something *absolutely given*. For at such times, "Meaning" (with a big "M") was "first of all an implicit *fact* of existence," "the logic of existence *as such*."[49] In the 19th century, the immediacy of and direct feeling for meaning and "worth of life" was no longer possible: "Man must have stepped out of his previous absolute containment in life [...] enabled and forced to view life as if from the outside [...]."[50] Ours is the reign of the "imitative arrangement," of the "just like [...] But isn't it, in reality just like nothing."[51]

Out of this historical rupture arises a reactionary longing for and search for meaning, for symbol, resulting historically in what Jung feared, our "feigning a legacy." Of which, psychology's collusion itself is not exempt. This "feigning" can be compared with what Nietzsche named as "incomplete nihilism," the attempt to seemingly overcome the *loss of meaning* and find a sense of "absolute containment." Note how in psychotherapy we often speak at the individual level of the need for "holding," for "containment." Nevertheless, ironically

---

[47] *Ibid.*

[48] Friedrich Nietzsche, *The Will to Power*, trans. W. Kaufmann (New York: Vintage Books, 1968), Aphorism 1, p. 7.

[49] Giegerich, *CEP* IV, pp. 191-192.

[50] *Ibid.*

[51] Bruckner, *The Triumph of the Slippers*, p. 23.

"incomplete nihilism" is a self-contradiction. The problem with attempting to overcome the loss of meaning, the loss of symbol, is that despite one's "noble" intentions at "restoration," one ends up doing the opposite, namely, one ends up reinforcing the very nihilistic condition that one is trying to surmount and escape from. Nietzsche's ironic eye foresaw the futility of trying to combat nihilism by such means. As he neatly put, "Incomplete nihilism; its forms: we live in the midst of it. Attempts to escape nihilism [...] produce the opposite, make the problem more acute."[52] "Incomplete nihilism" is, in other words, the self-contradictory attempt to escape meaninglessness "through the mere assigning of sense and meaning."[53] Meaning becomes no longer a *fact of existence*, the very logic of being as such, but becomes merely the work of the ego, conjuring up "meaning" in its own image and way of thinking, meaning-*making*.

The purpose of "incomplete nihilism" is to find a "Why," a "For what?" It is the demand for "*another* authority that can speak *unconditionally* and *command* goals and tasks."[54] Such occurs in psychology with its attempt at "re-enchantment." This is the attempt to give sense and purpose, to fill the metaphysical vacuum. It is the soul's resistance and ours, too, to the metaphysical nakedness of our "bare life." Yet, simultaneously, it is the soul's counter-work against its own self-negation, self-emptying, precisely within the core of and by means of simulation. For, nevertheless, the soul poignant in its absence can be "understood as the first immediacy of the fact that the soul's fundamental quality of absolute negativity has now at long last come home to the soul, become syntactical and explicit."[55]

The demand for an *absolute* that can speak *unconditionally* installs within psychology itself *fake* or *simulated* absolutes, certain forms of sovereign principle, an *archē*, a "beginning" or "first principle." The notion of the soul coming home to itself describes the movement from substance to "soul-as-subject." "Soul-as-subject" contains the psychological difference within itself, the difference between the psychology of the soul and the psychology of the individual

---

[52] Nietzsche, *The Will to Power*, Aphorism 28, p. 19.
[53] Heidegger, *The Question Concerning Technology and Other Essays*, pp. 53-54.
[54] Nietzsche, *The Will to Power*, Aphorism 20, p. 16.
[55] Giegerich, *What Is Soul?* p. 164.

personality.[56] Psychology, however, in its present-day *substantializing, positivizing* form, conversely recognises only one side of the "soul-as-subject." It determines the meaning of the "soul-as-subject" solely as the empirical individual's personal psyche and personality. This becomes its "absolute principle," its "unconditional principle." To hold this position, though, is to *reduce* the "soul-as-subject" and hence psychology itself to the "theory *about* people's inner."[57] Psychology's deflected stance is no longer a *working with soul*, rather it has been misdirected into becoming "a long-range *cultic effort* whose function it is to defend and celebrate, by way of *simulation*, the old form of substance against the new truth of the soul, and this even while itself already inescapably being *on* the new level of 'the subject' that it wants to prevent."[58] Psychology has accordingly lost sight of its true subject-matter, the soul, and regressed to the "cultic" restoration of a metaphysics of "substance," a veneration of the human personality. Thereby, psychology forsakes its own truth of the realization of its and our metaphysical nakedness.

The Parable of the Mandala

Jung in his own way described an analogous situation regarding simulation in the transmission of psychology, its "feigning a legacy," which he titled "the parable of the mandala." We could also speak of it as the "parable of the simulacrum":

> There was once a queer old man who lived in a cave, where he had sought refuge from the noise of the villages. He was reputed

---

[56] *Ibid.*, p. 298: "The soul as subject is I. However, the I or subject is within itself, the dialectical unity and difference between itself as that function primarily oriented towards 'survival' in the most general sense, in other words, the pragmatic, technical I (in the sense of the one side of the subject-object opposition), on the one hand, *and* the internal not-I as the subject of true knowing, the organ of truth and of the syntactical or logical form, on the other. The latter is 'not-I' because it is the *objective* subject, *experienced* by the ego-personality as an internal other with an intentionality (and often impelling necessity) of its own. We could also say an autonomous other, however one that despite its otherness is nevertheless also I (me)."

[57] *Ibid.*, p. 294.

[58] *Ibid.*, p. 295.

to be a sorcerer, and therefore he had disciples who hoped to learn the art of sorcery from him. But he himself was not thinking of any such thing. He was only seeking to know what it was that he did not know, but which, he felt certain, was always happening. After meditating for a very long time on that which is beyond meditation, he saw no other way of escape from his predicament than to take a piece of red chalk and draw all kinds of diagrams on the walls of his cave, in order to find out what that which he did not know might look like. After many attempts he hit on the circle. 'That's right,' he felt, 'and now for a quadrangle inside of it!'—which made it better still. His disciples were curious; but all they could make out was that the old man was up to something, and they would have given anything to know what he was doing. But when they asked him: 'What are you doing there?' he made no reply. Then they discovered the diagrams on the wall and said: 'That's it!'—and they all imitated the diagrams. But in doing so they turned the whole process upside down, without noticing it: they anticipated the result in the hope of making the process repeat itself which has led to that result. That is how it happened then and how it still happens today.[59]

Jung's parable points us to the difference, imperative to realise in thought and practice, between authentic and simulated soul phenomena. Psychology is still in the throes of needing to work out the mercurial duplicity and duplexity of the soul's simulations. Or, to quote Jung again, psychology "still has a vast amount to unlearn and relearn. [...] [I]t must cease thinking neurotically and see the psychic processes in true perspective."[60] And as Jung remarked, it "still happens today." It is the task of psychology caught in this trap of the "regressive restoration" of soul truths long ago surpassed, to reflect upon itself and learn to exercise the discernments of a refined *feeling* function.

---

[59] Jung, *CW* 9i § 233.
[60] Jung, *CW* 10 § 369.

11

A Journey to Infinity: Bridging Consciousness across Traditions

JOSEP M. MORENO ALAVEDRA

This paper employs a phenomenological methodology, mirroring Wolfgang Giegerich's approach in *Pitfalls in Comparing Buddhist and Western Psychology*,[1] to delve into the concept of consciousness. A comparative analysis between Western thought and the divergent worldview of Ancient Mexican shamanism, as presented in Carlos Castaneda's anthropological works, serves as the foundation for this exploration. Castaneda's accounts offer a window into the experiences of an ancient tradition that discovered and navigated dimensions of consciousness unfamiliar to Westerners, challenging our conventional notions of this concept. My thesis advocates for a broader appreciation of diverse cultural narratives, suggesting that such engagement can deepen our understanding of our subject matter. By confronting the complexities of consciousness and its inseparable counterpart, the universe, the thesis emphasizes the necessity of a critical examination of this concept within the framework of Psychology as the Discipline of Interiority (PDI), one that acknowledges its potential for illumination while remaining mindful of its limitations.

Castaneda[2] was an anthropologist who encountered a lineage of shamans during his fieldwork. He became a renowned author, known for his early works exploring psychotropic plants and their resulting

---

[1] Wolfgang Giegerich, *Pitfalls in Comparing Buddhist and Western Psychology: A Contribution to Psychology's Self-clarification* (London, ON: Dusk Owl Books, 2018).

[2] For more on him, and the controversy that his work generated, see the extended note in the box on the next page.

altered states of consciousness. I agree with Giegerich's criticism that such explorations, together with their influence on the modern fascination with "non-ordinary reality," reflect some of the deeper cultural and existential anxieties of our time. It is true, many followers and spiritual seekers find solace in a nihilistic or neurotic manner, but interpreting Castaneda's work solely through that lens is a reductive oversimplification. Such a reductionist perspective fails to capture the complexity and depth of his contribution. Castaneda's later, more mature, works—often overshadowed by his early ethnographic writings—offer a more nuanced understanding. When considered in its entirety, Castaneda's oeuvre represents a unique and multifaceted body

> Much of the debate surrounding Castaneda's early works focused on whether he was an anthropologist or a fiction writer. Authors such as Baron,[1] Silverman,[2] and De Mille,[3] for example, debated the authenticity of Castaneda's accounts and the existence of his shaman teacher, don Juan. However, later works by Donner-Grau[4] and Abelar[5] presented experiences congruent with Castaneda's, complicating this debate. This raises a significant question: Are these authors presenting truthful accounts of difficult-to-accept realities, or are they perpetuating an elaborate fabrication?
>
> While acknowledging the controversy, this paper proceeds on the assumption that these works convey genuine experiences. In the spirit of *the psychological difference*, which prioritizes the content of the work over the author's motivations, I will refrain from engaging in *ad hominem* arguments and instead focus on the insights presented in Castaneda's oeuvre.

[1] Larry Baron et al., "Slipping inside the Crack between the Worlds: Carlos Castaneda, Alfred Schutz, and the Theory of Multiple Realities," *Journal of Humanistic Psychology*, 23, no. 2 (1983), pp.52-69, https://doi.org/10.1177/0022167883232007.

[2] David Silverman, *Reading Castaneda: A Prologue to the Social Sciences* (London: Routledge, 1975/2015).

[3] Richard de Mille, *Castaneda's Journey: The Power and the Allegory* (Santa Barbara, CA: Capra Press, 1976).

[4] Florinda Donner, *Being-in-Dreaming: An Initiation into the Sorcerers' World* (New York: HarperSanFrancisco, 1991).

[5] Taisha Abelar, *The Sorcerer's Crossing: A Woman's Journey* (New York: Penguin Books, 1992).

of work that invites a more profound and comprehensive exploration. I assert that the true "Otherness" of our concept of soul, as understood in PDI, resides in the type, scope, and form of consciousness that the seers of Ancient Mexico possessed and cultivated. A form and status of consciousness that cannot be fully understood if we interpret it strictly within the parameters of our cultural tradition.

Following Giegerich's theoretical orientation, we operate under the fundamental epistemological assumption that knowledge, language, and thought are inextricably linked. This premise underpins not only my methodological framework but also the broader epistemological current of Western philosophy and science. I intentionally adopt a methodological reductionist approach to examine the concept of consciousness[3] that has shaped and continues to shape our entire tradition—psychological, philosophical, and scientific. This perspective centers on a fundamental structure of our consciousness: the reasoning, logical, and speaking consciousness.

Language, Reason, and Perception

In a conversation between Castaneda and don Juan, his shaman teacher, we read: "He was really trying to tell me something, something I either could not grasp or which could not be told completely. "Knowledge and language are separate" […]."[4] The notion of knowledge existing without words or thoughts is, indeed, unconventional. Could the notion of a separation between knowledge and language be a vestige of a bygone era? Or does it perhaps hint at an unexplored dimension of consciousness within our tradition? Unexplored but perhaps sensed, intuited in the criticisms of some of our most eminent thinkers.

A cursory examination of philosophers who signaled a pivotal shift in philosophical discourse concerning language reveals a critique of the

---

[3] While the terms "consciousness" and "awareness" are used interchangeably in this context, they possess distinct meanings in various domains, particularly spirituality and philosophy. Similarly, the terms "sorcerers," "shamans," "men of knowledge," and "seers" are treated as synonymous here, although they may carry subtle nuances.

[4] Carlos Castaneda, *The Power of Silence: Further Lessons of Don Juan* (New York: Simon & Schuster, 1987), p. 37.

notion that truth is exclusively accessible through reason and language. Nietzsche's influence is evident in the growing skepticism towards Logos and rational argumentation. David Silverman observes that language games are deeply embedded in our cultural and social practices; "as Wittgenstein tells us, in playing our language games, we always do more than merely 'happen' to choose a useful convention. Language-games have as their bedrock a form of life, a mode of existence."[5]

Wittgenstein and Heidegger assert that language itself is the crux of the matter. Their proposed solution involves a paradoxical self-deconstruction of language, akin to using language as a metaphorical ladder to ascend to a higher understanding, only to discard the ladder upon reaching one's destination. Jacques Derrida analyses the complex interplay between language, philosophy, and the institutions that shape our understanding of the world. His deconstructive approach challenges traditional assumptions about language and meaning, opening new avenues for philosophical inquiry. Similarly, Blanchot's concept of "the outside" refers to the ineffable as that which transcends language and conceptualization. For Blanchot, language is not merely a tool but a force that shapes and even distorts our understanding of the world. Derrida and Blanchot agree that language and philosophy have inherent limitations in their ability to represent reality fully. They explore the tension between the particularity of language and the universal aspirations of philosophical thought. Following Nietzsche, these thinkers criticize the naive belief that we control language, asserting instead that language shapes our understanding. They challenge the idea that we speak a language, the truth being that we are spoken by it. Castaneda would agree with Nietzsche: in our tradition we have freed ourselves from God, but we remain slaves to grammar. According to Hoffman,

> the language of our perceptions—including space, time, shape [...]— cannot describe reality as it is when no one looks. It's not simply that this or that perception is wrong. It's that none of our perceptions, being couched in this language, could possibly be right. [...] Space, time, and physical objects are not objective reality. They are simply the virtual world delivered by our senses

---

[5] David Silverman, *Reading Castaneda: A Prologue to the Social Sciences* (London: Routledge & Kegan Paul, 1975), p. 95.

to help us play the game of life. [...] [P]hysicists admit that space, time, and objects are not fundamental; they're rubbing their chins red trying to divine what might replace them. [...] Perhaps the universe itself is a massive social network of conscious agents that experience, decide, and act. If so, consciousness does not arise from matter; this is a big claim [...]. Instead, matter and spacetime arise from consciousness—as a perceptual interface.[6]

However, I must fully assume Derrida's criticism exposing the limitations and contradictions encountered in any critique of language-based discipline (such as philosophy), insofar as the critiques by philosophers are dependent on concepts that belong to the very ideas being critiqued. "[W]e cannot utter a single proposition which has not already slipped into the form, the logic, and the implicit postulations of precisely what it seeks to contest."[7] How pertinent this is to Castaneda's claim that the syntax of any language refers *only* to the perceptual possibilities that are part of the world in which we live!

According to sorcerers, the subjectivity of everyday life is dictated by the syntax of our language. It necessitates guidelines, and teachers, who, by means of well-placed traditional commands that seem to be the product of our historical growth, begin to direct us, from the instant of our birth, to perceive the world. The intersubjectivity resulting from this syntax-guided rearing is, naturally, ruled by syntactical description-commands [...] [O]n the other hand, the subjectivity resulting from perceiving energy directly as it flows in the universe is not guided by syntax. It does not necessitate guidelines and teachers to point out this or that by commentary or command. The resulting intersubjectivity among sorcerers exists by means of something which they call power, which is the total of all the intending brought together by an individual. Since such intersubjectivity is not elicited through the aid of syntactical commands or solicitations.[8]

---

[6] Donald Hoffman, *The Case against Reality: Why Evolution Hid the Truth from Our Eyes* (W. W. Norton & Company, 2019), p. xviii.

[7] Quoted in Daniel Anderson, "Deconstruction and the Modern Self," in: Jennifer M. Sandoval, Coleen El-Bejjani, and Pamela Power, eds., *Essays on "The Soul's Logical Life" in the Work of Wolfgang Giegerich* (London and New York: Routledge, 2024), p.157.

[8] Carlos Castaneda, *Readers of Infinity: A Journal of Applied Hermeneutics*, 1, no. 4 (April 1996): 3.

For sorcerers, perception is not a mental act that allows us to capture what there is by means of categories of understanding; it is a process that creates a world and encloses us in it as in a perceptual "bubble." Put another way, the sorcerers' perception is tantamount to an unmediated visionary power that encompasses both an empirical description of reality and the underlying parameters and logical rules of rationality and thought. These constituent elements shape the lens through which reality is perceived, creating a self-contained world within which human existence unfolds.

According to Castaneda's sorcerer guide, don Juan "men of ancient times had a very realistic view of perception and awareness because their view stemmed from their observations of the universe around them. Modern men, in contrast, have an absurdly unrealistic view of perception and awareness because their view stems from their observations of the social order and from their dealings with it."[9] This difference in perceptual understanding highlights a fundamental divergence between the sorcerers' worldview and the modern perspective. While ancient man grounded his understanding of perception in the observation of the natural world, modern man derives his understanding from social structures and interactions. This shift, according to sorcerers, has led to a distorted and "unreal" vision of perception and consciousness in the modern world. "We are perceptors,"[10] says don Juan, whose basic orientation is perceiving:

> [...] [H]uman beings as organisms perform a stupendous maneuver which, unfortunately, gives perception a false front; they take the influx of sheer energy and turn it into sensory data, which they interpret following a strict system of interpretation which sorcerers call the human form. This magical act of interpreting pure energy gives rise to the false front: the peculiar conviction on our part that that our interpretation system is all that exists.[11]

Human beings have the ability to perceive the flow of energy directly. Consequently, "shaman practitioners judged the world from

---

[9] Carlos Castaneda, *The Art of Dreaming* (New York: HarperCollins 1993), p. 170.

[10] Carlos Castaneda, *The Warriors' Way: A Journal of Applied Hermeneutics*, 1, no. 1 (January 1996): 2.

[11] *Ibid.*

points of view which were indescribable to our conceptualization devices. For instance, they perceived energy as it flowed freely in the universe, energy free from the bindings of socialization and syntax, pure vibratory energy. They called this act *seeing.*"[12]

The world of the sorcerers of ancient Mexico was different from ours, not in a shallow way, but different in the way in which the process of cognition was arranged. According to Castaneda's guide, don Juan, the universe is composed of an infinite number of energy fields that exist in the universe at large as luminous filaments. Those luminous filaments converge on human beings and pass through them. Our response is to turn those energy fields into sensory data. The sensory data is then interpreted, and that interpretation becomes our cognitive system.[13] By cognitive system, don Juan meant the standard definition of cognition: the process responsible for the awareness of everyday life, processes that include memory, experience, perception, and the expert use of any given syntax. He explained: "[...] [O]ur cognition, which is in essence an interpretation system, [...] curtails our resources. Our interpretation system is what tells us what the parameters of our possibilities are, and since we have been using that system of interpretation all our lives, we cannot possibly dare to go against its dictums."[14]

Don Juan claimed that the shamans of ancient Mexico had, indeed, a different cognitive system from that of the average person. In the sorcerer's world, the phenomenology of thinking implies the necessity of suspending judgment,[15] which for them is not

> [...] the desired beginning of any philosophical-spiritual inquiry, but the necessity of every shamanistic practice. Sorcerers expand the parameters of what they can perceive to the point that they

---

[12] Carlos Castaneda, *The Wheel of Time: The Shamans of Ancient Mexico, Their Thoughts about Life, Death, and the Universe* (Los Angeles, CA: LA Eidolona Press, 1998), p. 3-4.

[13] Carlos Castaneda, *The Active Side of Infinity* (New York: HarperCollins, 1998), p. 147.

[14] *Ibid.*, p. 199.

[15] *Epoché*, or bracketing of meaning, in its fullest and absolute expression.

systematically perceive the unknown. To realize this feat, they
have to suspend the effect of their normal interpretation system.[16]

In their cognitive system, sorcerers are not concerned with creating
classification systems. Rather, as don Juan explained to Castaneda,
they work with an "arrangement of concepts," which should not be
taken as mere sorcerers' "theories," since "it was an arrangement
formulated by the shamans of ancient Mexico as a result of *seeing*
energy directly as it flows in the universe."[17] Castaneda notes:

> Human beings are two-sided. The right side encompasses
> everything the intellect can conceive of. The left side is a realm of
> indescribable features: a realm impossible to contain in words. The
> left side is perhaps comprehended, if comprehension is what takes
> place, with the total body; thus its resistance to conceptualization.[18]

There is a form of consciousness called *silent knowledge,* a state of
human awareness in which everything pertinent to man is instantly
revealed, not to the mind or the intellect, but to the entire being.
Through the cancellation of the interpretation system, it is possible
to achieve the kind of *silent knowledge,* "in which sorcerers obtained
knowledge directly from *intent,* without the distracting intervention
of spoken language."[19] By doing this, they "discombobulate [our]
trust in the normal system of cognition that makes the world around
us comprehensible to us."[20] Don Juan defined *inner silence* as:

> [...] a natural state of human perception in which thoughts are
> blocked off and all of man's faculties function from a level of
> awareness which doesn't require the functioning of our daily
> cognitive system. [...] The body functions as usual, but awareness
> becomes sharper. Decisions are instantaneous, and they seem to

---

[16] Castaneda, *Readers of Infinity: A Journal of Applied Hermeneutics,* 1, no. 3
(March 1996), p. 2.

[17] Castaneda, *The Active Side of Infinity,* p. 146.

[18] Castaneda, *The Wheel of Time,* p. 198.

[19] Castaneda, *The Power of Silence,* p. xiii. This concept is intrinsically linked
to inner silence, which necessitates a transformative experience often
referred to as "canceling the interpretation system." This metaphorically
equates to pausing the ceaseless flow of thought and perception.

[20] Castaneda, *The Wheel of Time,* p. 3.

stem from a special sort of knowledge which is deprived of thought-verbalizations.[21]

Castaneda wrote: "Whenever the internal dialogue stops, the world collapses, and extraordinary facets of ourselves surface, as though they had been kept heavily guarded by our words."[22] Following the conviction of the shamans, he was convinced that *inner silence* is the matrix that is needed to perform a gigantic evolutionary leap towards *silent knowledge*. Castaneda describes silent knowledge in these terms:

> Silent knowledge is a state of human awareness where knowing is automatic and instantaneous. Knowledge in this state is not the product of cerebral cogitations or logical inductions and deductions, or of generalizations based on similarities and dissimilarities. In silent knowledge, there is nothing a priori, nothing that could constitute a body of knowledge. For silent knowledge, everything is imminently <u>now</u>. Complex pieces of information can be grasped without any preliminaries.[23]

Since we are trying to highlight the bridge between the concepts of consciousness we have been comparing, I must add (following the sorcerer's guidelines) that "the one-way bridge from silent knowledge to reason was called *concern*. That is, the concern that true men of silent knowledge had about the source of what they knew. And the other one-way bridge, from reason to silent knowledge, was called *pure understanding*. That is, the recognition that told the man of reason that reason was only one island in an endless sea of islands."[24]

Dreaming

In her book on dreaming in the sorcerers' world, Florinda Donner-Grau says that "the woman who taught me to dream could maintain two hundred dreams."[25] A radical expression of the absolute strangeness of the shamanic cognitive system is the conceptualization

[21] Carlos Castaneda, *Silent Knowledge* (Los Angeles: Cleargreen, 1996), p. 33.
[22] Castaneda, *The Wheel of Time,* p. 128.
[23] Castaneda, *Silent Knowledge,* p. 33.
[24] Castaneda, *The Power of Silence,* pp. 241.
[25] Florinda Donner, *Being-in-Dreaming: An Initiation into the Sorcerers' World* (New York: HarperSanFrancisco, 1991), p. 46.

and pragmatic use of dreams. While, for our tradition, dreams are mere neurological byproducts (positivism), messages from the unconscious (psychoanalysis), or the soul speaking to itself (PDI), for the shamans dreams are areas of experience as real as ordinary reality. This is evident in the shamans' practice of transforming their dreams into areas of action, interaction, exploration, and discovery of unfathomable worlds beyond our cognitive parameters. Castaneda tells us through the mouth of don Juan that "[…] ordinary dreams are the honing devices used to train the assemblage point to reach the position that creates this energy-generating condition we call dreaming."[26] Ancient sorcerers developed a series of practices designed to recondition our energetic abilities of perception. Don Juan called this series of practices *the art of dreaming,* and stipulated further that it refers to "[…] the capacity to utilize one's ordinary dreams and transform them into controlled awareness by virtue of a specialized form of attention called the *dreaming attention*."[27] According to Castaneda, the shamans of Ancient Mexico discovered that there are two kinds of dreams. One class is the dreams that we are familiar with, in which there are ghostly elements, something that we could categorize as the product of our mentality, our psyche, perhaps something that is related to our neurological structure. The other kind of dreams are what shamans call energy-generating dreams. Don Juan said that those shamans of ancient times had dreams that were not dreams but true visits, made in a dream-like state, to genuine places that were not in this world.

The path from ordinary dreams to lucid dreams by which to finally reach *dreaming,* leads on to extraordinary discoveries for explorers of consciousness. The dimension of consciousness related to *dreaming* is a "two-way hatch" between our world and other worlds.

The Western Soul and Its Others

Two central ideas have presided throughout our cultural tradition: the human mind's capacity to grasp the universe and the idea that the human mind can grasp itself. Hedda Hassel Mørch suggests that these ideas historically align with distinct historical perspectives on the

---

[26] Castaneda, *The Art of Dreaming,* p. 174.
[27] Castaneda, *The Active Side of Infinity,* p. 187.

mind-world relationship.[28] The ancient Greeks envisioned a rationally structured universe, wherein rationality is inherent in both mind and cosmos. Descartes, at the dawn of modernity, posited thought as the fundamental basis of consciousness and existence. Echoing Plato's idealism, the primacy of this form of consciousness later led to enduring dualisms, such as mind/body and subject/object, in the thought of prominent thinkers in philosophy and science. This philosophical kind of dualism was severely criticized by the Mexican shamans. Writing about don Juan, Castaneda says:

> He had asserted that the physical body and the *energy body* were the only counterbalanced energy configurations in our realm as human beings. He accepted, therefore, no other dualism than the one between these two. The dualism between body and mind, spirit and flesh, he considered to be a mere concatenation of the mind, emanating from it without any energetic foundation.[29]

The advent of the scientific and technological revolution shifted focus towards the object, relegating the subject to the periphery of scientific inquiry. Yet, interest in consciousness reemerged, with figures such as Bertrand Russell grappling with the relationship between mind and matter[30] in a manner echoing that of Leibniz, Kant, and Schopenhauer. Today, we operate within the framework of PDI, assuming a self-referential dialogue of the soul accessible through an absolute interiority that excludes any external influence. This approach, we argue, transcends the dichotomous subject/ object split of positivism, situating itself in a *realm* of reflexivity beyond ontological considerations. It aligns with the Hegelian principle that *the real is the rational*, affirming that dialectical thought, or psychological consciousness, represents the pinnacle of contemporary consciousness.

---

[28] Hedda Hassel Mørch, "Panpsychism and Causation: A New Argument and a Solution to the Combination Problem" (PhD diss., University of Oslo, 2014), p. 14ff.

[29] Castaneda, *The Active Side of Infinity* (New York: HarperCollins, 1998), p. 216.

[30] See: Bertrand Russell, *My Philosophical Development* (London and New York: Routledge, 1959/2022).

While Giegerich argues, and I agree with him about this, that the Western psyche dominates the world as an objective suprapersonal psychological reality, I propose a different perspective: all the historical changes and developments within our tradition, as Giegerich envisions and conceptualizes them, belong to the same "world," dominated by a single form of consciousness, that confines us within a "hermetically self-enclosed—and linguistic—consciousness."[31] This limitation, I argue, hampers our understanding.

In comparing the Western historical and Mexican shamanic traditions, I have chosen to avoid geographical or historical assumptions. Time (History) and space (Geography) are categories belonging to a form of Western consciousness that according to the shamans limits our understanding. While Giegerich states that "[r]eal history is found in datable documented events, institutions and actual determinable epochs of cultural development,"[32] I argue that such a perspective runs the risk of mistaking certain cultural artefacts ("documents of the soul") for the pinnacle of that era's awareness. Giegerich, in other words, may be misinterpreting past eras by assuming that their documents fully capture their most advanced consciousness. To understand the contributions of the seers of Ancient Mexico to the understanding of consciousness, we need to look beyond those obtained by historians.[33] Castaneda asserts: "For the American Indian, perhaps for thousands of years, the vague phenomenon we call sorcery has been a serious bona fide practice, comparable to that of our science. Our difficulty in understanding it stems, no doubt, from the alien units of meaning with which it deals."[34] These achievements have reached us through various paths. Here, I highlighted the one that came through the testimony of a lineage of modern practitioners who have been able to remain faithful

---

[31] Giegerich, *Pitfalls in Comparing Buddhist and Western Psychology*, p. 24.

[32] Giegerich, *CEP*, III, p. 26.

[33] According to these testimonies, the social, material, sacred, ritual, etc. functions of the Shamanic practices are misunderstood by modern hermeneutic speculations. The objectives and maneuvers of the ancient shamans involved a type of consciousness that had nothing to do with the naive concepts of contemporary historians.

[34] Castaneda, *A Separate Reality: Further Conversations with Don Juan* (New York: Simon & Schuster, 1971), p. 10.

to the accumulated teachings and experiences lived from ancient times to the present day. Through complex maneuvers of consciousness resulting from a perfected discipline, they were able to make unimaginable journeys to other worlds and historical epochs. Therefore, their concepts of the universe, life, and consciousness were of a sophistication that we today can barely intuit.

Final Reflections

> We need this sense of fundamental otherness so that psychology can come home to itself to a much higher degree than before. [35]

—Wolfgang Giegerich

This inquiry analyzed and critiqued the concept of consciousness, challenging the assumption, sometimes explicit, but often implicit, that our Western understanding of truth and consciousness encompasses all of reality. Just as we cannot understand Christianity solely through the behavior of Christians, the interpretations of its exegetes, or the doctrines of the Church, we must apply the same criterion when attempting to apprehend the meaning and "truth" of Castaneda's work, which transmits the testimony of *seers* who know about ancient times through direct experience in their journeys of consciousness.

Our epoch has produced two unique flowerings of this topic: the works of Giegerich and Castaneda. Both are intended to be expressions of the most sophisticated forms of consciousness. Castaneda's revelations suggest that our Western tradition confines itself within a *perceptual bubble* that limits the possibilities of human consciousness. Our system of interpretation, in which language and the type of knowledge relative to it play a decisive role with respect to illuminating the world, is blind to its limitations, imprisoning us in a kind of Plato's Cave.

The *Opus Magnum* of the soul, it follows, must be considered both a power (in the sense of a process constitutive of the cultural and psychological reality of each historical era) and as a limiting *constraint* of the same. It envelops the human being in a psychological structure or form of consciousness that impoverishes and forecloses his or her

---

[35] Giegerich, *CEP*, III, p. 270.

emancipatory potential. The contradiction between emancipation and subjection is therefore a *mysterium tremendum et fascinans*.

Consciousness not only thinks and speaks to itself, but also and perhaps more primordially, perceives in a manner that makes it a medium for "navigation." Sorcerers' experiences were not merely physical journeys, but expeditions of consciousness, utilizing awareness as a vessel to navigate the cosmos. Just as water carries us through the physical world, awareness serves as a medium, facilitating encounters with beings from distant corners of the universe. This highlights the existence of consciousness beyond Logos, and it is not a primitive, archaic, or obsolete consciousness, but a form with the potential for unfolding within our civilization. This may be the only way, according to don Juan, to emancipate ourselves from the current human condition of the "suicidal egomaniac," which prevails globally and threatens our very existence.

While this potential, born witness to by Castaneda and the shamans, currently interests only a few, its emancipatory possibilities remain vitally significant. As Christopher Lauer argues, "[t]o prevent a system of reason from overstepping its bounds, we must allow reason's self-certainty to come into question through its confrontation with something it genuinely cannot encompass."[36]

Both PDI and Castaneda's work posit the existence of a dimension that is neither empirical, metaphysical, nor positivist. In PDI, this dimension is inhabited by the pre-existing logic of the cultural process and its dialectical changes. For Castaneda, it involves the awareness of energy as it flows directly in the universe, accessed through a type of consciousness irreducible to metaphysical or positivist frameworks. Wittgenstein's aphorism, "The limits of my language mean the limits of my world,"[37] resonates with Castaneda's accounts. If reason and language constitute but one "center of gravity" among many within the vast landscape of consciousness, then the call to silence, to the dismantling of interpretive systems,

---

[36] Christopher Lauer, *The Suspension of Reason in Hegel and Schelling*, (London and New York: Continuum International, 2010, p. 176.

[37] Ludwig Wittgenstein, *Tractatus Logico-Philosophicus*, trans. D. F. Pears & B. F. McGuinnes (London and New York: Routledge & Kegan Paul, 1961), 5.6, 5.62, p. 68.

becomes an invitation to explore our full potential. We must remember that our discipline should engage with "a deeper principle," "a more difficult subject matter," and a "material richer in compass."[38]

Positivist science, philosophy, and psychology are enclosed within tautologies that are at once their strength and their limitation. Physics, with its foundational motto that a physical phenomenon can be explained only by another physical phenomenon, and our discipline, founded on absolute interiority, share a linguistic-rational approach to perceiving and interpreting phenomena. This approach reflects an unbroken identity with a specific form of consciousness and a particular way of being-in-*a*-world.

The works of Giegerich and Castaneda stand out as unique anomalies—*rara avis*—in the landscape of contemporary culture. Giegerich's psychological theory faces ongoing debate, with some arguing that it is merely a "hobby"[39] (a thesis, be it noted, that has been shrewdly criticized by Barreto[40]). Similarly, Castaneda's work remains controversial, sparking discussions about its status as either literary fiction or ethnography. As mentioned, critics often dismiss it as catering to a niche audience neurotically seeking esoteric meaning.

However, both Giegerich and Castaneda deviate significantly from mainstream ideas (positivistic psychologies, New Age movements) and challenge the prevailing doctrines and practices within their respective fields. They stand as pioneers—*primus inter pares*—seeking to illuminate the nature, experience, and meaning of their central themes: soul and consciousness. In essence, both are proponents of revolutionary thought. Learning from them reveals an urgent need to thoroughly rethink the notion of consciousness.

The cognitive revolution implicit in Castaneda's texts and testimony is comparable to that represented by the texts of the New

---

[38] Giegerich, *CEP*, VI, p. 348.

[39] Giegerich writes, "Psychology has no higher status and collective significance than has a hobby or pastime. Just as hobby and pastime have their place in the private life of individuals, so psychology has its place only in the interiority." (*What Is Soul* [New Orleans, LA: Spring Journal Books, 2012], pp. 307-308.)

[40] See: Marco Heleno Barreto, *Psychology and Metaphysics: On the Logical Status of Psychology as the Discipline of Interiority* (New Orleans, LA: Spring Journal Books, 2021).

Testament and the project of Incarnation and *kenôsis,* which enabled the historical emergence of *psychological consciousness.* Castaneda's message requires a similarly long and complicated process, to which we metaphorically allude as the *aeon* of Aquarius, the emergence of the waters, in which we are invited to leave all previous forms of containment, all *inness,* to be able to use water (consciousness) as a means of navigation accessible to human experience.

Finally, I hope that this brief exploration of the Western Soul and its Others underscores the importance of engaging with alternative perspectives to achieve a comprehensive understanding of Consciousness in its Journey to Infinity. This engagement might contribute to Psychology's "necessary fundamental openness, which ought to be an openness that is capable of fearlessly embracing all prejudices. Nothing must be a priori excluded or avoided."[41]

---

[41] Giegerich, *What Is Soul,* p. 17.

12

Minamata Disease as a Negation of Japan as an Anima World: A Consideration from the Life of Dr. Hajime Hosokawa

Jun Kitayama

Introduction

Minamata disease in Japan is a result of toxic factory waste having been released into the environment after World War II. Regarded as an important event in modern Japanese history, it is routinely taught in Japanese primary schools. Recently, in 2020, a motion picture titled, "Minamata," was released. Starring the American actor Johnny Depp, the film relates its tragic story from the viewpoint of the acclaimed photojournalist, Eugene Smith, who came to the city of Minamata and took photographs of people afflicted with Minamata disease. Besides this film, the pollution case portrayed in it has been the subject of several literary works and documentaries. Additionally, academic research, surveys, and studies have been conducted from a wide variety of perspectives, including medicine, chemistry, law, sociology, anthropology, and environmental studies.

This essay focuses on Dr. Hajime Hosokawa, who was both the discoverer of Minamata disease and a physician active in treating many of its sufferers. Its aim, further to this, is to examine, from the perspective of psychology as the discipline of interiority, the process wherein a representative individual is prompted by a terrible negation to face up to a truth that for cultural reasons is difficult to acknowledge.

Summary of Minamata disease[1]

Minamata is a regional city located 1,000 km southwest of Tokyo. The Shiranui Sea, where Minamata disease occurred, is a lake-like natural inland sea with rich fishing grounds. In 1908, the Minamata factory of the Chisso Corporation[2] began operations. In 1932, the Minamata factory began producing acetaldehyde, a raw material for vinyl, plastics, and other chemical products. As vinyl and plastics have a great many applications, the Chisso Corporation readily grew into a conglomerate, supporting Japan's industries both before and after World War II. Tragically, insidiously, however, the effluent associated with this production process contained methylmercury, and it was this that was discharged into Minamata Bay.

Minamata disease is a toxic central nervous system disease that occurs in humans who have eaten fish containing methylmercury compounds discharged into the sea and rivers from the Chisso factory in Minamata. The main symptoms include sensory disturbances (numbness in the limbs), visual field narrowing, ataxia, and dysarthria (inability to speak well).

In 1956, several patients exhibited these symptoms. In 1959, Dr. Hosokawa observed that cats fed the Chisso factory effluent developed symptoms of Minamata disease. His subsequent research into the matter, however, was stopped by the Chisso Corporation's top management, and the findings he had made remained hidden and were not made public. The toxic wastewater continued to be discharged until 1968 when Chisso discontinued the production of

---

[1] In order to provide an overview of Minamata disease, the following references were consulted for this section: Masazumi Harada, *Minamata-Byou* (*Minamata Disease*) (Tokyo: Iwanami Shoten, 1972); Takeshi Takamine, *Minamata-Byou wo Shitte Imasuka* (*Do You Know Minamata Disease?*) (Tokyo: Iwanami Shoten, 2016); Soshisha, the Supporting Center for Minamata Disease, *Zukai Minamata-Byou* (*Illustration of Minamata Disease*) (Kumamoto: Soshisha, the Supporting Center for Minamata Disease, 2021); Sumio Arima and Makoto Uchida, (*Minamata-Byou*) *Jiken no Hassei Kakudai wa Boushi Dekita (The Occurrence and Spread of the Case of Minamata Disease Could Have Been Prevented)* (Fukuoka: Gen Shobo, 2022).

[2] The company name, "Chisso," is the Japanese word for "nitrogen." This name in itself shows that it is closely involved in the chemical industry.

acetaldehyde. Looking back on this period, it can readily be shown that the Minamata disease problem would not have become so serious if Chisso had stopped discharging the methylmercury-contaminated wastewater, or had taken some other preventative action, back in 1959, when the cause of the disease was first identified.

The Life of Dr. Hajime Hosokawa and Minamata Disease[3]

Dr. Hajime Hosokawa (1901-1970) was the person who first identified Minamata disease. After graduating from the University of Tokyo Faculty of Medicine and working at the University of Tokyo Hospital for eight years, he joined Chisso in 1936 and became Director of the Chisso Minamata Plant Hospital in 1947. He spent 26 years as a Chisso employee before retiring in 1962.

On May 1, 1956, Hosokawa reported cases to the Minamata Health Service after several patients appeared with symptoms such as numbness in the limbs and lips, gait disturbance, speech disorder, and afferent visual field constriction. As the cause of Minamata disease was unknown then, Hosokawa subsequently conducted extensive interviews with the patients, assisted by other doctors. The patients were concentrated in fishing villages a short distance outside the city of Minamata, in poor areas where mainly repatriates were living. Hosokawa visited houses in the villages, conducted careful interviews, and treated the villagers kindly as a physician. On discovering Minamata disease, Hosokawa said, "As a doctor, I had the joy of having discovered a new disease and the sadness of having discovered a terrible disease, which are strange feelings that are hard to describe."[4]

---

[3] The following literature on Dr. Hosokawa was consulted in composing the summary of him provided in this section: Hajime Hosokawa, *Ima dakara iu Minamata-Byou no Shinjitsu* (*Now I Can Tell the Truth about Minamata Disease*), *Bungei-Shunju,* 46, no. 13 (1968): 140-148; Kanji Irie, *Hosokawa Sensei no Hanashi: Irie Kanji Memo* (*A Story about Dr. Hosokawa: A Note by Kanji Irie*), *Minamata-Gaku Kenkyu* (*Journal of Minamata Studies*), 3 (2011): 125-146; Nobuo Miyazawa, *Irie Memo "Hosokawa Sensei no Hanashi" Kaidai* (*An Annotation of "A Story about Dr. Hosokawa: A Note by Kanji Irie"*), *Minamata-Gaku Kenkyu* (*Journal of Minamata Studies*), 3 (2011): 107-123.

[4] Hosokawa, *Now I Can Tell the Truth about Minamata Disease*, p. 144.

Hosokawa decided to organize a research group to identify the cause of the disease. He later recalled, "I wanted to know quickly whether our factory was black or white, because I am a factory doctor. In terms of the company's responsibility, to know if the factory was responsible or not was my basis."[5] As a physician, Hosokawa strongly emphasized and explained to the factory manager the ethical standpoint of "respect for the patient's life first." And he thought that it would be honorable for the company to determine whether the company was at fault or not, and to solve the problem quickly by taking preventative measures and providing relief to the victims.[6] The factory manager, however, was uncooperative, and imposed the condition that Hosokawa would not present the research results independently, but within a broader context as part of the company's unified position. Needless to say, for the factory manager, the main focus was on keeping production going uninterrupted.

Hosokawa tried to identify the source of contamination and the causative agent by feeding local fish and toxic feed to cats and rats to see if they developed symptoms of Minamata disease. In 1959, he conducted an experiment in which he administered Minamata factory effluent directly to cats. The cats developed the disease as a result, and Hosokawa confirmed, on October 7, 1959, that the factory effluent was the cause of Minamata disease. Since it was cat number 400 that developed the disease, it is known as the Cat 400 experiment.

Hosokawa reported the results of this experiment to his superiors and tried to continue with additional experiments to obtain proof, but the factory refused to allow him to collect the waste fluid, which he had previously been able to obtain as experimental samples. Hosokawa insisted that the company continue the experiment, but they disagreed. Hosokawa thought, "If I fight against the company here, I will not be able to carry out experiments in the future," so he decided to stop the research temporarily and wait for another opportunity.[7] Chisso Corporation continued to deny that they had any knowledge of the connection between the factory effluent and Minamata disease, until Hosokawa later testified at the trial.

---

[5] Irie, *A Story about Dr. Hosokawa: A Note by Kanji Irie*, p. 127.

[6] Arima and Uchida, *The Occurrence and Spread of the Case of Minamata Disease Could Have Been Prevented*, p. 23.

[7] Hosokawa, *Now I Can Tell the Truth about Minamata Disease*, p. 147.

Experiments with cats were resumed in August 1960 and Hosokawa and his colleagues continued their research into Minamata disease until his retirement on April 30, 1962. Yet, neither Hosokawa nor the Chisso Corporation ever revealed the results of this research. Hosokawa also kept his promise to the company and never published the results of his research. After his retirement, Hosokawa returned to his hometown and worked as a physician.

Published Memoir

In 1968, Hosokawa published a memoir in a famous Japanese literary magazine.[8] Commenting in this article on the background of the times, Hosokawa wrote: "Now that I think about it, I could have made an announcement of the results of the Cat 400 experiment at that time. However, I insisted on being accurate and precise."[9] "I judged that it would be dangerous to make a judgment based on only one example, number 400, and decided to expand the experiment further and proceed with careful research on both mass and quantity."[10] "At that time, the word 'pollution' had never been heard of, and not only the plant managers but also the section chiefs and ordinary employees thought that the best thing for the company was to make a profit."[11] "I have a deep attachment to Chisso because it was the company I worked at for more than 20 years. In those days, company managers in Japan generally had the lowest awareness of pollution problems, so it may be harsh to blame Chisso's management alone, but I think it is a problem that should be reflected upon in retrospect. I am now thinking that I myself should have reflected on this issue. Well, perhaps I should be satisfied that I was able to do all this while being inside the company."[12]

A Testimony from a Hospital Bed at the Inquiry

In 1970, while suffering from lung cancer and with limited time left to live, Hosokawa gave evidence at the Minamata disease trial

---

[8] *Ibid.*, pp. 140-148.
[9] *Ibid.*, p. 147.
[10] *Ibid.*
[11] *Ibid.*, p. 146.
[12] *Ibid.*, p. 148.

from his hospital room. He testified about the Cat 400 experiment and stated that he was surprised that the cat developed the disease and reported it to the company's technical department. This report resulted in the company discontinuing the experiment. His testimony made it clear that the results of the experiment had been reported to the company, allowing the plaintiffs to pursue liability for Chisso's negligence back to 1957.[13]

It is said that Hosokawa was careful in his trial testimony to avoid naming specific people. It appears that he did not want to hurt anyone from the company and endeavored to ensure that neither the Chisso Corporation, nor any individual there, was held responsible due to what he had to report in his answers.[14]

Dr. Hosokawa's Baptism and Death

According to the magazine, *The Catholic Graph*, it is reported that Dr. Hosokawa was baptized a Catholic in his last days.[15] In a letter to a friend from junior high school whom he met again a few years before his death, Hosokawa wrote: "I am tired of the troublesome human society." Concerned about Hosokawa's exhaustion, the friend introduced him to Bishop Eikichi Tanaka, another old friend from junior high school. At that point, Hosokawa's lung cancer had advanced considerably, but he hoped that if he recovered, he would be baptized as a Christian by Bishop Tanaka. Just before his death, Bishop Tanaka visited Hosokawa on his sickbed and baptized him while he was unconscious. The next day, Hosokawa regained slight consciousness and when his wife told him that he had been baptized, he said happily, "I understand well, now my heart is much easier." Hosokawa died on October 13, 1970, two days after his baptism.

---

[13] Katsuhiko Bando, *Hosokawa Hajime Sensei no Rinsho Jinmon (Clinical Examination of Dr. Hajime Hosokawa)*, Nigata-ken Bengoshi kai Kaishi (*Journal of Nigata Bar Association*), 10 (1987): 1-10.

[14] Miyazawa, *An Annotation of "A Story about Dr. Hosokawa: A Note by Kanji Irie,"* pp. 118-119.

[15] The Catholic Graph, *Minamata-Byou no Kenkyu ni hansei wo sasageta otto Hosokawa Hajime wo omou Tsuma no ki* (A private paper of a wife who loves her husband, Hajime Hosokawa, who devoted half his life to research on Minamata disease), *The Catholic Graph*, 10 (1971): 16-21.

Soul Movement in Modern Japan

Before and after World War II, the entire country of Japan was working to become an economically strong nation alongside the Western powers. Especially in Japan's post-war reconstruction period, the total impact of Chisso on Japanese industry, as a producer of raw materials for plastics and vinyl, was so great that the plant was in no condition to stop its operations. Not only that, but Chisso also had a corporate culture that was obsessed with company profits and did not take responsibility for the environment, nor did it attempt to take appropriate measures to deal with the medical conditions from which the local residents suffered.

The outbreak of Minamata disease may have been the beginning of this trend, which occurred 70 years ago. Giegerich has discussed a trend within modern society wherein productivity and profit are more authoritative than the individual. He writes:

> Not individuation, but *globalization* is the soul's *magnum opus* of today. And globalization means the elimination of personal identity as something in its own right and the logical subjugation of everything individual under the one great abstract goal of profit maximization: Profit must increase, but I must decrease.[16]

This suggests that maximization of profit is a powerful soul movement that transcends the interests and welfare of individuals. Psychologically, it is difficult to stop the operation of the factory, so structural has it become to life in modernity. I feel it is very important to recognize that individuals such as Dr. Hosokawa lived out their lives and practiced their careers within this sweeping and very powerful soul movement.

Anima World, Japan

Giegerich describes the characteristics of what he calls the "anima stage" of the soul's historical process as follows:

> Characteristic of the anima stage is a containment in the natural course of events, the pleroma of the soul, the surrender to that

---

[16] Giegerich, *CEP* V, p. 338.

which *is* and happens, the *participation mystique* and the sympathetic experience of the world, just as seduction, being seduced and fascinated by her, is essential to the anima as a figure. [17]

And on the topic of Japanese culture as compared with Western culture, Giegerich has stated:

> To the extent that on the soul level there is, grossly speaking, no *incisive* happening in Japan, one could say that the Japanese soul did not have a history, provided one means by "history" a serious rupture and real, decisive transformations. Japan certainly had a rich history in the ordinary sense, but it did its best to prevent having to undergo radical psychological reformations, revolutions, redefinitions of itself, changes that render previous beliefs and attitudes irrevocably obsolete, the way Roland Barthes said that "To be modern means to know what is no longer possible." In this sense the contrast between Europe and Japan would be that between a full-fledged soul *history* here and an *unbroken continuity* across the ages there. But with the same right one could, of course, also say that this unbroken continuity *is* precisely Japan's form of soul history. [18]

In general, Japanese people have a comparatively weak sense of clear-cut individuality and live their lives in a natural way, tuning in to and cooperating with others. Their focus is predominantly upon how best to get along within the family and other social groupings, rather than on asserting one's own will, and collective interests often set the final direction. Very telling with respect to the animating cultural ethos of the Japanese is the Japanese proverb, "A protruding nail will be hammered down." And thus it can be said that Japanese culture is characterized by the previously mentioned "anima stage," wherein harmonious envelopment with others is emphasized and self-determination via separation and singularity of purpose is difficult to establish.

Now, while bearing all this in mind, let us also recall from what was briefly discussed at the beginning of this paper, that the

---

[17] Giegerich, *CEP* III, p. 113.

[18] Wolfgang Giegerich, *Pitfalls in Comparing Buddhist and Western Psychology: A Contribution to Psychology's Self-clarification* (London, ON: Dusk Owl Books, 2018), p. 25.

Minamata area was a natural fishing ground, and the inland sea was teeming with fish. The fishermen regarded the fish as a blessing of nature, and they went fishing while praying to and thanking the gods. Munakata wrote regarding this, "For fishermen, the sea was more than mere physical nature. It was a fundamental frame of existence that was important in shaping a worldview, a religious world, in the fishermen's minds."[19] So the sea itself in Minamata was a sacred place, and the fishing was conducted under the protection of the sacred. The anima world unique to Japanese culture can be seen here: not only in the harmony that the people dwelt within, but in their identification with nature and with the divinity of nature itself.

In response to Munakata's statement, Japanese Jungian analyst Hayao Kawai suggested that "the implication [of the Chisso Corporation pollution disaster] is that we Japanese will no longer worship nature as a god. In the past, we lived our lives with a sense of oneness with nature as a subconscious religion. However, I believe that this incident was a very symbolic expression of the fact that such an era has come to an end."[20] Later in his remarks, Kawai simply reiterates that this is the case: "Perhaps we should say that 'nature' as the bearer of an ambiguous image of God for the Japanese is dead."[21] In other words, Minamata disease was an event that invaded and destroyed the sense of oneness with sacred nature and the unconscious religious image that the Japanese had previously held. The Minamata disease health tragedy, outwardly caused by the sacred sea being polluted by toxic industrial waste, may be viewed psychologically as a strong, innocence-sundering negation of Japan as an anima world.

---

[19] Iwao Munakata, *Minamata Mondai ni miru Shukyo* (*Religion in the Minamata Problem*), in: Kakichi Kadowaki & Kazuko Tsurumi, eds., *Nihon-Jin no Syukyo-shin* (*The Religious Sense of the Japanese People*) (Tokyo: Kodan-sha, 1983), pp. 173-194.

[20] As one of the symposiasts, Hayao Kawai responded to Munakata's statement in this way. *Touron: Ishiki suru Syukyo towa?* (*Discussion: What is Religion of Consciousness?*), in: *Nihon-Jin no Syukyo-shin* (*The Religious Sense of the Japanese People*) (Tokyo: Kodan-sha, 1983), p. 208.

[21] Hayao Kawai, *Syukyo to Kagaku no Setten* (*A Contact Point of Religion and Science*) (Tokyo: Iwanami Shoten, 1986), pp. 162-166.

Minamata Disease as a Negation of Japan

Dr. Hosokawa, who had lived in the anima world as a Japanese, obtained the results from the Cat 400 experiment. With this odious discovery, the dweller in what until then had been largely a state of oneness with the anima world was abruptly dislocated by a terrible other, the truth as negation. This negation, as we know, was meted out by the brutal fact that the factory effluent from the company where he had worked for many years was the cause of Minamata disease. A conflict then arose between the truth he had discovered and the harmony within the company he had worked at for many years. Expressed in the terms of our psychology, a syzygy of the anima and animus arose at this juncture, but the negation by the animus in this was not yet strong enough to penetrate the anima.

Giegerich has explained that the animus is pure negation, which means dependent upon some existing thing which it produces itself by critiquing or negating.[22] Further to this, he has characterized the animus as a logical property of action as follows:

> The animus is thus also the strength to stake one's life—this is a positing, too!—to put one's happiness and well-being at risk. He says: "And if you do not stake your life, life will never be won for you." He is the readiness to fight, to stand firm, to resist. He gives steadfastness as well as courage. He does not only want to assert his own interest and foist it on life, but also, while asserting himself, to preserve himself. In contrast to the anima's tendency to spend itself, to give itself over and let itself be carried away, the animus has an interest in the safeguarding of life. Often he shows himself also as a pragmatist and as the strength that is necessary for the realization of projects. He is the force behind the will to survive, to get through dangers. He teaches us to brave the storms of life. He feels challenged by what happens, accepts the challenge and wants to stand up to it. He does not simply put up with the given, but meets it with his "Stop!", his "No!" Thus, he is the archetype of opposition, of objection, of otherness; he is essentially adversary (Klages: *Der Geist als Widersacher der Seele* [The mind as adversary of the soul]). Only because, from the outset, he

---

[22] Wolfgang Giegerich, *Animus-Psychologie* (London, ON: Dusk Owl Books, 2021), p. 177.

experiences life from the standpoint of otherness and opposition can he feel challenged by all that happens.[23]

When the Cat 400 experiments made the unwelcome fact clear, the animus's demand to face the truth arose in the anima world of loyalty and conformity. However, still under the sway of his communal tradition, Dr. Hosokawa did not risk his life completely. That is to say, he did not fight against the company, did not say "No!" Instead, less courageously, he continued to conduct his research while maintaining harmony with the company as far as possible. It can be assumed, therefore, that the enveloping anima of harmony and stability was still very much dominant compared with the newly constellated animus.

Hosokawa Negated, but It Was Not Fully

Towards the end of his life, Dr. Hosokawa published a memoir. He also, during that late period, provided evidence at an inquest in which he finally made public the date and findings of his Cat 400 experiment, establishing thereby, as a legal fact, that the company knew at that much earlier stage about the relationship between Minamata disease and their factory's effluent. Through the writing of his memoirs and his testimony at the trial, he raised his voice and said "No!" This we may regard as an ethical uprising of the principled I, accomplished by means of a self-asserting act of putting himself on the line in the spirit of the animus.

Yet, for Dr. Hosokawa it seems that the ties to the company (these in the anima sense) were not completely severed. For, although there are words of self-criticism in his memoir, it is clear that his attachment and loyalty to the Chisso Corporation continued until his final years. Even in the forensic interrogation, he remained sensitive to workplace relationships, presenting the content of his replies in a way that did not hurt anyone in particular. If we were to find pure expression of an animus in his testimony, it would be a clear and truthful statement in the form of "this person did that," but instead, a slightly different consideration can be seen. In his memoir, Dr. Hosokawa talked about his attachment to the company and concluded, "Well, perhaps I should

---

[23] *Ibid.*, p. 226. The author thanks Dr. Giegerich for translating the passage into English for this volume.

be satisfied that I was able to do all this while being inside the company."[24] As a doctor who was an employee of the company that caused Minamata disease, and who was especially involved at the forefront of research and medical treatment of the disease, this reflection seems to show a sense of distance from the truth he knew. From this, one can sense his deep emotional connection to Chisso, the corporation to which he had belonged for so many years. But truth is simply truth, impersonal and completely abstract. Self-critically produced within the syzygy of the soul as its animus moment, it is not a humanistic concept, but an ego-transcending, insight that exists only through its being thought. Though at the trial and in his memoir, Dr Hosokawa did express the truth, it was not the complete truth, but one that contained cleverly hidden parts. Owing to this, it can be said that in essential regards he was not open to the truth, but rather evaded the full reach of the penetrating animus.

Again, Japan as Anima World

It has been already discussed that Japan has a culture that places extreme importance on "harmonization" within groups or organizations. In a society that places a high value on harmony, a high level of care, consideration, and avoiding disruption of the atmosphere is required. Additionally, breaking relationships with others or hurting anyone is avoided, when possible, to maintain harmony. From this perspective, Hosokawa's contaminated syzygy of anima and animus is not solely due to his own personality, but should be understood as reflecting a reticence that is traditional to the collective soul of the Japanese people. Whilst mediating the advent of the modern industrial era, the animus at the same time is what breaks the unity of the animistic soul. Even today in Japan, due to the great value that the society still attaches to harmony, it is very difficult for the individual, even in the service of a greater cause, to bet on himself, to assert himself, to rise up and say, "No!"

---

[24] Hosokawa, *Now I Can Tell the Truth about Minamata Disease*, p. 148.

Contrast between the West and the East: Ibsen's play "An Enemy of the People"[25]

According to Takamine,[26] Henrik Ibsen's play, "An Enemy of the People," was Dr. Hosokawa's favorite literary work. In Ibsen's play, a city tries to keep the presence of toxic substances in its hot springs a secret because of the city's economic situation and the high cost in time and money that would be required to repair the damage. The overlap with Minamata disease is obvious.

The twin of Dr. Hosokawa in the play is its main character, Dr. Stockmann. It is he who finds out the truth about the toxic hot springs and is determined to somehow make the facts public. Angrily, he tries to disclose the truth, even though his brother, the mayor, and the people of the town, oppose it. As a result, Dr. Stockmann and the townsfolk confront each other in the form of a public debate. There, Stockmann righteously declares, "A community based on lies and corruption deserves to be destroyed! Men who live on lies should be wiped out like a lot of vermin. This poison will spread throughout the country, and eventually the whole country will deserve to be destroyed; and, should it ever come to that, I'd say from the bottom of my heart: let it be destroyed, and let all its people perish!"[27] The audience, having none of this, says back to him, "[He's] an enemy of the people! He's a traitor to his country! He's against the People!"[28] Complicating this tense exchange, it then comes out that the toxic water comes from a factory run by a man named Kiil, who is Dr. Stockmann's father-in-law. Very important is Dr. Stockmann's willingness to share this painful truth, despite its involving his own relative. In response to this, the factory-owner father-in-law, Kiil, tries to hide the truth and manipulate Dr. Stockmann and his family with money. Stockmann, however, refuses the bribes he is offered and steadfastly chooses to continue to live with his family in the town,

---

[25] Henrik Ibsen, "An Enemy of the People," in: *Six Plays,* trans. Eva Le Gallienne (New York: The Modern Library, 1957), pp. 155-250.

[26] Takamine, *Do You Know Minamata Disease?*, p. 20. Takamine mentions only that this book was Hosokawa's favorite, but does not describe the reason for this or any references to this play by Hosokawa.

[27] Ibsen, "An Enemy of the People," p. 232.

[28] *Ibid.*

even though he has become an enemy of the people. At the end of this play, Dr. Stockmann resolutely declares, "The strongest man in the world is the man who stands alone."[29]

What is interesting when comparing Dr. Hosokawa's real-life story with Dr. Stockmann's in Ibsen's play is the difference in the ways each faced up to the truth of their having discovered the cause of a similar pollution problem. Dr. Hosokawa, as we have seen, is so inclined to maintain harmony with the others around him that he has difficulty dealing with the truth as it is. Dr. Stockmann, by contrast, stands firm in the face of the truth, no matter what anyone says or does, even if the people of the town all try to ostracize him. If this play, as is claimed, was Hosokawa's favorite literary work, he may have identified himself with Stockmann. However, the difference that distinguishes the two men is not merely a matter of the personality of each at the individual level, but is of a more collective nature. Dr. Stockmann, who is a Westerner, is not a resident of a predominantly Anima World. Right from the outset of his life and story, the animus moment of the syzygy is available to him, a part of his cultural heritage. Heir to this, he exists in society as an individual (i.e., already, but not yet as "the man who stands alone"). For Dr. Hosokawa, by contrast, the situation is different. As a Japanese person living in the world of anima, it is a bigger step, almost impossible to take due to the singularity this would require, to uphold the truth and reveal the animus in the face of his employer's and society's denial of the pollution hazard. This "difficulty of being alone" may also be considered a characteristic of Japanese people living in the world of anima.

Seeking the Catholic Faith

In his later years, Dr. Hosokawa took an interest in Christianity and was baptized two days before he died.[30] Although the record indicates that he was unconscious at the time of this baptism ritual, his wife and his old friend, Bishop Tanaka, seem to have been in no doubt that he wanted to be baptized, and they facilitated this happening. The question is: "Why did he want to become a Catholic?"

---

[29] *Ibid*, p. 250.
[30] The Catholic Graph, pp. 16-21.

The predominant religion in Japan is a mixture of Buddhism and Shintoism. The majority of Japanese people are rarely aware of belonging to a definite faith, such as being a Buddhist or a Shintoist. Yet even those who identify themselves as "non-religious" have faith as an integral part of their lives, displaying this in such actions as celebrating at a shrine the birth of a child or having a funeral involving a Buddhist ceremony. Japan is not a Christian country and Christians, including Catholics and Protestants, account for only about 1 percent of the total population. Why, then, did Dr. Hosokawa want to be baptized? As there is only very limited documentation available regarding the circumstances leading up to Hosokawa's baptism, my understanding of his baptism is based on my own speculation.

First of all, in line with a very common Christian doctrine, I believe it may well have been that, wounded and tormented by guilt, Dr. Hosokawa embraced Christianity, in the hours just prior to his death with the aim of obtaining forgiveness for his sins and peace before his conscience in the sanctuary of heaven. This, despite or in addition to the assurance already available to him from his Buddhist tradition, that he would be welcomed directly into its Paradise as into a world without suffering. Evidently, the Catholic Church's clear doctrine regarding "the forgiveness of sins" meant something to him and met a deep need.

Secondly, I also speculate that it must have been of great inner importance to Dr. Hosokawa that he proactively give voice to his desire to be baptized. The subtlety of this lies in the fact that if he were to die as a Buddhist, there would be no need or provision for him to personally come forward to proclaim his faith. Dying as a Christian, however, required this of him. So, it was very unusual and special, this choosing at the end of his life of a different faith from the majority of the Japanese people. In this can be seen a measure of openness to the animus aspect of his historical and cultural moment and the emergence of an inner voice quietly expressive of his discomfort with Japanese society. It would seem, then, that Japanese society and religion no longer wholly suited him. Dr. Hosokawa, I surmise, experienced the anima world of Japan's negation by Minamata disease, and to a small but significant extent stepped outside of Japanese society, with its values of harmony and conformity. I think, moreover, that his baptism brought healing, not only to the moral injury that his discoveries about Minamata disease had caused to him personally, but in addition to this, as a testimony to Japanese society that was helpful for its facing up to its own collective nature, as this had been impressed upon it via the negation it had had to sufferer via the terrible scourge of Minamata disease.

Conclusion

The existence of Minamata disease is the result of a huge historical accident, which even to the present day has not been medically overcome or psychologically assimilated. The difficulty that its discoverer, Dr. Hosokawa, had in facing up to its truth—this due to his striving to maintain at the same time harmony within the group—teaches us once again that Japan is an Anima World. Tearing this asunder, Minamata disease was a powerful negation which has subsequently required a rewriting of the values of Japanese society. This is why it caused such extraordinary pain, not only for its immediate victims, but for all involved and for the nation as a whole.[31]

---

[31] Obviously, in this essay, I did not want to evaluate the rightness or wrongness of Dr. Hosokawa's actions with respect to Minamata Disease. My purpose, rather, has been to examine the episode of his life having to do with that disease strictly for the sake of the light it sheds upon the larger movement of soul.

INDEX

2

2001: A Space Odyssey (Clark), 43

A

T

（

www.ingramcontent.com/pod-product-compliance
Lightning Source LLC
Chambersburg PA
CBHW031129270326
41929CB00011B/1556